COMMUNITY-BASED
ORGANIZATIONS

COMMUNITY-BASED ORGANIZATIONS

The Intersection of Social Capital and Local Context in Contemporary Urban Society

Edited by Robert Mark Silverman

WAYNE STATE UNIVERSITY PRESS   DETROIT

Community-based organizations : the intersection of social capital and local
context / edited by Robert Mark Silverman.
       p. cm.
Includes bibliographical references.
ISBN 0-8143-3157-2 (pbk. : alk. paper)
1. Community development—United States. 2. Community organization—
United States. 3. Social capital (Sociology)—United States. 4. Non-
governmental organizations—United States. I. Silverman, Robert Mark,
1967–

HN90.C6C645 2003
307.1'4'0973—dc21
2003009648

∞ The paper used in this publication meets the minimum requirements of
the American National Standard for Information Sciences—Permanence of
Paper for Printed Library Materials, ANSI Z39.48–1984.

To My Wife,
KELLY

———————

Contents

Part Three: The Effects of Race, Gender, and Religion

Acknowledgments

The book was the product of a collective effort on the part of several individuals. First and foremost, I wish to thank Judith DeSena, Ivan Light, Gina Neff, Kelly Patterson, Brian Sahd, Randy Stoecker, and Sherri Wallace for their work on chapters contributed to this book. I also want to thank the two external reviewers and the reviewer from the editorial board of Wayne State University Press for their comments on earlier version of the manuscript for this book. These comments were invaluable. They had a substantial influence on the final editing of this book and framing of the arguments concerning progressive reform. Additional thanks go to Jane Hoehner, director of Wayne State University Press, for her efforts to get the manuscript through the review process and ultimately published. Finally, I would like to thank Skye for her cooperation during the completion of this project.

1 Introduction

Social Capital and Community Development

Robert Mark Silverman

Social Capital as a Foundation for Grassroots Empowerment

A unique phenomenon has emerged in contemporary American society. Scholars, policymakers, and practitioners are concurrently engaged in public discourse concerning the importance of community. In one of its most distinct forms, this dialogue focuses on the importance of social capital to the production and maintenance of a healthy civic culture. However, the debate concerning social capital is part of a broader discussion which is surfacing nationally. This discussion concerns the degree to which issues such as civic engagement, community consensus, and citizen participation are necessary components of community development initiatives. In essence, Americans from a cross-section of society are beginning to reevaluate the role of democracy in their everyday lives. In the context of this movement, the social capital debate should be viewed as an effort to account for this shift in public sentiment and develop strategies for responding to it. As academics, elected officials, and administrators become more engrossed in the debate concerning social capital and civic engagement, they are finding that this dialogue merely scratches the surface of a larger movement to create mechanisms to empower citizens through democratic reform.

Undeniably, there is a great deal of contention among those engaged in this debate. For instance, academics dispute the manner in which social capital is defined, policymakers deliberate over proposals for infusing it in public programs, and administrators attempt to develop strategies for implementing community-centered initiatives. However,

1

one unifying theme among all of these actors is the recognition of an emerging popular appetite for a more tangible form of democratic governance. The authors of this edited volume explore the significance of the growing movement for local control and community-based development. In particular, each author critically examines how social capital is linked to organizational efforts to promote community development, and the institutional structures and constraints that shape them. Through this critical analysis, a progressive response to the social capital debate emerges. This response highlights three areas where reform is needed to make community-based organizations more effective.

First, greater attention needs to be paid to linking social capital to other elements of capital formation. In essence, community development strategies must focus on leveraging social capital, financial capital, and human capital in unison. In terms of reform, this critique identifies the need for an increased infusion of financial resources, technical assistance, job training, and other opportunities for educational attainment at the community level. Moreover, there is a need to design delivery systems that provide communities with stable and autonomous sources of such resources and opportunities. Progressive reform recognizes that the development of social capital is rooted in an environment where financial resources are stable and communities have access to information. In short, social capital is but one form of capital that is needed for community organizing and community building efforts to be successful.

Second, community-based organizations require greater decision-making power in the policy-making process and resource autonomy for policy implementation. In essence, there is a need for greater community representation in policy-making circles and stable sources of funding for grassroots organizations. In terms of reform, this critique argues for expanding the role of residents in local governance through formal representation in decision-making bodies and increasing the use of popular referendums to determine the fate of local development proposals. Progressive reform also advocates for direct funding of democratically governed grassroots organizations in order to promote fiscal stability and autonomy. Rather than being dependent on other organizations for grants and other forms of funding, a portion of existing revenues from property, sales, and income taxes should be earmarked to community-based organizations that are democratically governed. A core tenet of progressive reform is the link between achieving resource autonomy for community-based organizations and enhancing the power of residents in the decision-making processes of all organizations that impact the quality of life in local communities.

Finally, progressive reform requires that goals of inclusiveness be considered in community development strategies. This aspect of a progressive approach to leveraging social capital entails an inclusive community development process with a focus on empowering disenfranchised groups and the poor. In terms of reform, this critique identifies the need to define communities in an inclusive manner. In part, this would require community boundaries to be articulated in ways that encompass diverse populations along the lines of race, class, gender, and religion. Moreover, progressive reform would provide for the inclusion of underrepresented groups in local decision-making processes, allowing a broad cross-section of community residents to have a voice in community-based organizations. Among other benefits, this emphasis on inclusiveness and diversity would add strength to community organizing efforts and enlarge the pool of potential grassroots leaders. The principle of diversity would be promoted in all community development activities and outcomes in order to encourage the development of social capital across group boundaries and foster sustainable community development.

Through the examination of social capital in the chapters of this book, it is hoped that the broader issue of promoting democratic reform will be forwarded. With this in mind, each author critically examines the social capital debate as it relates to the elements of local development and community-based organizations identified above. In some instances, authors identify the limitations of social capital as a community development strategy, and argue for a more comprehensive approach to community-based development. In others, authors examine the institutional context in which current policies and programs that seek to leverage social capital are embedded, and they critically examine the degree to which progressive reforms can emerge from this milieu. Still other authors examine the multiple platforms from which social capital can be mobilized, with a particular emphasis on community development strategies grounded in networks based on race, class, gender, and religious identity.

In the following sections of this introductory chapter, dimensions of the social capital debate are elaborated upon and linked to issues related to grassroots empowerment and community development. This discussion begins with an examination of the conceptualization of social capital in academic circles. The purpose of this section is to develop a progressive response to the manner in which scholars define social capital. This section is followed by a review of themes found in empirical studies focusing on measurements of social capital linked to community characteristics and ascriptive traits. This section is included in order to illuminate the many ways in which social capital can be expressed, and to raise questions about the relationship between particular forms of social capital and the more general conceptualization of civic culture. Finally, a section focusing on the role of social capital in community-based organizations is presented. This section is designed to connect the discussion of social capital to broader issues of community development and citizen empowerment. Through this framework readers will be able to construct a general perspective from which to view the individual chapters in the book, as well as the relationship between the chapters and broader movement in society for a reformulation of democratic governance in daily life.

A Progressive Response to the Conceptualization of Social Capital

One of the purposes of this book is to forward a progressive response to the discussion of social capital in scholarly circles. In part, this response is voiced in the critiques of many of the authors. One unifying theme throughout the chapters is the emphasis on how the role of social capital has been reified in past scholarship. As a result, the authors attempt to frame the discussion of social capital within respective institutional and organizational contexts. Moreover, the formulation of a progressive response to the conceptualization of social capital among scholars is presented here in order to provide an audience of general interest readers with a medium for transcending rhetorical debates concerning the definition of social capital. As a result, the principal goals of the progressive response to the social capital debate are to generate a basic understanding of how social capital is shaped by local context, and to delineate the degree to which social capital fits into a broader movement for grassroots empowerment. Although there are many nuances to a progressive response to the social capital debate, this book sets out to establish a foundation upon which future efforts to promote progressive reform can be built. That foundation includes an emphasis on creating mechanisms for enhancing grassroots decision-making in local policymaking, expanding community control of resources for local development, empowering community-based organizations through capacity building and technical training, and including disenfranchised groups in core activities related to community development.

This approach, which frames social capital in the context of progressive reform, expands upon previous discussions of this concept in the scholarly literature. While earlier discussions of social capital focus on conceptualizing how social networks, norms, and reciprocity facilitate coordination and cooperation in society, the progressive response to this discussion emphasizes how these elements can be mobilized to promote the development of democratic governance in community-based organizations. To some extent other scholars have examined this relationship. For example, in *Making Democracy Work* (1993), Putnam identifies the link between social capital and the cultivation and growth of democratic institutions. Yet, in subsequent works published in 1995 and 2000, Putnam's focus becomes more restricted. In essence, he confines his discussion of the relationship between social capital and civic participation to the measurement of trends in traditional civic institutions. As a result, an investigation into the extent to which new forms of democratic governance have emerged in contemporary society remains underdeveloped in the literature.

Despite this limitation, Putnam's work spurred considerable debate among scholars, policymakers, and practitioners. However, much of the response to his work focused on two issues. First, a number of scholars concentrated their efforts on debating the degree to which Putnam accurately conceptualized social capital. Second, another group of scholars and pundits inquired about how well Putnam had measured trends in civic engagement through traditional institutions. With respect to the first issue, a considerable rift has emerged along disciplinary lines in the social sciences concerning how social capital should be conceptualized (Foley and Edwards 1999). For instance, political scientists and urban planners argued for a general definition of social capital, focusing on its role in producing cohesion at the societal level (Putnam 1993, 1995; Chang 1997; Wilson 1997; Dionne 1998; Gittell and Vidal 1998; Wallis 1998; Wallis, Crocker and Schechter 1998; Woolcock 1998; Dasgupta and Serageldin 1999; Putnam 2000). In contrast, sociologists argued for a more particularistic conceptualization of social capital, emphasizing the manner in which social networks are embedded in specific social structures (Portes 1998; Wacquant 1998; Portes and Landolt 2000). Much of this critique is grounded in the theoretical work of Bourdieu (1980, 1986), Burt (1992), Coleman (1988, 1990), and Granovetter (1972, 1985). The progressive response to the debate concerning the conceptualization of social capital focuses on integrating these two perspectives. In essence, a progressive stance is cognizant of the need for social capital to be embedded in parochial networks, while also maintaining a focus on cultivating social capital that facilitates the integration of local communities through a shared investment in democratically governed, community-based organizations.

Of course, designing public policy based on the progressive stance appears problematic given Putnam's (1995, 2000) observations concerning trends in civic participation. If Putnam is correct, and civic participation is on the decline, then efforts to promote the development of democratically governed community-based organizations could be implausible. However, just as scholars have reexamined Putnam's conceptualization of social capital, others have raised issues about his analysis of trends in civic engagement. The most notable example of this line of inquiry is found in Paxton's (1999) research which assesses trends in social capital. Her analysis offers mixed evidence for Putnam's conclusions related to a decline in social capital in American society. Although Paxton finds support for a general decline in the degree to which Americans trust individuals, she does not find evidence supporting a similar decline in associations or trust in institutions. Similarly, Wuthnow's (1998) research on civic engagement contradicts Putnam's (1995, 2000). Although Putnam is correct in asserting that civic participation is declining in traditional institutions, Wuthnow (1998) highlights the degree to which individuals continue to engage in civic culture through emergent institutions in society. Paxton and Wuthnow's findings add credence to the progressive response to the social capital debate. The continued role of associations and institutions in the daily lives of Americans and their willingness to participate in civic organizations complements progressive goals of mobilizing social capital to promote the further democratization of local institutions.

Community Characteristics and Ascribed Dimensions of Social Capital

Another dimension of the social capital debate requiring further development involves the degree to which analyses involving dimensions of race, class, gender, religion, and urban communities are integrated. Although each of these dimensions is examined individually in the literature concerning social capital, few studies have approached them in a holistic manner. In order to develop a progressive response to the social capital debate, strategies for mobilizing social capital in the context of an increasingly diverse society are needed. In part, this is an issue concerning equity. However, to a greater extent, there is a need to examine issues of diversity in a holistic manner to ensure that all groups are incorporated into emerging democratic institutions. Moreover, diversity concerns are most pronounced in urban settings. In these settings a progressive response to the social capital debate is highly salient, since a diverse urban context presents opportunities for cultivating an assortment of social networks that share a common investment in democratically governed community-based organizations.

Until recently, much of the existing literature examining issues related to diversity lacked a progressive emphasis. Instead, it remains highly fragmented in its approach to the examination of social capital and diverse groups in society. For example, much of the literature examining social capital and race is found in highly specialized research which lacks a connection to other aspects of diversity in society (Portes and Bach 1985; Waldinger 1996; Bates 1997; Portney and Berry 1997; Orr 1999; Silverman 1999; Light and Gold 2000). Similarly, the emerging literature, which focuses on the relationship between gender and the mobilization of social capital, is primarily concerned with the manner in which women leverage parochial networks (Naples 1998; Gittell, Ortega-Bustamante and Steffy 2000). Likewise, examinations of social capital as it relates to religious networks remain parochial in their focus (Greeley 1997; Wood 1997). The progressive response to the social capital debate argues for a more integrated approach to analysis concerning race, gender, class, and religious networks in the community development process.

Despite the trend toward parochialism, an integrated focus on multiple sources of social capital has remained a part of the academic literature. This is most apparent in the literature dealing with social capital in urban settings. For example, Sampson, Morenoff and Earls (1999) integrate aspects of race and urban structure in their comparative analysis of social capital at the neighborhood level. Similarly, Fernandez Kelly (1994, 1995) integrates the same dimensions in here analysis of the impact of neighborhood and community characteristics on the life- cycle of African American women. Moreover, other scholars have examined issues related to social capital in community studies dealing with the intersection of race, class, gender, religion and local context (Pardo 1998; Duncan 1999; Hartigan 1999; Patillo-McCoy 1999). In order for a progressive response to the social capital debate to develop further, additional research that aims to integrate the analysis of community characteristics and ascriptive groups is needed. A holistic and dynamic approach to the examination of social capital is necessary if community-based organizations are to have the ability to develop participatory structures capable of incorporating diverse groups in society into the democratic process.

Social Capital in Organizational Context

Fundamentally, a progressive response to the social capital debate requires a strategy for revitalizing urban communities and implementing democratic reform. Community-based organizations are considered to be a core component of such a strategy (Grogan and Proscio 2000). This is because of the potential for developing these organizations as nodes for planning neighborhood renewal and expanding citizen participation. Although some existing community-based organizations include a blend of neighborhood revitalization and citizen participation in their agendas, many do not. A progressive approach would seek to develop means by which social capital could be leveraged to enhance the role of citizen participation in the revitalization activities of all local organizations. By focusing on the local level, members of diverse groups in society would have increased opportunities to become invested in the democratic process. The development of these democratic nodes would stimulate popular debate in society, and create an organizational mechanism to inform municipal, regional, state, and federal bodies.

To some degree, community-based organizations have begun to move in this direction. However, the manner in which social capital is mobilized in these organizations varies widely, and this issue becomes more complex due to the assortment of functions these organizations fill in local communities. Moreover, community-based organizations face constraints due to both the institutional context in which they are embedded and limitations in organizational capacity. For instance, Stoutland (1999) places community-based organization at the bottom of an institutional hierarchy in the community development field. Given this position, these organizations are considered to be at a disadvantage in the policymaking process, despite their relative grassroots orientation. This thesis is developed further in a recent study of community development corporations (CDCs) (Silverman 2001). In this analysis, it is argued that organizations like CDCs are embedded in an institutional context where they lack full access to the policymaking process and subsequently end up focusing on program implementation. These constraints are compounded by resource instability and the limited organizational capacity of many community-based organizations. For instance, Stoecker (1997) indicates that local organizations often sacrifice community organizing for program implementation due to such constraints. Likewise, Glickman and Servon (1998) indicate that community-based organizations often face constraints due to limited capacity and uneven power relations in the institutional settings in which they are embedded. In order for the mobilization of social capital to complement progressive reform, community-based organizations must be assisted in developing greater capacity and the institutional settings where they are embedded must become less hierarchically oriented.

In this book, the aforementioned issues related to social capital are examined in the context of four distinct types of community- based organizations: microfinance programs, CDCs, religious organizations, and neighborhood associations. Each type of organization is examined in order to further the articulation of a progressive approach to community development. This approach focuses on mobilizing social capital to forge a reformulation of democratic governance in daily life. Of course, this is not a comprehensive list of community-based organizations, but it comprises entities which focus on core functions filled by economic, political, and cultural institutions. An examination of the role of social capital in each of these institutional contexts is essential for the development of progressive alternatives.

In addition to examining community-based organizations that operate in various institutional settings, this book also focuses on organizational types that are fairly well established in society. As a result, the organizations examined here are part of broader institutional networks. This scenario makes the analysis of the mobilization of social capital in these organizations of particular interest for two reasons. First, this analysis will give readers insight into the current manner in which social capital is mobilized in existing institutional networks. Second, this analysis will facilitate the development of concrete recommendations for adapting existing organizational structures in a manner that enhances their responsiveness to the emerging movement for grassroots empowerment in society. Consequently, this book builds on a large body of research concerning microfinance, community development, faith-based, and neighborhood-based organizations.

By infusing the social capital debate with the organizational types examined, this book initiates a dialogue in which this nexus can be used to construct a progressive framework for further research and policy development. For instance, this book builds upon existing research concerning community economic development and microfinance programs (Perry 1987; Taub 1988; Servon 1999). In particular, it examines how social capital currently fits into the economic development activities of community-based organizations and explores ways in which these activities can be harnessed to further democratic reform. Similarly, this book informs existing debates concerning the role of social capital and citizen empowerment in CDCs and faith-based organizations (Thomas and Blake 1996; Stoecker 1997; Vidal 1997; Gittell and Vidal 1998; Ferguson and Dickens 1999; Rubin 2000). In the context of these organizations, inquiry concerning the relationship between organizational form and the level of access diverse groups have to the community development process is considered. Moreover, at the most parochial level, this book expands the literature concerning the role of social capital in neighborhood organizations (Dilger 1992; Barton and Silverman 1994; McKenzie 1996; Portney and Berry 1997; Stabile 2000). This analysis is of specific interest given the potential for these organizations to cultivate grassroots leaders.

Outline of the Book

Individual chapters of this book examine social capital in the context of community-based organizations. Consequently, the manner in which social capital is framed and discussed in each chapter should be considered in the context of the local setting focused upon. This approach to the discussion of social capital is informative, since it reconciles some of the disputes over the conceptualization of this concept by highlighting the degree to which the parameters of social capital are responsive to the context in which it is embedded. Similarly, the framing of social capital in this book is a reflection of the disciplinary leanings of the authors of individual chapters. In addition to examining social capital in different social contexts, this book also presents the discussion of social capital in community-based organizations from multiple academic perspectives. Despite these contextual and disciplinary distinctions, this book presents a coherent picture of the manner in which social capital is viewed in contemporary scholarship and practice. From this foundation, a progressive framework for the mobilization of social capital is developed. This framework is built on critical analysis and emphasizes three dimension of progressive reform: institutionalizing community control of local public policy-making, creating autonomous resources and a grassroots knowledge base for community-based organizations, and empowering the poor and other disenfranchised groups in the local community development process.

The development of this framework is build upon an examination of three dimensions of the current social capital debate. In the first section of this book, the role of social capital in poverty alleviation and community economic development is explored. This aspect of the social capital debate is first examined from a theoretical perspective in chapter 2. In this chapter, Ivan Light examines the underpinnings of social capital and their relationship to the capital formation process. His emphasis is on the interdependence of social capital, financial capital, human capital, and cultural capital. Following this discussion, Gina Neff's analysis in chapter 3 focuses on microfinance programs and the manner in which institutions leverage social capital in the community economic development process. Her main findings are that the parameters of microfinance activities and social capital formation are largely structured by a small group of funding agencies. Together, these chapters outline the parameters in which social capital is currently mobilized for economic development purposes, as well as a framework for constructing a progressive model for community-based development.

This theme is built upon in the second section of this book, which focuses on the interaction of social capital and institutional structures. This section is divided into three chapters, each focusing on a different dimension of this nexus. In chapter 4, Randy Stoecker examines the degree to which the current social capital debate has emerged in response to governmental retrenchment in urban policy. From this perspective, it is argued that the importance of social capital is overstated in contemporary policy debates, and that this emphasis overshadows the need for other forms of capital to stimulate community development. This chapter is followed by others that examine the effects of institutional structure on the development of two forms of community-based organizations: homeowners associations and CDCs. In chapter 5, Kelly Patterson and I examine the political and economic structures that shaped the genesis of a homeowners association in suburban Detroit, Michigan. This case study highlights how the mobilization of social capital is shaped and constrained by institutional networks. Finally, chapter 6 examines the manner in which the mobilization of social capital has changed historically in New York City's CDCs. This analysis follows the development of several CDCs in the city over time, identifying how the nature of grassroots organizing has responded to structural change. Combined, these three chapters illuminate the nexus between social capital and institutional structure. The addition of this dimension in the analysis assists in the development of a progressive framework for mobilizing social capital which recognizes the interrelationship between local context and broader societal processes.

Finally, the third section of this book focuses on the effects of race, gender, religion, and class on the mobilization of social capital in community-based organizations. This section is divided into three chapters, each juxtaposing the mobilization of various forms of social capital among groups involved in community development. In chapter 7, I examine the role of race in the community development process in Jackson, Mississippi. This analysis focuses on the role of social capital based on race in CDCs and voluntary organizations, and its implications for collaborative action aimed at promoting social change. In chapter 8, this theme is reexamined in the context of the Black church in Buffalo, New York. Here, Sherri Wallace discusses how social capital based on race, religion, and gender are mobilized for grassroots empowerment. Finally, chapter 9 examines this aspect of the social capital debate in relation to the role of gender and class. In this chapter, Judith DeSena describes how social capital was mobilized in Brooklyn, New York in a multi-ethnic, multiracial community organizing effort led by women. This chapter also provides an example of how social capital cannot sustain community development efforts after financial resources and institutional support are withdrawn from local communities. Each of the chapters in this section focus on how the articulation of social capital is shaped by group identity, local context, and institutional influences. Through these discussions, insights are gained concerning the mobilization of social capital to promote the development of inclusive community development processes.

In the light of discussions in the three sections of this book, chapter 10 focuses on three interrelated issues. First, themes from the preceding chapters of the book are synthesized. Second, these themes are used to develop recommendations for mobilizing social capital in a manner that addresses local economic and community development needs while remaining sensitive to emerging democratic impulses in society. Finally, from these elements, a model is outlined for mobilizing social capital through community-based organizations in a manner that enhances civic engagement and promotes grassroots empowerment. It is argued that this model should be applied to future inquiry and public policy that impacts local communities.

References

Bates, Timothy. 1997. *Race, Self-Employment, and Upward Mobility: An Illusive American Dream.* Baltimore: Johns Hopkins University Press.
Bourdieu, Pierre. 1980. "Le Capital social." *Actes de la recherche en sciences sociales,* 31:2–3.
Bourdieu, Pierre. 1986. "The Forms of Capital." In *Handbook of Theory and*

Research for the Sociology of Education, ed. John G. Richardson, 241–258. New York: Greenwood Press.

Burt, Ronald S. 1992. *Structural Holes: The Social Structure of Competition.* Cambridge: Harvard University Press.

Chang, Hedy Nai-Lin. 1997. "Democracy, Diversity, and Social Capital." *National Civic Review,* 86.2:141–147.

Coleman, James S. 1988. "Social Capital in the Creation of Human Capital." *American Journal of Sociology,* 94S:S95–S120.

Coleman, James S. 1990. *Foundations of Social Theory.* Cambridge: Harvard University Press.

Dasgupta, Partha, and Ismail Serageldin, eds. 1999. *Social Capital: A Multifaceted Perspective.* Washington, DC: World Bank.

Dilger, Robert Jay. 1992. *Neighborhood Politics: Residential Community Associations in American Governance.* New York: New York University Press.

Dionne, E. J. Jr., ed. 1998. *Community Works: The Revival of Civil Society in America,* Washington, DC: Brookings Institution Press.

Duncan, Cynthia M. 1999. *Worlds Apart: Why Poverty Persists in Rural America.* New Haven, CT: Yale University Press.

Fernandez Kelly, M. Patricia. 1994. "Towanda's Triumph: Social and Cultural Capital in the Transition to Adulthood in the Urban Ghetto." *International Journal of Urban and Regional Research,* 18.1:88–111.

Fernandez Kelly, M. Patricia. 1995. "Social and Cultural Capital in the Urban Ghetto: Implications for the Economic Sociology of Immigration." In *The Economic Sociology of Immigration: Essays on Networks, Ethnicity, and Entrepreneurship,* ed. Alejandro Portes, 213–247. New York: Russell Sage Foundation.

Foley, Michael W., and Bob Edwards. 1999. "Is it Time to Disinvest in Social Capital?" *Journal of Public Policy,* 19.2:141–173.

Ferguson, Ronald F., and William T. Dickens, eds. 1999. *Urban Problems and Community Development.* Washington, DC: Brookings Institute Press.

Gittell, Marilyn, Isolda Ortega-Bustamante, and Tracy Steffy. 2000. "Social Capital and Social Change: Women's Community Activism." *Urban Affairs Review,* 36.2:123–147.

Gittell, Ross, and Avis Vidal. 1998. *Community Organizing, Building Social Capital as a Development Strategy.* Newbury Park, CA: Sage.

Glickman, Norman J., and Lisa Servon. 1998. "More than Bricks and Sticks: Five Components of Community Development Corporation Capacity." *Housing Policy Debate,* 9.3:497–539.

Granovetter, Mark S. 1972. "The Strength of Weak Ties." *American Journal of Sociology,* 78.6:1360–1380.

Granovetter, Mark S. 1985. "Economic Action and Social Structure: The Problem of Embeddedness." *American Journal of Sociology,* 91.3:481–510.

Greeley, Andrew. 1997. "Coleman Revisited, Religious Structures as a Source of Social Capital." *American Behavioral Scientist,* 40.5:587–594.

Grogan, Paul S., and Tony Proscio. 2000. *Comeback Cities: A Blueprint for Urban Neighborhood Revival.* Boulder, CO: Westview Press.

Hartigan, John. 1999. *Racial Situations: Class Predicaments of Whiteness in Detroit.* Princeton, NJ: Princeton University Press.

Light, Ivan, and Steven J. Gold. 2000. *Ethnic Economies.* New York: Academic Press.

McKenzie, Evan. 1996. *Privatopia: Homeowner Associations and the Rise of Residential Private Government.* New Haven, CT: Yale University Press.

Naples, Nancy A. 1998. *Grassroots Warriors: Activist Mothering, Community Work, and the War on Poverty.* New York: Routledge.

Orr, Marion. 1999. *Black Social Capital: The Politics of School Reform in Baltimore, 1986–1998.* Lawrence: University Press of Kansas.

Pardo, Mary S. 1998. *Mexican American Women Activists: Identity and Resistance in Two Los Angeles Communities.* Philadelphia: Temple University Press.

Pattillo-McCoy, Mary. 1999. *Black Picket Fences: Privilege and Peril smong the Black Middle Class.* Chicago: University of Chicago Press.

Paxton, Pamela. "Is Social Capital Declining in the United States? A Multiple Indicator Assessment." *American Journal of Sociology,* 105.1:88–127.

Perry, Stewart E. 1987. *Communities on the Way: Rebuilding Local Economies in the United States and Canada.* Albany: State University of New York Press.

Portes, Alejandro. 1998. "Social Capital: Its Origins and Applications in Modern Sociology." *Annual Review of Sociology,* 24:1–24.

Portes, Alejandro, and Patricia Landolt. 2000. "Social Capital: Promise and Pitfall of its Role in Development." *Journal of Latin American Studies,* 32:529–547.

Portes Alejandro, and R. Bach. 1985. *Latin Journey: Cuban and Mexican Immigrants in the United States.* Berkeley: University of California Press.

Portney, Kent E., and Jeffrey M. Berry. 1997. "Mobilizing Minority Communities: Social Capital and Participation in Urban Neighborhoods." *American Behavioral Scientist,* 40.5:632–644.

Putnam, Robert D. 1993. *Making Democracy Work: Civic Traditions in Modern Italy.* Princeton, NJ: Princeton University Press.

Putnam, Robert D. 1995. "Bowling Alone: America's Declining Social Capital." *Journal of Democracy,* 6.1:65–78.

Putnam, Robert D. 2000. *Bowling Alone: The Collapse and Revival of American Community.* New York: Simon and Schuster.

Rubin, Herbert J. 2000. *Renewing Hope within Communities of Despair: The Community-Based Development Model.* Albany: State University of New York Press.

Sampson, Robert J., Jeffrey D. Morenoff, and Felton Earls. 1999. "Beyond Social Capital: Spacial Dynamics of Collective Efficacy for Children." *American Sociological Review,* 64:633–660.

Servon, Lisa J. 1999. *Bootstrap Capital: Microenterprise and the American Poor.* Washington DC: Brookings Institution Press.

Silverman, Robert Mark. 1999. "Black Business, Group Resources, and the Economic Detour: Contemporary Black Manufacturers in Chicago's Ethnic Beauty Aids Industry." *Journal of Black Studies,* 30.2:232–258.

Silverman, Robert Mark. 2001. "Neighborhood Characteristics, CDC Emergence and the Community Development Industry System: A Case Study of the American Deep South." *Community Development Journal,* 36.3:234–245.

Stabile, Donald L. 2000. *Community Associations: The Emergence and Acceptance of a Quiet Innovation in Housing.* Westport, CT: Greenwood Press.

Stoecker, Randy. 1997. "The CDC Model of Urban Redevelopment: A Critique and an Alternative." *Journal of Urban Affairs,* 19.1:1–22.

Stoutland, Sara E. 1999. "Levels of the Community Development System: A

Framework for Research and Practice." *Urban Anthropology and Studies of Cultural Systems and World Economic Development,* 28.2:165–191.

Taub, Richard P. 1988. *Community Capitalism: The Southshore Bank's Strategy for Neighborhood Revitalization.* Cambridge: Harvard University Press.

Thomas, June Manning, and Reynard N. Blake, Jr. "Faith-Based Community Development and African-American Neighborhoods." In *Revitalizing Urban Neighborhoods,* ed. W. Dennis Keating, Norman Krumholz, and Philip Star, 131–143. Lawrence: University Press of Kansas, 1996.

Vidal, Avis C. 1997. "Can Community Development Re-Invent Itself? The Challenge of Strengthening Neighborhoods in the 21st Century." *Journal of the American Planning Association,* 63.4:429–438.

Wacquant, Loic. 1998. "Negative Social Capital: State Breakdown and Social Destitution in America's Urban Core." *Netherlands Journal of Housing and the Built Environment,* 13.1:25–40.

Waldinger, Roger. 1999. *Still the Promised City?: African-Americans and New Immigrants in Postindustrial New York.* Cambridge: Harvard University Press.

Wallis, Allan, Jarle P. Crocker, and Bill Schechter. 1998. "Social Capital and Community Building: Part One." *National Civic Review,* 87.3:253–271.

Wilson, Patricia. 1997. "Building Social Capital: A Learning Agenda for the Twenty-First Century." *Urban Studies,* 34.5/6:745–760.

Wood, Richard L. 1997. "Social Capital and Political Culture: God Meets Politics in the Inner-City." *American Behavioral Scientist,* 40.5:595–605.

Woolcock, Michael. 1998. "Social Capital and Economic Development: Toward a Theoretical Synthesis and Policy Framework." *Theory and Society,* 27:151–208.

Wuthnow, Robert. 1998. *Loose Connections: Joining Together in America's Fragmented Communities.* Cambridge: Harvard University Press.

Social Capital as a Tool
for Empowering the Poor

2 Social Capital for What?

Ivan Light

Introduction

Nineteenth-century economists, including Karl Marx, thought that financial and physical capital were the only forms of capital (Woolcock 1998:154). In the last quarter century, social science research has awakened interest in novel forms of capital, greatly expanding the forms of capital beyond what the classical economists would have recognized.[1] The current literature of social science identifies, in addition to financial capital and physical capital, three new forms of capital. These forms are cultural capital, social capital, and human capital (Table 2.1). Each can be understood independently of the other, but they are best understood in their interconnection. Also, the researchers who developed social and cultural capital were aware of human capital, and this awareness later became reciprocal. Finally, the value of social capital lies precisely in its conversion into other desirable resources. Therefore, to understand social capital, one needs also to understand the neighbor concepts (financial capital, physical capital, human capital, cultural capital) that emerged in tandem with it and into which social capital transmutes and from which it is in turn transmuted.

Human capital means an individual's investment in training that increases his or her productivity and therewith earns a money return (Becker 1993, 1996).[2] Since training costs money, whether through tuition payments, opportunity costs, or both, an individual's human capital represents an income-generating, reliable, long-term investment. Therefore, economists understand an individual's repertoire of trained skills as a capital reserve analogous to financial capital. "Education and training are the most important investments in human capital."[3] Human capital resides in the owner's person, not in the owner's bank. One invests money in a business inventory in the expectation of a money return, and one invests in education for the same reason. The chief promoter and most visible theorist of human capital, Gary Becker, received a Nobel prize in economics for this contribution.

The related concept of cultural capital originated in the work of the late Pierre Bourdieu (1979:10,12)[4] who defined cultural capital as high cultural knowledge that ultimately redounds to the owner's advantage, non-financial as well as financial (Erickson 1998:217). An example would be knowing how to dress for success. This is a kind of cultural knowledge. Fortune 500 corporations hire executives who dress appropriately. As a result, a job-seeker's sartorial knowledge commands a salary bonus above and beyond what his or her expected productivity would have commanded alone. That is, the well-dressed candidate gets a salary bonus unattributable to her productivity. Therefore, the knowledge of how to dress for success earns a bonus reserved for those who have the right cultural knowledge. Most people do not know how to dress for success. For this reason, the acquisition of high cultural knowledge and style, including stylish dress, table manners, golf, and arty chit-chat, is a capital resource of the owner, vested in the owner, but it is not human capital. An executive may have human capital without cultural capital, or, more commonly, cultural capital without human capital. In principle, one might acquire cultural capital as an adult by hiring a tutor as did Moliere's Bourgeois Gentilhomme. However, cultural capital is prohibitively inconvenient and expensive to buy that way. In reality, people normally acquire cultural capital informally when they grow to maturity in privileged, upper-class backgrounds.

In contrast to human capital and cultural capital, social capital means relationships of trust embedded in social networks.[5] Jane Jacobs (1961) is usually credited with authorship of the concept.[6] Nonetheless, social capital's current prominence and formal definition stems most centrally from the work of the late James Coleman (1988).[7] Social relationships become capital, a store of value, Coleman argued, when and because participants can rely upon one another to uphold social norms and to reciprocate favors. Diamond merchants in Amsterdam utilize social capital when they turn over priceless packets of cut diamonds to one another for inspection without any prior inventory. In so doing they rely upon a community norm ("don't steal!") to obtain time-saving flexibility in their business. Farmers exploit their social capital when they turn out to build another farmer's barn in the expectation that someday the other farmer will return the favor.

Coleman's development of the concept of social capital exhibited explicit familiarity with Becker's concept of human capital. Coleman (1988) showed that human capital formation often depended

Table 2.1. Forms of Capital, Capsule Definitions

Form of Capital	Definition
Capital	A store of value that facilitates action
Financial Capital	Money available for investment
Physical Capital	Real estate, equipment, and infrastructure of production
Human Capital	Training that increases productivity on the job
Cultural Capital	High cultural knowledge that confers economic and social advantage
Social Capital	Relationships of trust embedded in social networks

upon prior social capital. The research context was Coleman's study of parochial schools. Finding that parochial schools had lower drop-out rates than public schools, Coleman concluded that the social capital of the parochial schools permitted parents to impose a rigorous discipline upon their school-age children.[8] In that sense, an individual student's human capital could be decomposed into the social relationships that had permitted the individual to acquire them in the first place. This origin does not diminish the independent impact of having productive skills, an unassailable resource, but it specifies a metamorphosis in which social capital first becomes human capital, and human capital later becomes financial capital. Ultimately, social capital became financial capital through this sequence.

Capital's Properties

All forms of capital should share all or most properties of financial and physical capital to merit designation as capital. Social, cultural, and human capital do share the most important features of financial and physical capital (Table 2.2). One shared feature is storability. Physical capital and financial capital can be stored for protracted periods, but there is depreciation and risk when so doing. When storing physical capital, one encounters depreciation caused by normal wear as well as the hazards of arson, vandalism, and natural catastrophes. When storing financial capital, one encounters depreciation caused by taxes as well as the risks of inflation, theft, embezzlement, bankruptcy, revolution, and war. Owners can store social, human, and cultural capital too, albeit at some risk. One's store of human and cultural capital is a store of knowledge. One's store of social capital is a store of dependable relationships. Storing knowledge encounters the risks of obsolescence, personal loss of memory, infirmities that inhibit the knowledge's utilization, fashion change, public education, and the like. Storing relationships encounters the risks of death, divorce, emigration, religious or political conversions, imprisonment, and so forth.[9] That is, some reliable friend, who owes one a favor, might die, divorce her spouse and move far away, enter a cloister, or receive a life sentence to prison. The same fates could befall ego. In either case, ego will never receive back the favor owed so the social capital will be lost.

Mutual Metamorphosis

A second and possibly the most important property of capital's various forms is mutual metamorphosis. Bourdieu emphasized this feature, and this discussion follows him on that important point (Brubaker 1985; Bourdieu 1986; Portes 1998:4). Metamorphosis means that the forms of capital change into one another and back again over time. Physical and financial capital metamorphose into one another. This is an essential property of these forms of capital. When merchants buy inventory, they change their financial capital into physical capital. A million dollars becomes 100 box cars loaded with beans. When merchants sell the beans, they change the physical capital back into financial capital. If we represent financial capital as F and physical capital as P, then we can represent this transaction schematically as: F1 becomes P, which becomes F2. First, the merchant has F1, then F1 becomes P, and finally P returns to F2. Here F1 exceeds F2, indicating that when the merchant sold his inventory, and reconverted his assets to money form, she had more financial capital than when she originally converted her money into inventory. The merchant earned a profit on this transaction. This is not invariable, but it is the goal of trading capital.

In the same sense, social, human, and cultural capital metamorphose into one another and into financial and physical capital (Johannisson 2000; Bourdieu 1986). The archives of social science bulge with evidence.[10] To illustrate, let us consider the metamorphosis of social, human, and cultural capital into financial capital. When someone acquires human capital, and later gets a high-paying job on the strength of it, the person's human capital has produced financial capital. Without the prior human capital (an education), the financial capital (a salary) would not have been obtained. One might say that the costs of education, a financial capital investment, turned into the human capital. Becker would illustrate the process as follows where H is human capital and F is money capital: Here, as before, F2 exceeds F1, indicating that the costs of the investor's education were less than the lifetime earnings increment that the investor received as a result of his or her education.

When a manager lands a high-paying job thanks to a network referral, which research finds is the best way to get a good job (Sandefur and Laumann 1998:486), then the job-seeker's social capital has metamorphosed into financial capital. That is, the job seeker started with a social network, then converted that network into a high salary: money. If the network the seeker utilized derived from her college days, then the same financial capital that paid for the job seeker's human capital also obtained the job seeker's social capital. When the job seeker's prestige diploma additionally secures a high-paying job for her, then the graduate's cultural capital has metamorphosed into her financial capital (Farkas 1996; Borocz and Southworth 1996). Financial investment in this job seeker's education obtained more than human capital. In fact, it obtained three forms of capital (not just one!) that in tandem permitted the job seeker's ultimate valorization on the labor market: human capital, social capital, and cultural capital. We might diagram this relationship as follows, where F1 is the initial financial investment, C is cultural capital, S is social capital, H is human capital, and F2 is the good job that results. Note that one cannot go directly from F1 to F2. The transaction requires that F1 metamorphose into S, C, and H in which form it can then again metamorphose into F2.

Metamorphic sequences need not begin with F. Consider the metamorphosis of human, social, and cultural capital into one another. When an applicant's personal references from well-connected alumnae obtain or, at least, facilitate her admission into a college, then the applicant's social capital has metamorphosed into human capital in that, having been admitted, she can now learn what the college teaches. Four years later she will emerge from college knowing more than she earlier did, a store of human capital that exists in part because her social network secured her admission. If, additionally, the college enjoys social prestige, then the applicant's social capital, her alumnae network, has metamorphosed into cultural capital as well as human capital. Should a graduate's occupational productivity, arty savoir-faire, or both awaken the interest and respect of others, who then join her social network, the graduate will have translated human capital or cultural capital into social capital that can, of course, later be reconverted into financial capital. When the Nobel Committee awarded the Nobel Prize in Economics to Gary S. Becker, Becker obtained the prize money as a return on his human capital. Additionally, thanks to the Nobel prize, a prestigious award, the economist's human capital became cultural capital on the strength of which the celebrated economist was offered higher pay, an additional financial reward.

Finally, consider how financial and physical capital can meta-morphose into social, human, and cultural capital. Affluent persons give swank parties that introduce them to an expanded social network, thus translating their financial capital into social capital. If they hire tutors or attend a respected college, affluent people can turn their financial capital into human capital and even into cultural capital. Owning a yacht or a lavish country estate, both forms of physical capital, affords the wealthy the capability of giving parties that will not only expand their social network, but also introduce them to cultured celebrities, includ-ing opera stars, painters, and poets, whose companionship enhances their cultural capital. By hanging out with opera stars, painters, and poets, millionaires may, if they choose, embellish their conversational repartee with marks of cultural distinction.

Social Capital's Relative Abundance

In general, the metamorphosis of any form of capital into any other form of capital requires a preliminary capital stock to initiate the pro-cess. Nothing comes of nothing so those who have nothing can get nothing more from it. They are stuck at the gate. In this maxim we encounter a socio-economic obstacle that limits access to capital trad-ing by poor people. If people have even modest capital of any form, they can, with skill and luck, parlay what they have into the other forms as well. Having education, one can get a high-paying job; having cul-tural capital, one can get into the country club, and the social contacts made there will enable one to get a good job, etc. In principle, any form of capital can become any other over the course of the life cycle. However, all metamorphoses are not equally easy.[11] Depending on cir-cumstances, which vary empirically, some metamorphoses will prove harder than others. For example, absent other resources, it is probably harder for adults past school age to turn financial capital into human capital than it is for them to turn human capital into financial capital. Both transformations are possible, but one trade is harder than the other. After all, the acquisition of human capital requires 12 to 20 years of education. Adults past the school-leaving age cannot afford the huge investment of time required to build human capital that will yield an adequate return.[12] It is easier and more lucrative for adults to translate their existing human capital, even when skimpy, into financial capital by getting a job. In other words, even though any transformation is theoretically possible at any time, what form or forms of capital a person initially has influences the likelihood of that person's successful obtaining others with it. All forms of capital are not equivalently valuable at every stage of the life cycle, nor do they equally well metamorphose into every other form.

Those unfortunates without any capital of any form cannot enter the trading system at all. They cannot obtain financial capital from social, or vice-versa, as they have nothing in their hand to initiate the process. To trade, one must initially have something to exchange. Suppose a person has no money, no alumnae connections, no high culture knowledge, and no high school diploma. How shall she obtain admission to a prestigious college? Capital indigents lack that minimal stake, which opens the trading system. They cannot enter the system. For this reason, capital's potentially profitable metamorphoses exclude the homeless, the indigent, the illiterate, the uncultivated, and the friendless from participation in the trading process. The homeless have no physical capital; the indigent have no financial capital; the illiterate no human capital; the uncultivated no cultural capital; and the friendless no social capital. Someone who is all of these has no capital to access the system.

Happily, four back doors mostly obviate this absolute exclusion from capital metamorphosis of even the most impoverished. The first is the minimal availability of capitals in human populations. Even in the poorest countries, hardly anyone has no capital of any kind. After all, what would it mean that a person or persons have no form of capital? A feral man, naked in the wilderness, like Tarzan of the Apes, has arguably no capital of any form: no money, no home, no friends, no education, and no language. If our sociology is correct, Tarzan of the Apes could not obtain a job, make friends, get into college, or even eat in a restaurant. However, aside from fiction, even the most destitute adults normally have some capital. For example, if they own their own clothing, homeless beggars have at least that physical capital. If, additionally, the beggars are literate, they have this human capital as well. Even the lowest derelict normally has some resource. Technically, this capital stake opens the metamorphic system to these beggars; how much that actually helps them is an empirical question.

The second back door is relative capital advantage. Even those who have very little capital of any kind are unlikely to have exactly the same negligible amount of all capitals. One form of capital will normally be somewhat more abundant than the others in their capital profile. Poor in every form of capital, illiterate beggar A is relatively more endowed with financial capital than his starving but literate neighbor, B. Even these most wretched individuals, who plumb the bottom of the

Table 2.2. Properties of Capital

	Popular Access	Taxable	Storable	Metamorphic
Financial	No	Yes	Yes	Yes
Physical	No	Yes	Yes	Yes
Human	No	No	Yes	Yes
Cultural	No	No	Yes	Yes
Social	Yes	No	Yes	Yes

class hierarchy, actually have slightly different profiles of capital deprivation. Moreover, each one has a relative advantage in some form of capital. Their strongest capital suit is their relative capital advantage. Relative advantage in some form of capital facilitates the process of bringing the less abundant forms of capital up to the level of the most abundant form. If literate beggar B can find employment reading to the blind, he need no longer beg. He has a job thanks to his human capital. If affluent beggar A can buy some pencils to sell on the corner, he can become a small business owner and ex-beggar.

The third back door is the ability of the impoverished person to trade on her relatively most abundant capital in order to bring the other forms of capital up to that level. If one has friends who will vote as directed, a form of social capital, one can become a ward heeler in a political machine, obtaining beer and holiday turkeys in compensation.

Individual and Collective Capital Advantage

Impoverished and downtrodden individuals can enjoy relative capital advantage, but so can impoverished and downtrodden collectivities. When comparing collectivities in respect to the amount and forms of capital they control, a researcher can in principle obtain their average scores on each. Thus, a researcher could compute for collectivity A, B, and C each one's average scores for financial, physical, human, cultural, and social capital. Even if the three collectivities were mightily deprived in all forms, it is unlikely that all would be equally deprived in each and every form of capital. A might have a higher average score in financial capital than do B and C; B might have a higher average score in physical capital than do A and C; and C might have a higher score in human capital than do A and B. Additionally, even if these collectivities were severely deprived in all forms of capital, it is unlikely than any one collectivity would be equally deprived in all forms of capital. Deprived and downtrodden collectivity B might have relatively more human capital than other forms of capital whereas A and C have relatively more social capital.

Addressing the probable social trajectories of these deprived and downtrodden collectivities, such as slums or immigrants, a researcher would expect their successful agency, if any, to develop around that capital form in which the slum dwellers were relatively least disadvantaged. If a slum's population is relatively well educated, then the slum's best chances would lie in the exploitation of their human capital to acquire more of the relatively less abundant forms of capital. If the slum has relatively high income, relative to other slums, then income would be its strong suit for metamorphoses that yield long-term increase in other, even less abundant forms of capital. Like individuals, collectivities may pursue transactional strategies that permit them to exchange what they have in greatest abundance for what they most grievously lack. The success of various strategies depends partially on exogenous factors that change the value of initial resources, but also on the initial capital profile, and relative capital advantage of each collectivity. For instance, if immigrants speak a foreign language whose financial and cultural value increases thanks to the improvement of their homeland's stature in the world system, then the exchange value of their cultural resource would increase, allowing the immigrants to obtain more financial, social, and cultural capital in exchange for their language skill.

The Unique Accessibility of Social Capital

The system of capital metamorphoses has a fourth extremely important back door. If we ask, in what capital resource are poor people, individually and collectively, most likely to have a relative advantage, we ask around what relative capital strength is their agency most likely to prove effective? This is not a formula for naive optimism as the severely deprived have little chance to affect anything by their own agency because, in point of fact, their most abundant capital resource is negligible. Nonetheless, the practical question is only around what resource is their agency most likely to materialize? The answer would be: their relative capital advantage offers the best chance for this deprived collectivity's members, individually and collectively, to escape poverty. Of course, any negligible capital resource of the poor may be relatively abundant. One can find numerous historical illustrations of poor people, individually and collectively, who have had unusual capital profiles. After the Russian Revolution, Russian aristocrats waited on tables in Paris. Their relative capital advantage was clearly cultural capital, not financial, and many Russian waiters married into bourgeois families eager to acquire a patina of aristocracy. But few poor communities have cultural capital as their relative capital advantage. In general, for reasons that are obvious, impoverished and downtrodden collectivities are most likely to enjoy a relative capital advantage in social capital even when they are desperately lack all forms of capital. They do not own property, they have no money, they are uneducated, and they lack high culture, but they do trust one another.

This access privileges social capital in this impoverished context. Except for social capital, all other forms of capital exclude the poor, illiterate, unpropertied, and downtrodden.[13] The rich have the most money, property, culture, and education. The poor and unpropertied do not have much of these.[14] In effect, the poor and downtrodden, whom Mohammed Yunus (1998) calls "the poorest of the poor," lack money, property, education, and high culture virtually by definition. Lacking all four, they lack the minimal stake that permits individuals or collectivities to enter the system of interdependent capitals, to make profits on capital's transmutations, and gradually, with luck, persistence, and shrewdness, to ascend the social hierarchy. Lacking system access, the truly indigent have no prospect for improving their lot insofar improvement depends upon an initial endowment of money, property, education, or high culture with which one acquires other values.

However, the poor do have social capital when they have working families and cohesive neighborhoods (Lin 2000:788). In fact, these are essential resources of poor people. "In poor areas, many people rely on their social and family ties for economic survival" (Portes and Landolt 1996:20). Poor people have additionally in many cases, the ability to create additional social capital by utilizing the social capital they already have because the more social capital is used, the more of it one has. The essential claim is not that the downtrodden poor have as much social capital as all others. That would be quite untrue. We have known for decades that social capital is inversely related to social-economic status. The more voluntary associations people report, the higher is their average socio-economic status. Attempting to measure social capital, Yanjie Bian (2001) reports that high-ranking Chinese executives had more than 200 visitors during China's Spring Festival whereas some manual workers had only two, a measure of their unequal social capital.

Nonetheless, compared to other, even less accessible forms of capital, social capital is relatively more accessible to the humblest (Nee and Sanders 2001:390). This possibility defines social capital's uniquely popular and democratic accessibility. A barrio resident who is penniless, without property, illiterate, and uncultivated need not also be a social isolate (Hernandez-Leon 2000:216). Cohesive communities have lower unemployment rates than less cohesive ones (Lichter and Oliver

2000:240). Poor but cohesive communities exist aplenty (Zhou and Bankston 1998). It is not necessary to claim that the impoverished have solidarity the wealthy lack, romantic clap-trap, in order to recognize that occasionally residents of poor but cohesive communities actually do have more social capital than the wealthy. Pennsylvania Amish people have 80 to 100 first cousins living within 15 miles, a social capital no wealthy community can match (Kraybill and Knolt 1995).

The rotating savings and credit association (ROSCA) illustrates the metamorphosis of social capital into financial capital. Even those too poor to obtain a bank account can operate a ROSCA and obtain the credit and savings facilities it provides if only they have the requisite social capital (Light and Gold 2000:220; Yoo 2000). Just as the ROSCA makes financial capital available to poor individuals, so ROSCAs make capital available to redlined and shunned communities, permitting them to promote more small business and more home ownership than would otherwise have been possible (Immergluck 1999). In this manner, ROSCAs enable poor individuals and poor communities to obtain resources otherwise unobtainable, possibly even to escape poverty in a generation or two (Light 1972). ROSCAs depend on social capital; ultimately, then, social capital offers poor communities the possibility for trading out of poverty in the long-term (Synghal 1994).

The Grameen Bank of Bangladesh provides a related but slightly different experience. A social movement that targets the poorest people in a poor country, the Grameen Bank improves the material lot of the poor, F2, by first enabling the poor to improve their human capital and their social capital (Yunus 1998). Just giving the poor money, F2, would not endow them with the human and social capital that must be owned for subsequent metamorphosis if sustained income acquisition and economic independence is the desired outcome. The poor are capable of acquiring social and human capital, and when they have done so, they have brought their resource stock up to a level that permits them to obtain increased income. The success of the Grameen Bank suggests that abolishing poverty requires upgrading the capital resources of the poor.

Conclusion

This essay has identified five forms of capital (financial, physical, human, cultural, social) that actors can transpose into one another and back again, often with advantage. Sometimes requiring generations to accomplish, these capital metamorphoses enable individual and collective social mobility, including mobility from poverty to low-income status. However, all capital metamorphoses require an initial capital stock to initiate the process. Lacking that initial capital stock, a collectivity or an individual lacks the wherewithal to enter the system, thence obtaining augmented and new resources from initially available resources. No capitals means no possibilities for agency; limited capitals means limited possibilities for agency. This qualification highlights the special problems of poverty.

That said, both individuals and collectivities usually have some amount, however negligible, of some form of capital. Moreover, one of these forms of capital is likely to be relatively more abundant than the others. The possibilities for agency of those most deprived of all forms of capital then revolve around that capital form in which they are relatively best endowed. This resource can be utilized to obtain other, initially less abundant resources, thus permitting the individual or collectivity, over time, to parlay what little it has of one capital resource into a greater abundance of many resources.

In general, severely deprived communities and individuals are better endowed in social capital than in other forms of capital. True, the deprived are poorly endowed even in social capital when compared to the privileged individuals and communities in their own society. However, social capital is a democratic resource that is likely to be the relatively most abundant form of capital that poor communities possess. Therefore, social capital usually powers the agency of the most deprived who, possessing this resource, can obtain on its account greater values of all the other capitals, thus improving their welfare.

Thus understood, social capital is a kind of philosopher's stone in that, costing no money and available even to the humble, it can metamorphose into rare and precious values.[15] The medieval alchemists sought to change lead into gold. They hoped to turn something valueless into something precious. They failed. It appears, however, that in social capital, the world has a capital resource that metamorphoses into money, property, education, and even into high culture. Social capital's uniquely democratic accessibility identifies it as the usual start-up motor of agency in the most necessitous communities.

Notes

1. Economists do not agree about this issue. Becker (1996) wants to add social capital to human capital; Bates (1998) wishes to recognize human capital but exclude social capital; Bowles (1999) argues that social capital is not capital. Knack and Kiefer (1997) use the concept of social capital to explain international differences in growth.

2.   "Expenditures on education, training, medical care, etc. are investments in capital." Becker (1993), 16.

3.   Becker (1993), 17.

4.   For a review of the career, publications, and ideas of Bourdieu, see Wacquant 1998.

5.   "An individual's potential stock of social capital consists of the collection and pattern of relationships in which she is involved and to which she has access, and further to the location and patterning of her associations in larger social space. That is, her potential social capital is both the contacts she herself holds and the way in which those contacts link her to other patterns of relations" (Sandefur and Lauman 1998:484).

6.   Hanifan (1920:78) is the first to have used the term "social capital" with approximately its current meaning. Nonetheless, Jacobs' work was unquestionably more influential than Hanifan's.

7.   For a review of social capital, see Portes 1998.

8.   If one does favors for others, in the expectation of later repayment, and then dies before the repayment is made, one's investment in the relationship has been in vain.

9.   Zhou and Bankston (1998) also develop this idea.

10.   Some of this evidence is reviewed in chapter 4 of Light and Gold (2000).

11.   Strictly speaking, any form of capital increases the odds of obtaining any other. There is always the risk of non-success. Exactly which risks are greatest is an interesting question that awaits research.

12.   Adults are limited by their expected length of life which may not even extend long enough to permit them to complete their education.

13.   "Differential access to social capital deserves much greater research attention. It is conceivable that social groups (gender, race) have different access to social capital because of their advantaged or disadvantaged structural positions and social networks" (Lin 1999:483).

14.   Public education lowers the cost of human capital to the student, making its acquisition more accessible to the poor. Nineteenth century reformers thought that public education would endow the poor with cost-free skills enabling them to escape poverty. Sometimes this strategy does work. However, it does not always work. Those for whom this strategy did not work become educated poor adults for whom social capital is the only resource they possess.

15.   Costing no money, social capital is not absolutely free. It takes effort and work to build and maintain social capital. The effort and work is the cost of having or maintaining social capital. Happily, anyone can perform the requisite work. The capital thus created can then metamorphose into money such that when the poor build social capital, they can obtain money returns on their effort.

References

Bates, Timothy. 1997. *Race, Self-Employment, and Upward Mobility.* Baltimore: Johns Hopkins University.

Becker, Gary S. 1993 [1964]. *Human Capital.* 3d ed. Chicago: University of Chicago.

Becker, Gary S. 1996. *Accounting for Tastes.* Cambridge: Harvard University.

Bian, Yanjie. 2001. "Family Social Capital in Urban China: A Network

Measurement." Paper presented at the University of California, Los Angeles, Mar. 15.

Bourdieu, Pierre. 1979. *La Distinction: Critique sociale du jugement.* Paris: Editions de Minuit.

Bourdieu, Pierre. 1986. "The Forms of Capital." In *Handbook of Theory and Research for the Sociology of Education,* ed. John G. Richardson, 241–251. New York: Greenwood Press.

Borocz, Jozsef, and Caleb Southworth. 1996. "Decomposing the Intellectuals' Class Power: Conversion of Cultural Capital to Income in Hungary, 1986." *Social Forces,* 74:797–821.

Bowles, Samuel. 1999. "Social Capital and Community Governance." *Focus,* 20:6–10.

Brubaker, Rogers. 1985. "Rethinking Classical Theory." *Theory and Society,* 14:745–775.

Coleman, James S. 1988. "Social Capital in the Creation of Human Capital." *The American Journal of Sociology,* 94:95–120.

Counts, Alex. 1996. *Give Us Credit.* New York: Random House.

Erickson, Bonnie H. 1996. "Culture, Class, and Connections." *American Journal of Sociology,* 102:217–251.

Farkas, George. 1996. *Human Capital or Cultural Capital?* Hawthorne, NY: Aldine de Gruyter.

Hanifan, L. J. 1920. *The Community Center.* Boston: Silver, Burdett and Company.

Hernandez-Leon, Reuben. 2000. "Urban Origin Migration from Mexico to the United States: The Case of the Monterrey Metropolitan Area." Ph.D. Dissertation. State University of New York, Binghamton Unversity.

Immergluck, Daniel. 1999. "Intrametropolitan Patterns of Small-Business Lending." *Journal of Urban Affairs,* 34:787–804.

Jacobs, Jane. 1961. *Death and Life of Great American Cities.* New York: Vintage.

Johannisson, Bengt. 2000. "A Tripolar Model of New-Venture Capitalising: Financial, Human and Social Capital." Paper presented at the 11th Nordic Conference on Small Business Research, Aarhus, Denmark, June 18.

Knack, Stephen, and Philip Keefer. 1997. "Does Social Capital Have an Economic Payoff? A Cross Country Investigation." *Quarterly Journal of Economics,* 112:1253–1287.

Kraybill, Donald B., and Steven M. Nolt. 1995. *Amish Enterprise.* Baltimore: Johns Hopkins University Press.

Lichter, Michael I., and Melvin L. Oliver. 2000. "Racial Differences in Labor Force Participation and Long-Term Joblessness Among Less-Educated Men." In *Prismatic Metropolis, Inequality in Los Angeles,* ed. Lawrence D. Bobo, Melvin L. Oliver, and James H. Johnson, 220–248. New York: Russell Sage Foundation.

Light, Ivan. 1972. *Ethnic Enterprise in America.* Los Angeles: University of California.

Light, Ivan, and Steven Gold. 2000. *Ethnic Economies.* San Diego: Academic Press.

Lin, Nan. 1999. "Social Networks and Status Attainment." *Annual Review of Sociology,* 25:467–487.

Lin, Nan. 2000. "Inequality in Social Capital." *Contemporary Sociology,* 29:785–795.

Massey, Douglas S. 1999. "Why Does Immigration Occur? A Theoretical Synthesis." In *The Handbook of International Migration,* ed. Charles

Hirschman, Philip Kasinitz, and Josh DeWind, 34–52. New York: Russell Sage Foundation.

Nee, Victor, and Jimy Sanders. 2001. Trust in Ethnic Ties: Social Capital and Immigrants." In *Trust in Society,* ed. Karen S. Cook, 374–392. New York: Russell Sage Foundation.

Portes, Alejandro. 1998. "Social Capital: Its Origins and Applications in Contemporary Sociology." *Annual Review of Sociology,* 24:1–24.

Portes, Alejandro, and Patricia Landolt. 1996. "The Downside of Social Capitalism." *American Prospect,* 26. May–June:18–21.

Sandefur, Rebecca L. and Edward O. Laumann. 1998. "A Paradigm for Social Capital." *Rationality and Society,* 10:481–501.

Synghal, Sudarshan. 1994. "How in the World Can We Lend to the Poor? A Case Study of Group Lending among the Urban Poor in the U.S." Ph.D. dissertation, Boston University

Wacquant, Loic. 1998. "Pierre Bourdieu." In *Key Sociological Thinkers,* ed. R. Stone, 1–24. New York: Macmillan.

Woolcock, Michael. 1998. "Social Capital and Economic Development: Toward a Theoretical Synthesis and Policy Framework." *Theory and Society,* 27:151–208.

Yoo, Jin-Kyung. 2000. Utilization of Social Networks for Immigrant Entrepreneurship: A Case Study of Korean Immigrants in the Atlanta Area. *International Review of Sociology,* 10:347–363.

Yunus, Muhammed, with Alan Jolis. 1998. *Banker to the Poor.* London: Aurum Press.

Zhou, Min, and Carl L. Bankston. 1998. *Growing Up American: How Vietnamese Children Adapt to Life in the United States.* New York: Russell Sage.

3 The Failure of Funding Social Capital

An Evaluation of Microfinance Funding in the United States, 1996-1999

Gina Neff

Introduction

Microcredit and microenterprise emerged as ways to distribute loans and banking services to those not traditionally serviced by mainstream financial institutions. Typically, these include programs serving the very small businesses that mainstream financial institutions overlook. One of the oldest and most visible of these programs is the Grameen Bank in Bangladesh, founded by Muhammad Yunus (Yunus 1999). Grameen lends money secured by a form of social collateral to a clientele largely comprised of poor women. Instead of traditional collateral, these "microloans" are secured by the honor and credit lines of a peer group so that if one woman defaults no one else in her lending group will receive another loan. Grameen's success has led to replication around the world, including programs in the United States.

American policymakers from across the political spectrum have taken an interest in microcredit. In an era of a return to personal responsibility, micorcredit represents the ultimate in market solutions to poverty. The can-do enthusiasm of targeting the poor meshes nicely with the shredding of the safety net, and, indeed provisions for supporting microcredit programs for former welfare recipients were included in the Personal Responsibilty Act of 1996. But microcredit's effectiveness as an anti-poverty strategy in the United States is beginning to be challenged. Bhatt, Painter and Tang (1999) quoted a survey of 341 microenterprise programs in the United States in which only 29 percent listed "poverty alleviation/individual income increase" as their first priority, while 44 percent of programs ranked "job creation/business development" first. In their own survey of Southern Californian programs, they note operational inefficiency, cost ineffectiveness, and lack of breadth as problems currently facing microcredit funders. And in contrast to programs in developing countries, U.S. programs have a higher overhead and higher default rate than their overseas counterparts. One of the pioneering programs in their survey, the Women's Development Association, reported average costs per loan of nearly $8,500 more than the average loan size (1999:19), and one of the oldest microloan demonstration projects lost nearly 60 percent of its loans for the 1988–1995 period (1999:20).

Lisa Servon (1999) studied four programs in the United States. She noted that "access to credit and training are two of the ingredients most lacking in U.S. areas with persistently high poverty levels" (1999:3). But in addition to countering these problems, Servon added, microcredit also helps communities to form social capital:

> [A]lthough the programs do not exhibit outstanding numbers in terms of traditional economic development indicators—jobs created, income generated, and so on—they have the potential to produce strong second- and third-order outcomes. These include the formation of social and human capital, the spread of economic literacy, and the transformation of disenfranchised people into economic actors. Blurring the boundaries allows investment in social capital to help people become self-sufficient in the long run rather maintain them in the short run. (1999:76)

Servon concludes that, "Microenterprise programs build on the reality of current economic conditions. They target disenfranchised groups and strengthen the attachment of their clients to the economy" (1999:127). These second-order effects are among the reasons microcredit programs have been funded as part of foundations' initiatives in poverty alleviation programs and community development.

Social Capital

It is through increasing social capital that microcredit programs transform borrowers into economic actors with increased attachment to the economy. There are two problems, however, with the assumption that microcredit builds social capital. First, there is some question of what is meant by the term social capital, and this bears on how microcredit programs can be evaluated. Specifically, sociologists and political scientists have defined social capital in different ways, both as an asset for individuals to use and as a public good. Below a few of these theories are compared. Second, there is the question of whether individual-level loans can increase a collective good, namely social capital. While I do not intend to address empirically the second question, I hope to raise some questions about the priorities of U.S. foundations for funding those programs that emphasize social capital formation.

Among theorists there is some controversy about whether social capital is a collective or an individual asset. Perhaps one of the most widely cited definitions of the term is Robert Putnam's: "'Social capital' refers to the features of social organizations such as networks, norms, and social trust that facilitate coordination and cooperation for mutual benefit"(1995:67). Putnam's research in Italy and the United States focused on the effectiveness of government and the relationship to civic engagement. Networks of "organized reciprocity and civic solidarity" are a precondition for socioeconomic modernization (1995:66). "Civic norms and networks are not simply froth on the ways of economic progress" (Putnam 1993:162)—they form the very basis for economic programs. Cooperation learned in dense networks of civic engagement in communities is translatable into political and economic development.

James Coleman also thought of social capital as an asset that a group can utilize (1988). Coleman's example of trust among diamond merchants illustrates how close, dense networks of ties can be used by a group for market efficiency and education gains for the group. What connects these two theories is that, while there are still individual benefits for those in groups with social capital, social capital itself is accrued by groups and held by groups. Association is an active phenomenon that benefits a group.

Still others have less focus on the associative aspects of social capital. For many in economic sociology, social capital is an asset that individuals use within a group for individual gain. Nan Lin, a social network theorist, considers "social capital as assets in networks" (1999:5). Social capital is "investment in social relations with expected returns," and although Lin states those profits can be accrued for "the group or for the individuals" (1995:5), it is clear that his perspective is more individually oriented than, say, Putnam's. For network theorists, the theoretical inquiry into social capital involve not evaluating the effectiveness of the collective action, but on the structure of the community. Ron Burt, for example, examined the structural holes that provide opportunities for power brokers to connect isolated groups of people and argues that social capital is contingent upon position within a network (1997). Neither of these approaches emphasize civic engagement like Putnam and Coleman do.

There is also literature in economic sociology on the connection between community and market. In "Markets as Politics," Neil Fligstein uses political metaphors to examine the creation and maintenance of markets and concludes that "networks are at the core of markets to the degree that they reflect social relations between actors" (1996:657). Like Putnam, Fligstein argues that conditions for market stability are built through non-market processes, although he likens these to state-building: "Capitalist firms could not operate without collective sets of rules governing interaction." The institutions of shared rules "held in place by custom, explicit . . . or tacit agreement" support market interactions (Fligstein 1996:658). Avner Greif also examined how *community* supports *market*. In his examination of the transition from a community responsibility system to individual legal responsibility among late medieval traders Greif challenged the notion that communities are those in which exchange is governed by impersonal, repeated relationships and markets are those relationship governed by the legal system (1999). The existing communities of traders and the social structure determined the scope of the impersonal market. Intra- community relationships secured intercommunity trading. Gittell and Thompson (1999) also focus on the relationship between market and community in their study of New York's Neighborhood Entrepreneur Program. Using Granovetter's notion of "weak ties" and Burt's idea of "structural holes," Gittell and Thompson find that while inner-city businesses often have an advantage in terms of social networks, many communities lack "bridging capital," the capital ties outside the community, which are important to the expansion of inner-city enterprise (1999).

Community Capital

Part of the problem of evaluating microcredit programs in the United States is the conflation of the goals of building social capital, of providing for social welfare and of developing business and job opportunities. Microcredit programs abroad often ask borrowers to use their preexisting social capital to enforce loan repayment, capitalizing community ties. When targeting poor populations, microcredit is a poverty alleviation strategy; in inner-cities it becomes an inner-city business development strategy; in rural Bangladesh, an international development model. On the one hand, microcredit programs have encouraged social capital formation in poor communities and among non-poor entrepreneurs. On

the other, though, microcredit programs encourage a pro-market definition of the problems of poor, would- be entrepreneurs, and by extension,
of poverty alleviation. On a larger scale, microcredit represents the notion
that full economic participation is equal to ownership and much of the
rhetoric of empowerment surrounding such programs in the U.S. and
abroad make this connection. Rather than challenge the notions of alienation from mainstream economic life, microcredit seeks to resolve that
alienation by bringing small and often informal businesses into the mainstream, formal economy. Consistent with Ulrich Beck's (1992) theory of
the increasing perception of risk as an individual, as opposed to a social
phenomenon, microcredit challenges economic disenfranchisement
through a process of "individualization." The alleviation of poverty
through microcredit programs relies on the concept of poverty as a lack
of access to other opportunity; the programs are designed to rectify the
lack of access to the opportunity to borrow start-up capital. In this policy construction, poverty is no longer seen as a process of social, group,
or class forces. Rather, problems of imperfect information, bottlenecks in
the credit process, and barriers to the mainstream economy are all solv-
able within this economic development framework.

In addition to linking poverty alleviation with market forces, the
microcredit phenomenon links risk and poverty. If the way out of
poverty is self-employment, what does this say about the root causes of
poverty? One reason for the attention paid to microcredit by policymakers and the media is that it fits nicely with prevailing American prej-
udices toward local, rather than national, programs and individual,
rather than collective, approaches. Even in the beneficial secondary
effects of building social capital through these programs, market
approaches are frequently emphasized over civil and social concerns. No
longer concerned with associative democracy as Putnam (2000) outlined, this form of social capital is banked in the self-interest of market-
oriented, calculating individuals. Providing assets for individuals is seen
as a mechanism for creating a collective good.

Foundation Capital

Although many microcredit organizations obtain funding from governmental and private sources, foundation funding is a vital part of their
budgets. In their study of Southern Californian microenterprise programs, Bhatt et al. found that approximately 36 percent of the funding
for those organizations was obtained through private donors and foundations (1999:8). Despite its prominence, foundation funding is often

treated as neutral, and foundations are argued to "provide an independent, countervailing force to big business and government, [serving] as a channel of access for citizens/consumers which is more open and participatory" (Arnove 1980:17). Through a network examination of board of directors memberships, grants, and membership in other clubs among foundations and their recipient organizations, Colwell found an "interconnected foundation club not immediately visible to the outside observer among foundations involved in public policy grants" which is "heavily connected with the major policy organizations" (1980:430). Examining foundation involvement in policy is necessary for understanding "the exercise of power and the process of decision-making in public policy" (Colwell 1980:434).

American philanthropic foundations have long been interested in community-based finance as a mechanism for community development. The Ford Foundation provided funding that was "vital to the lift-off" of Community Development Corporations and funded the most visible of the first generation of CDCs, such as the Bedford-Stuyvesant Restoration Corporation, The Woodlawn Organization, Watts Labor Community Action Committee, and Rev. Leon Sullivan's Zion Baptist Church CDC (Peirce and Steinbach 1987). In 1983, the Ford Foundation formed the Community Development Partnership Strategy to pool the resources of private sector, foundations and government agencies. Ford has invested $30 million to created 20 public-private partnerships that assist 150 CDCs (Ford 1998).

Ford has also been instrumental in funding for microcredit programs. Muhammad Yunus began the Grameen Bank in 1977 with support from the Ford Foundation, and in 1981 the Grameen Bank was able to expand their reach to 100 branches with the help of a Ford Foundation Program-Related Investment: Ford provided $770,000 in loan guarantees which enabled Grameen to expand through the commercial bank system in Bangladesh. This loan allowed Grameen to become an autonomous financial institution in 1983 (Ford 1991). As we will see below, Ford is still the largest funder of microcredit programs in the United States, both in terms of the amount of money granted and the number of grants made.

Data Analysis

To examine funding for microcredit programs I examined funding for members of the Association for Enterprise Opportunity (AEO), the main trade organization for microcredit and community-based lending orga-

Table 3.1: Total Amounts Granted and Received, 1996–1999

Number of AEO members getting grants 1996–1999	168
Number of foundations granting to AEO members	235
Number of grants made	1,009
Average grant size	$107,936
Median grant size	$35,000
Average total amount granted per foundation	$463,434
Median total amount granted per foundation	$73,000
Average total amount received per organization	$648,256
Median total amount received per organization	$200,000
Number of organizations receiving only 1 grant	47
Average amount to organizations receiving only 1 grant	$68,120
Average amount to organizations receiving more than 1 grant	$879,328

nizations, using the AEO's Directory of Microenterprise Development Programs. I then obtained information on grants to these organizations from the Foundation Center database of tax-return information for non-profit organizations. This resulted in information on 1,009 grants made to 168 AEO member organizations from 1996 to 1999 by 235 American foundations.[1] This does not cover all microenterprise programs in the United States as there are several that are not AEO members; nor does it exhaust American foundations' funding for microcredit, as smaller foundations are not included in the Foundation Center database. Nor are international grants included. Grants to Grameen Bank, for example, are not included in the sample, although grants to its newly formed U.S.-based Grameen Foundation USA are. Local and state government agencies are listed among AEO's microcredit development programs, but not eligible for foundation funding and thus not included in the sample. Organizations listed in the directory but for which no grants were listed in the Foundation Center Directory were also excluded. In the resulting sample, foundations and AEO member organizations were ranked by the total amounts granted and received, respectively, over the three-year sample period. This data is presented in Table 3.1.

Of AEO member organizations receiving funding, 121 organizations received more than one grant, and among the 235 foundations in the sample 190 made more than one grant over the period sampled. The average grant size was just over $100,000, while half of the grants made were $35,000 or below. The median contribution that a foundation granted to AEO members was $73,000, and the median total amount that the organizations received from all foundations was $200,000.

Before any network analysis was done, organizations and foundations were ranked by grant size. This data is presented in Table 3.2

Table 3.2. Top Fifteen Foundations by Total Grants Made

Foundation	Total Granted	Number of Top 30 Organizations Receiving Grants	Number of Grants to the Top 30 Organizations	Total Number of Grants to AEO Members
Ford Foundation	$27,703,500	17	54	66
Charles Stewart Mott Foundation	$14,640,664	14	39	61
W. K. Kellogg Foundation	$8,065,262	12	19	21
Pew Charitable Trusts	$4,447,500	2	9	13
McKnight Foundation	$2,829,000	2	2	12
Citigroup Foundation	$2,634,000	9	22	47
Surdna Foundation	$2,210,000	7	9	19
William Penn Foundation	$2,113,950	1	9	13
Northwest Area Foundation	$2,060,520	3	5	7
John D. and Catherine T. MacArthur Foundation	$1,824,250	3	5	9
San Francisco Foundation	$1,532,000	3	6	13
F.B. Heron Foundation	$1,500,000	9	20	29
U S WEST Foundation	$1,440,000	4	5	8
Annie E. Casey Foundation	$1,361,949	3	8	11
Doris Duke Charitable Foundation	$1,300,000	1	1	1

and Table 3.3. Not terribly surprising, the 15 foundations that granted the most to AEO members are represented among the funders of the top 15 grant recipients. Only four of top funders made fewer than half of their grants to organizations not among the top 30 recipients, pointing to a concentration on these organizations by the philanthropic lead-

Table 3.3: Top Fifteen Organizations by Total Funding Amount

Organization	Total Amount
First Nations Development Institute	$7,739,061
Delaware Valley Community Reinvestment Fund	$7,101,450
Self Employment Loan Fund	$7,055,000
Corporation for Enterprise Development (CFED)	$6,729,688
Aspen Institute	$4,509,822
Center for Rural Affairs	$4,112,251
Community Reinvestment Fund of Minnesota	$4,052,010
Shorebank Enterprise Group Pacific	$3,638,000
Coastal Enterprises	$2,894,000
National Foundation for Teaching Entrepreneurship to Disadvantaged and Handicapped Youth	$2,597,180
ACCION International	$2,591,300
Northern Economic Initiatives Corporation	$2,214,000
Women's Housing and Economic Development Corporation	$2,117,500
Self-Help Ventures Fund	$2,000,000
National Community Capital Association	$1,750,000

ers. The Ford Foundation alone made 9 of the 30 largest grants, and made 82 percent of their grants to the 30 largest organizations. The Kellogg Foundation made 90 percent of their grants to these largest organizations.

Using network analysis, indirect links between organizations and funders can be observed. Certainly as the largest funders in this field, Ford, Mott, and Kellogg are important, but how their grants relate to one another as well as to those to the other funders is less obvious. I created a sub-sample of all the grants made to the top 15 microcredit organizations. One hundred seventeen foundations made over $64 million in grants to these organizations. Using UCINET IV, a social network analysis package (Borgatti, et al. 1991) and Krackplot, a social networks visualization package (Krackhardt, et al. 1994), I created a map of these organizations and the foundations from which they receive funding.

This allowed for examining the centrality of both organizations and foundations and controlled for grants that may be split over multiple years and large one-time infusions of capital. In Table 3.4 the centrality scores for microfinance organizations are presented. This table clearly illustrates that many of these institutions receive very large capital

Table 3.4. Centrality Scores for Microfinance Organizations

	Out Degree	Normal Out Deg
First	22.000	18.966
Del	15.000	12.931
SELP	3.000	2.586
CFED	17.000	14.655
Aspen	5.000	4.310
CRA	10.000	8.621
CRFM	5.000	4.310
Shorebank	4.000	3.448
Costal	6.000	5.172
NFTEDHY	32.000	27.586
Accionall	24.000	20.690
NEIC	4.000	3.448
WHEDC	18.000	15.517
Selfhelp	2.000	1.724
NCCA	5.000	4.310

infusions and they do not skew the centrality scores. What the centrality scores indicate are merely the number of ties to foundations in the first column and those ties normalized by the mean of the total network in the second. For example, NFTEDHY, the National Foundation for Teaching Entrepreneurship to Disadvantaged and Handicapped Youth, has received grants from 32 foundations, Accion has received grants from 24 foundations and First, or the First Nations Development Institute received grants from 22 foundations. Just by counting the number of organizations to which these foundations are tied, we could conclude that these are the most central microcredit institutions.

However, looking at how the foundations grant in tandem to the same organizations demonstrates another way these groups might be tied. Using k-plexes, one can examine groups in which every member is tied to all others, except for k number of ties. For example if four organizations are in a 2-plex, then each organization is tied to 2 others (Wasserman and Faust 1994:266). For these data, there are 187 2-plexes of size four. This measure is useful for these data since the organizations themselves have no direct ties of funding to other microenterprise programs. Examples can be seen in Table 3.6 and Table 3.7: For example the group "First," or the First Nations Development Institute, is in several 2-plexes with "NFTEDHY," or the National Foundation for Teaching

Table 3.5. Clusters of Foundations and Organizations

	Ford	Mott	Surdna	Morgan	Heron
Accion	$700,000	$465,000	0	$90,000	0
WHEDC	0	$50,000	$200,000	$40,000	0
CFED	$1,620,000	$1,666,000	$15,000	0	$225,000
NFTEDHY	0	0	0	$15,000	0
First	$2,610,000	$1,000,000	$50,000	0	$200,000

Entrepreneurship to Disadvantaged and Handicapped Youth. In fact, First and NFTEDHY share several foundations in common: Dreyfus, FannieMae, Kellogg, and "SF" or the San Francisco Foundation. These are easily identified by using 2-plexes. But it is another pair of organizations that emerge as more connected when mapped this way. Both First and NFTEDHY have high centrality scores but their funders contain several *isolates,* or foundations that only fund them. Accion and WHEDC, or the Women's Housing and Economic Development Corporation, emerge high when the *k*-plexes are hierarchically clustered. Ford and Mott are the highest clustered foundations, pointing to the fact that they often fund the same organizations. Morgan, Heron and Surdna join Ford and Mott at the second clustering along with the organizations CFED, or the Corporation for Enterprise Development, NFTEDHY and First as the ten most "inter-connected" organizations.

From the data in Table 3.6 we can see that Accion shares many of the same funders as WHEDC, CFED and NFTEDHY, while First shares many of the same as CFED and NFTEDHY. NFTEDHY and First now seem less well connected compared to the rest of these groups, although their centrality scores—the number of total grants made—are

Table 3.6. Number of Shared Membership in 4 Group, 2–Plexes of Organizations

	Accion	WHEDC	CFED	NFTEDHY	First
Accion	—	28	10	15	1
WHEDC	28	—	3	3	1
CFED	10	3	—	6	21
NFTEDHY	15	3	6	—	6
First	1	1	21	6	—

Table 3.7. Number of Shared Membership in 4 Group, 2–Plexes of Organizations

	Ford	Mott	Surdna	Morgan	Heron
Ford	—	5	10	1	10
Mott	15	—	3	1	3
Surdna	10	3	—	1	6
Morgan	1	1	1	—	0
Heron	10	3	6	0	—

high. This is because foundations that fund NFTEDHY do not tend to fund other microenterprise groups.

Similarly, Ford, Mott, and Heron made several grants to the same organizations. Again, the number of 2-plexes is related, but not the same as the number of similar grants. These relationships can perhaps be best understood with a more in-depth examination of the social network of foundations and organizations. For instance, such an analysis reveals that Accion and WHEDC were both funded by the American Express Foundation, the J.P. Morgan Foundation, the New York Community Foundation, the Clark Foundation, the Ferris Booth Foundation, Deutsche Bank Foundation, the Merck Foundations, and the Charles Stewart Mott Foundation.

What is also clear from a more in-depth examination of the social network of foundations and organizations is that the First Nations Development Institute and NFTEDHY obtain most of their grants from foundations that do not fund other microcredit organizations. They could be identified as "power brokers" in Burt's sense by serving as a bridge for these foundations, but also as being able to garner resources from outside of the mainstream of microcredit funding.

This poses an interesting question: both First Nations and NFTEDHY are national policy and clearinghouse organizations for smaller groups that serve primarily poor and disadvantaged populations, and they are outside of the mainstream of the funding priorities. The largest grants, too, point to mainstream CDC, Reinvestment Funds, and policy organizations. Few grassroots groups are among these.

Conclusion

It should not be surprising that the major organizations receiving microcredit funding are not community-based, local groups, but national and international policy groups, nor that there is a cohesion among the major donors on what kinds of projects to fund.

While the rhetoric of empowerment of microcredit points to economic democracy and the link to ownership of assets, the association of these organizations points to a different kind of structure: one in which there is little diversity in ties between the large funders and large organizations. This may seem counterintuitive, but the concentration of major funding to a handful of organizations demonstrates a concentration of power among a few voices in the community capital movement.

The larger question remains: What does it mean that participation in the economy has been linked to ownership, and that entrepreneurial activity is linked to participatory democracy? Given that there are many strategies for economic development and many different problems facing poor communities, there is a tension over models for development. While microenterprise may offer the poor more autonomy, it does so at the cost of an increased burden of risk. Obviously, collective association through individual-level loans cannot create the same kinds of positive social capital benefits as does voluntary association. Microcredit programs may be effective in linking businesses, and while that certainly can help solve problems of inefficiency within market relations, it may not necessarily lead to civic- or community-mindedness among the individuals borrowing. The benefits of microcredit strategy need to be reexamined in the light of the issues of power at stake.

Notes

1. There were only 26 grants listed for 1999. These were included in the analysis, even though 1999 information was not available for most organizations. Also, where applicable, only grants for microcredit programs were counted for larger organizations, such as university centers or the Ms. Foundation for Women which obviously receive funding for other projects as well. Where these grants were not discernable they were omitted from the sample.

References

Arnove, Robert F., ed. 1980. *Philanthropy and Cultural Imperialism.* Boston: G. K. Hall.

Bates, Timothy. 1989. "Small Business Viability in the Urban Ghetto." *Journal of Regional Science,* 29.4:625–643.

Beck, Ulrich. 1992. *Risk Society: Towards a New Modernity.* London: Sage.

Bhatt, Nitin, Gary Painter, and Shui-Yan Tang. 1999. "Microcredit Programs in the United States: The Challenges of Outreach and Sustainability." Presented at the Twenty-first Annual Conference on Public Policy Analysis and Management in Washington, DC, November 4–6.

Borgatti, Stephen P., Martin G. Everett, and Linton C. Freeman. 1991. *UCINET,* Version 4, Columbia, SC: Analytic Technology.

Bowles, Samuel. 1999. "Social Capital and Community Governance." *Focus* (University of Wisconsin–Madison, Institute for Research on Poverty), 20.3:6–10.

Burt, Ronald. 1997. "The Contingent Value of Social Capital." *Administrative Science Quarterly,* 42 (June):339–365.

Colewell, Mary Anna Culleton. 1980. "The Foundation Connection: Links among Foundations and Recipient Organizations." In *Philanthropy and Cultural Imperialism,* ed. Robert F. Arnove. Boston: G. K. Hall.

Coleman, James S. 1988. "Social Capital in the Creation of Human Capital." *American Journal of Sociology,* 94.S:95–S120.

Durlauf, Steven N. 1999. "The Case 'Against' Social Capital." *Focus* (University of Wisconsin–Madison, Institute for Research on Poverty), 20.3:1–5.

Fligstein, Neil. 1996. "Markets as Politics: A Political-Cultural Approach to Market Institutions." *American Sociological Review,* 61.3:656–673.

Ford Foundation. 1998. *Seizing Opportunities: The Role of CDCs in Urban Economic Development.* New York: Ford Foundation. (April).

Ford Foundation. 1991. *Investing for Social Gain: Reflections on two decades of Program-Related Investments.* New York: Ford Foundation.

Gittell, Ross, and Phillip J. Thompson. 1999. "Inner-City Business Development and Entrepreneurship: New Frontiers for Policy and Research." In *Urban Problems and Community Development,* ed. Ronald F. Ferguson and William T. Dickens. Washington: Brookings Institution Press.

Granovetter, Mark S. 1973. "The Strength of Weak Ties." *American Journal of Sociology* 78.6:1360–80.

Greif, Avener. 1999. "Impersonal Exchange and the Origins of the Market: From the Community Responsibility System to Individual Legal Responsibility." Unpublished m.s.

Indergaard, Michael 1997. "Community-based Restructuring? Institution Building in the Industrial Midwest." *Urban Affairs Review,* 32:5:662–682.

Krackhardt, David, Jim Blythe, and Cathleen McGrath. 1994. "Krackplot 3.0: An Improved Network Drawing Program." *Connections,* 17.2:53–55.

Lin, Nan. 1999. "Building a Network Theory of Social Capital." Delivered at the 1999 Sunbelt Social Networks Conference.

Pierce, Neal R., and Carol F. Steinbach. 1987. *Corrective Capitalism: The Rise of Community Development Corporations—A Report to the Ford Foundation.* New York: Ford Foundation.

Portes, Alejandro. 1998. "Social Capital: Its Origins and Applications in Modern Sociology." *Annual Review of Sociology,* 24:1–24.

Putnam, Robert D. 1993. *Making Democracy Work.* Princeton, NJ: Princeton University Press.

Putnam, Robert D. 1995. "Bowling Alone: America's Declining Social Capital." *Journal of Democracy,* 6:65–78.

Putnam, Robert D. 2000. *Bowling Alone.* New York: Simon and Schuster.

Servon, Lisa J. 1999. *Bootstrap Capital: Microenterprises and the American Poor* Washington: Brookings.

Servon, Lisa J. 1999b. "The Intersection of Social Capital and Identity: Thoughts on Closure, Participation, and Access to Resources." Presented at The Conference on Civic Participation and Civil Society, Bellagio, Italy, April 6–10.

Servon, Lisa J., and Timothy Bates. 1998. "Microenterprise as an Exit Route From Poverty: Recommendations for Programs and Policy Makers." *Journal of Urban Affairs,* 20.4:419–441.

Wasserman, Stanley, and Katherine Faust. 1994. *Social Network Analysis: Methods and Applications.* Cambridge: Cambridge University Press.

2

Structural Barriers and the Context of Building Social Capital

The Mystery of the Missing Social Capital and the Ghost of Social Structure

Why Community Development Can't Win

Randy Stoecker

Introduction

Those of you familiar with the original Scooby-Doo cartoon series know how this troupe of teens and their nearly talking dog fall into mystery after mystery, all seemingly involving the supernatural. But in each episode we also find out that behind each apparent supernatural apparition lurks a flesh-and-blood villain.

So it is with "social capital." If Scooby-Doo and friends happened upon one of the country's downtrodden neighborhoods today, the mystery they would confront is why the parks are not filled with laughing children, why the commercial strips are vacant, why the housing is falling, down, why only the drug dealers are hanging out on the sidewalks and porches.

Now, if they listened to the adults, rather than following their instincts, they would be told to start investigating the missing social capital. They would be told the problem is the lack of social networks, the lack of neighborliness, the lack of "community."

Fortunately, our young friends and their nosy dog are smarter than the average adult and far smarter than the average academic at

An earlier version of this paper was prepared for the American Sociological Association Annual Meetings, 2001. It is part of a larger project studying the relationship between community organizing and community development, supported by a grant from the University of Toledo Urban Affairs Center.

sniffing out the mystery behind the mystery. And eventually they would notice the apparent apparitions lurking in the shadows—the ghost we call social structure. If it is a typical happy-ending Scooby-Doo episode, eventually the teens will unmask the real villain behind the ghost of social structure. And it ain't the people in the neighborhood.

This paper explores the problematic concept of "social capital," particularly as it is used in relation to community-based development, to expose the ghost of social structure and the villains behind it.

Social Capital

The concept of social capital is one of those academic ideas that has been de-theorized and morphed to the point where conservatives use it as much as liberals. So popular has the concept become that even the World Bank decided to sponsor a social capital initiative (Munro n.d.). The hair-splitting over its definition has been intense (Requier-Desjardins 1999). As it is used in the U.S. today, in contrast to the more theoretical European formulation (DeFilippis 2001), the term describes social networks that build trust among people, thus supposedly enhancing the productivity and quality of life of the people involved in those social networks (Siriani and Friedland 2001). In addition, the concept is often defined as the social norms and rules that make cooperation possible (Requier-Desjardins 1999.)

But why come up with yet another fancy new academic term, when it seems "social networks" would do? Well, the argument is that the social networks are "capital" in the sense that they enhance productivity. But attempts to actually make the metaphor hold are weak at best and misinformed at worst. The first problem is defining what "capital" means in this context. Siriani and Friedland (2001) say, for example, "two farmers exchanging tools can get more work done with less physical capital." Yes, but if neither of them had any tools their relationship would be pretty useless from a productivity standpoint (Portes and Landolt 1996). So, social capital in and of itself may have no relationship whatsoever to physical capital.

Trying to finesse a distinction between social capital and other forms of capital, the Michigan State University Social Capital Interest Group (n.d.) says:

> An important feature of social capital, compared with other forms of capital, is that it is social in origin. Financial capital originates in financial markets. Human capital originates in educational training settings in which human skills and talents are taught and learned. Physical capital

originates in the employment of physical goods crafted to produce services. Social capital originates from social relations.

The problem here is that all forms of capital are social. All forms of capital are established in exchange relationships which, by their very nature, are social relationships. Now, those other forms of capital may not be based in trust relationships. Indeed, the fact that we need to build massive government bureaucracies to address the disputes that arise from those relationships attests to the lack of trust.

This issue of trust seems to be the main thing distinguishing social capital and the other forms of capital. Robert Putnam (1993), one of the favored proponents of the concept of social capital, remains caught in the metaphor: "A society that relies on generalized reciprocity is more efficient than a distrustful society, for the same reason that money is more efficient than barter. Trust lubricates social life." Essentially, Putnam is arguing at first that non-monetary relationships are more efficient, while then arguing the opposite. It ends up sounding like monetary relationships are just like non-monetary relationships.

The difficulties these authors exhibit trying to deal with this convoluted concept can be understood by going back to the roots of the idea. Looking at Bourdieu's (1985) work on the concept of cultural capital, we can begin to understand what is going on. Interpreting Bourdieu is risky at best. But we can safely say that he was attempting to move beyond a strict structural Marxism, and thus was trying to go beyond the notion that all relationships are rooted in structural, physical, capital. And perhaps that's where the difficulty started.

To really make something useful of the convoluted mess of this concept requires going back to Marx himself. For Marx, capital was created as part of an exchange relationship and, for all practical purposes, an antagonistic relationship. Capital, then, has "exchange" value. By its very nature as exchange value, it undermines rather than supports the development of community. In this context, then, the popularized used of "social capital" is an inherent contradiction. In fact, perhaps the clearest examples we can imagine of social capital are those traditional or indigenous communities forced to sell their community on the tourism market, or those small communities forced to market their "community feeling" in hopes of bringing in new taxpaying residents and industry. And, of course when the tourists flock in, or the middle-class migrants flock in, they disrupt the social capital that had value to begin with.

This undermining of community by selling it is the quintessential example of the contradiction between use value and exchange value that Marx described. Use values, in contrast to exchange values, are created for one's own use. It is the garden you plant yourself, the clothes you sew yourself, the art you create for your own enjoyment. At the community level (though Marx did not develop this), it is the community garden, the community park, the community concert, and the other community amenities residents create for their own use, rather than for exchange in a market context. But as soon as these things begin to be "commodified"—sold as exchange in the capitalist market—they become subject to the controls of the market rather than the controls of the community. And the community relationships that maintained them as use value are no longer as important as the external relationships that can keep them profitable as exchange values.

Social capital, then, is an internally contradictory concept that conflates the distinction between use value and exchange value. As an explanatory model, it is worthless. However, it is fascinating to consider its influence as a cultural idea that has had considerable policy impact.

The Mystery of the Missing Social Capital

Now back to our mystery. The mystery most of you by now know— Robert Putnam's (2000) famous "bowling alone" thesis—has asserted that much of the social capital we used to have is now missing. This should have left us all wondering where the social capital has gone. But what is it that Putnam and others think is missing—is it the social part (the use value), or the capital part (the exchange value)?

It is pretty clear that the mystery of the missing social capital focuses on the social part. Putnam's (2000) evidence emphasizes the decline of involvement in voluntary associations, which he uses as indicators of a decline in "community."

As Putnam came out with this decline-of-community thesis, the community development corporation model of urban redevelopment was also gaining ascendancy. Particularly influential has been Kretzman and McKnight's (1993) asset-based community development (ABCD) model. The ABCD model is particularly important because it illustrates the conflation of exchange values and use values in the social capital concept. Community development is ultimately about enhancing exchange values—raising housing values, bringing businesses back, creating employable residents, and so on. But in the ABCD model, the strategy for enhancing exchange values is by developing a community's assets, which requires building use value social relationships that can deploy those assets.

In this model of CDCs, ABCD, and social capital, the Scooby-Doo mystery is defined as the lack of strong relationships that can develop local capital and help the community to compete in the marketplace. The problem is that the promoters of this mystery do not propose to solve it, only to repair its aftermath. Unlike the average capitalist who would have the police out looking for any physical capital that went missing, few seem to be very interested in finding out where the missing social capital went. Instead, the focus seems to be on how to replace the missing social capital, rather than find out how it wound up missing in the first place.

Now Scooby-Doo and his friends wouldn't be content leaving a good mystery unsolved, and we shouldn't either. But lacking their luck of stumbling onto the mystery even when they're not looking for it, we imagination-impaired academics need to be more deliberate in our investigation. We can take a lesson from Scooby by first investigating the ghost that everyone seems so scared of. The apparition seems to lurk outside the walls of every home on the streets, the sidewalks, the social clubs, and especially the bowling alleys. It is the ghost that killed Kitty Genovese in 1964. It is the ghost that killed Jeffrey Dahmer's victims in 1991. It is the ghost that caused the annual spring bloodbaths in U.S. high schools.

The ghost, the cause, has to be inferred from analysts today, who only focus on what we should do about the problem rather than on what caused it. But their solutions lend powerful clues to the nature of the ghost they fear. These analysts, whether they propose the CDC model of development, the ABCD model, the community building model, or the consensus "organizing" model, all focus on the community and its individuals (see Stoecker 2001). The community must develop its assets, build its relationships, develop its own economy and housing, and train its individuals to function successfully within the system. The cause of the problem that we must infer from these proposed solutions is that there is something wrong with the community (or its individuals) that is their own fault. If they must create, resource, and deploy their own solution, then they also must be held responsible for their continuing impoverishment if they don't.

This is the perfect ghost. It absolves the rest of us from any responsibility. If poor people stay poor—if poor communities stay poor—it's because they haven't mobilized their assets, built an effectively managed CDC, or trained themselves to get a job. This ghost is just a more sophisticated version of the old victim-blaming argument (Ryan 1976) so popular in U.S. capitalism. This ghost is feared by all. Holding up poor communities as responsible for their own fate keeps the rest of us in fear of being like them—so we work hard, build networks, and don't rock the boat to protect our privileged positions. This ghost keeps wages down by dividing the unemployed from the underemployed. It maintains segregation by defining the poor as "not-white" and personally deficient. Ultimately, this ghost keeps us—those of us who are white, middle-class, with homes in safe neighborhoods—under control.

Once we begin to understand the victim-blaming aspects of the social capital concept, we begin to understand why the analysts are not digging deeper. Digging deeper requires confronting the ghost and we are all scared of ghosts. Those of you know Scooby-Doo and his pal Shaggy know that the last thing they ever want to do is confront the ghost. But the curiosity of their companions always wins out and sooner or later they come face to face with the phantom.

So let's drag the social capital concept into confronting the ghost. And, since we are moving deeper into the mystery, let's name the ghost for what it really is—social structure.

The Ghost of Social Structure

One of the things that we seem to have lost track of in the rush to postmodern cultural analysis and concepts such as social capital is the fact of social structure. Social structure is like natural gas. It's odorless and colorless, so you have to add something to it to make it stink in order to know it's there. And if you don't, it could kill you.

How does social structure matter here? It actually matters in contrast to social capital, whose convoluted conflation of use value and exchange value has confused rather than clarified. DeFillippis (2001) brings together the many critiques around the concept of social capital, showing the lack of connection between social capital and economic development. He shows how social capital is not connected to wealth, both because many poor communities have social capital but are still poor, and because many wealthy communities lack social capital but are still rich. So what is going on here, if so many rich communities don't have a sense of community and so many poor communities do?

There are actually two simultaneous processes at play. The first, and most important, is a fundamental contradiction between community and capital (Feagin and Parker 1990; Logan and Molotch 1987; Mollenkopf 1981; Capek and Gilderbloom 1992; Swanstrom 1993; Bluestone and Harrison 1982; Stoecker 1994; 1997; 1998). Here we return to our earlier discussion about use values and exchange values.

Consider, for a moment, that there may in fact be two kinds of "social networks," which I will use in place of the term social capital. First, there are use-value networks. Those are the places we call "communities." The social networks of those groups are developed and maintained for the purpose of the group. They help the group maintain its identity. They help the group care for its members. These are the groups that those who lament the "decline" of community long for. Whether or not there has been a historical change in the proportion of groups who exhibit these use-value community characteristics is debatable, but we do know that there are groups who do have these characteristics. The most important case, in fact, of use-value communities are communities of resistance, which we will discuss a bit later. Other cases include urban ethnic enclaves—the Chinatowns, little Italys, and other urban ethnic neighborhoods that are often impoverished but rich with social networks that link new and old immigrants (Abrahamson 1996).

The second kind of social networks are exchange value networks. These are the kinds of networks found among elites, who connect socially for the purpose of exchange relations to improve or maintain their elite status. These are networks not based on giving but on getting. These are the networks of every daytime or nighttime soap opera you have ever watched. These are the networks of TV's "Survivor" and and all its copiers. They are the "bad" form of social capital mentioned but un-theorized by the critics, since they are based on cheating, stealing, lying, exploiting, and doing all the other things capitalists do.

Use-value social networks tend to be more place-based. That is both because elites are more mobile and can maintain social networks over expensive distances, and because use-value networks require "free spaces" (Evans and Boyte 1986) that maintain a buffer between the community and its powerful elite enemies and depend on community member support to survive.

These kinds of networks play out in social structure in important ways. The tendency of capitalism is to "commodify" everything in its path—that is, to transform use values into exchange values. That's why middle class people don't grow gardens, sew clothes, clean their own homes, mow their own lawns, or talk to their neighbors over the back fence. Elites, embedded in exchange value networks, then see community space in terms of its exchange value, setting up an inherent antagonism. Where use-value communities see a park, exchange value network members see a parking lot. Where use-value communities see affordable housing, exchange value network members see unregulated apartment buildings. Where use-value communities see a community center, or a church, or a historical site, exchange value network members see a high-rise, high-rent office tower.

Exchange value networks are thus inherently antagonistic to use-value networks, since use-value communities see space and relationships in ways that prevent making a profit. Thus, in order to make a profit, exchange value networks must destroy use-value networks by removing their institutions, and even removing their members. No more famous example of this tendency exists than when the Detroit community of Poletown was removed to make way for a General Motors Cadillac plant in 1981 (Wylie 1989), but it occurred even more recently in Toledo, Ohio, when another community was removed for a Chrysler plant.

Now, of course, exchange networks have a structural advantage, as their members control the decision-making machinery and ultimately control bigger guns if it comes down to that. And they play the structure to their advantage, attempting to disrupt use-value social networks as much as possible. They strategize to divide the working class by pitting white workers against black workers, the unemployed against the barely employed. They move manufacturing facilities willy-nilly whenever too many local use-value networks develop among their workers. For use-value communities stand as the most powerful point of resistance against them, both structurally and culturally.

So here's the rub: if social capital is supposed to help develop economic capital, it can only be as exchange-value social capital, which wipes out use-value social capital, and undermines the purpose in the first place. And here is the problem of community development.

Our Scooby-Doo friends have discovered the ghost. And now they must capture it. But what to do?

Community Development

You cartoon junkies out there know what happens next. The villain tries to misdirect the Scooby gang. But our persistent heroes keep their noses to the trail, especially Scooby, and eventually come up with an elaborate strategy to lure, distract, overpower, and eventually capture the ghost. But still afraid of the ghost because they think it is a ghost, Scooby and Shaggy mess up the plan.

Such is the strategy of community development and its associated strategies of consensus organizing and community-building.

Please do not misunderstand. My analysis here is not of the community development workers, who are every bit as committed as the

Scooby gang to solving the mystery, and every bit as good at it. My analysis is of the model they are forced to work with.

What is this model? From the beginning CDCs were to accomplish bottom-up, comprehensive redevelopment, following the principles of supply-side economic models and "free"-market philosophy (Stoecker 1997).

This CDC model is very popular with elites, especially government and foundations. The U.S. federal government has set aside special funds for CDCs in Empowerment Zones and other federal housing programs. The Ford Foundation created a monster program to promote CDC-based comprehensive community initiatives (Smock 1997). Foundations, United Ways, and other elite-connected organizations have been particularly entranced with the "asset-based community development" promoted by Kretzmann and McKnight (1993), which they've interpreted as a "pull-yourself-by-your-bootstraps" poverty reduction strategy.

The reality is, however, much as CDC advocates would prefer to have it otherwise, that much of the emphasis on comprehensive development has been reduced to housing development. This is understandable, since part of the "comprehensive" characteristic emphasizes rebuilding use-value social networks that are incompatible with the overall exchange-value production mission of CDCs.

Undeterred by, or unknowledgeable of, the fundamental contradiction between use values and exchange values, the community development advocates continued on to develop new models to try and push the use-value network-building part of the mission. So "community building" and "consensus organizing" came to the fore. Doug Hess (1999) defines community building as "projects which seek to build new relationships among members in a community and develop change out of the connections these relationships provide for solving member-defined problems." Linked to Kretzmann and McKnight's (1993) asset-based community development model, and to communitarianism (Smock 1997), the emphasis in community building is creating and restoring relationships between community residents. The focus is internal, finding and building the community's own "assets" or "social capital" rather than confronting or negotiating with external power and resource holders. Ultimately, the goal of community building is community self-sufficiency (Smock 1997).

Consensus organizing includes the relationship-building focus of community building, but is broader in also focusing on moving people from welfare to work, improving school achievement, promoting inner-city reinvestment, and developing housing and businesses, among other things. Michael Eichler (1998), the founder of consensus organizing, specifically opposes the "us vs. them" model of community organizing: "today's landlord may be on the board of the community development corporation. Today's mayor may be a major advocate in improving the public schools; and today's corporate leader may be hiring and training welfare recipients while damaging the environment and paying solicited kickbacks to the mayor." The purpose of consensus organizing is to build cooperative relationships between community leaders and business and government to improve poor communities (Consensus Organizing Institute 2000).

The problem is, of course, that none of these models seem to be able to show much. Sure, CDCs build housing, but it's not clear they build housing any cheaper or better than for-profits. And yes, the other models do a lot of social programming, but so far no one has shown significant improvements in crime, infant mortality, marital stability, neighboring, or any of the other measures of "social capital" that would have occurred anyway with the improvement in the economy over the last decade.

There is even evidence that the development done by CDCs actually disrupts use-value relationships—pitting neighbor against neighbor for control over what happens in the neighborhood, and improving conditions just enough that longtime residents are able to leave and new individuals want to come in (Stoecker 1994; 1997). This is understandable, given the incompatibility of use values and exchange values.

The worst part of this model is, just like the villain in the Scooby-Doo mystery that tries to misdirect the Scooby kids, how blatantly hegemonic it is. Now we have privileged high-status academics (see Gittell and Vidal 1998) promoting non-conflict "community organizing" models and contributing to the mystification of structural inequalities. For all of these models can only work for building use value social networks if there was no pressure to transform them into exchange value relationships, which would require ending capitalism itself. And this is where Putnam (1993) and the others are confused when they argue that "investments in physical capital, financial capital, human capital, and social capital are complementary, not competing alternatives." Just like for consensus organizing, DeFillippis (2001) notes that "Putnam's [social capital] view is only possible if you erase the very real material interests that divide us (and even then, it is still highly questionable), and therefore create a vision of civil society as being solely constituted by people and groups with mutual interests."

The main problem is, just like the U.S. version of the social capital concept, how un-theorized the community development model is. The model is at best a superficial attempt to bandage a deep, broad, and infected wound. But it never tries to discover how the wound got there to begin with and whether the wound will recur because no one thought to remove the rusty nails sticking up from the ground. The model, and its definition of the mystery of the missing social capital, completely ignores the missing external physical capital, the theft of which caused the problem in the first place. As such, it is in danger of reproducing the same consequences that caused the problem to begin with. The best solution the community development advocates can come up with, then, is to create use value relationships inside the community and transform them into exchange value relationships outside the community. And just like we've created a society where people don't know how to grow their own food, sew their own clothes, or repair their own homes, as soon as we transform social bonds into exchange relationships and market them, we lose control over them.

The villain who stole the previous social capital, knowing we aren't even investigating the disappearance, will find any replacement social capital just as easy pickings. This is why community development can't win.

So what's a Scooby dog to do?

Communities of Resistance

We've reached the conclusion, the only place left to go, just like our Scooby-Doo heroes. For every time the toon-time teens lay their trap to catch the ghost, something goes wrong. All the technical planning, the sophisticated problem-solving, and the good intentions fall apart at the climax. But they catch the villain anyway. And the reason is that they are a team based in use-value relationships. Yes, they mobilize their assets, and they develop a solution. But when it all falls apart, they win because they take care of and protect and defend each other. They organize.

And this is what poor communities do. The most illustrative example comes from the civil rights movement. They understood what they were up against, and they understood the villain. They tried the nice and polite "consensus" route, and recognized it as a way to demobilize and disempower them. The civil rights movement, along with Saul Alinsky (1969, 1971) is the crucial source of community organizing. Its influence on community organizing practice has been as profound as Alinsky's but has been historically neglected. The accepted founding event of the movement, the Montgomery Bus Boycott, was coordinated through local African American networks and organizations and created a model that would be used in locality-based actions throughout the south. The efforts of the Student Nonviolent Coordinating Committee in organizing African American communities in the south for voting rights and integration are perhaps the most unrecognized influence on community organizing. Out of the efforts of these and other civil rights organizers grew the welfare rights movement (Piven and Cloward 1979) and eventually the famous Association of Community Organizations for Reform Now (ACORN) (Delgado 1986; Russell 2000).

The example of the civil rights movement is also illustrative not just because of the success it showed, but also because of the failure it showed. Because when the movement's use-value networks began to weaken, and the exchange-value policy of affirmative action was able to drive wedges between middle-class and poor African Americans, and between African Americans and whites, the movement faltered. The shift to development in the civil rights movement, like the shift to development in many more localized community organizing efforts, catalyzed the contradiction between use values and exchange values.

The only thing standing in the way of complete capitalist domination is use-value-based community. Because, ultimately, use-value relationships are stronger than exchange-value relationships. Because elites operate through exchange value-based networks, they always have to watch their backs and trust is never complete. Because of this, individual villains can be isolated, and factions of capital can be pitted against each other, creating the possibility for communities to win, and sometimes win big.

Even some CDCs are beginning to understand this. The $1.5 million Ricanne Hadrian Initiative for Community Organizing (RHICO), sponsored through the Massachusetts Association of CDCs and the Neighborhood Development Support Collaborative, supports and trains CDCs throughout Massachusetts to do community organizing. In some cases the organizing they do involves hard-core, in your face, confrontational tactics that forces elites to actually respond to community-designed programs, rather than force funder-driven programs down their throats. I have helped with a similar though smaller program in Toledo, and one of our participating CDCs recently won half a million dollars in city capital improvement funds through its enhanced organizing skill.

Now it's all fine and good to focus on rebuilding community relationships and developing community assets. But let's understand the truly radical implications of doing this correctly. Doing this in a way that maintains community relationships as assets and use values requires going up against capitalism and the ghost of social structure. And when we do it right, we will no longer have to fight over the crumbs of the Scooby snack.

References

Abrahamson, Mark. 1996. *Urban Enclaves: Identity and Place in America.* New York: St. Martin's Press.

Alinsky, Saul. 1969. *Reveille for Radicals.* New York: Vintage.

Alinsky, Saul. 1971. *Rules for Radicals.* New York: Vintage.

Bluestone, Barry, and Bennett Harrison. 1982. *The Deindustrialization of America: Plant Closings, Community Abandonment, and the Dismantling of Basic Industry.* New York: Basic.

Bourdieu, Pierre. 1985. "The Forms of Capital." In *Handbook of Theory and Research for the Sociology of Education,* ed. J. G.Richardson. New York: Greenwood.

Capek, Stella M., and John I. Gilderbloom. 1992. *Community Versus Commodity Tenants and the American City.* Albany: State University of New York Press.

Consensus Organizing Institute. 2000. <http://www.consensusorganizing.com>.

DeFilippis, James. 2001. "The Myth of Social Capital in Community Development." *Housing Policy Debate,* 12.4:781–806.

Delgado, Gary. 1986. *Organizing the Movement: The Roots and Growth of ACORN.* Philadelphia: Temple University Press.

Eichler, Michael. 1998. "Organizing's Past, Present, and Future." *Shelterforce Online.* <http://www.nhi.org/online/issues/101/eichler.html>.

Evans, Sara M., and Harry C. Boyte. 1986. *Free Spaces: The Sources of Democratic Change in America.* New York: Harper and Row.

Feagin, Joe R., and Robert Parker. 1990. *Building American Cities: The Urban Real Estate Game.* New York: Prentice Hall.

Gittell, Ross, and Avis Vidal.1998. *Community Organizing: Building Social Capital as a Development Strategy.* Thousand Oaks, CA: Sage.

Hess, Doug. 1999. "Community Organizing, Building and Developing: Their Relationship to Comprehensive Community Initiatives." Paper presented on *COMM-ORG: The On-Line Conference on Community Organizing and Development.* <http://comm-org.utoledo.edu/papers.htm>.

Kretzman, John P., and John L. McKnight. 1993. *Building Communities from the Inside Out: A Path Toward Finding and Mobilizing Community Assets.* Chicago: ACTA.

Logan, John R., and Harvey L. Molotch. 1987. *Urban Fortunes: the Political Economy of Place.* Berkeley: University of California Press.

Mollenkopf, John H. 1981. "Community and Accumulation." In *Urbanization and Urban Planning in Capitalist Society,* ed. Michael Dear and Allen J. Scott, 319–338. New York: Methuen.

Munro, Jenifer. n.d. The World Bank's Initiative on Defining, Monitoring and Measuring Social Capital. <http://www.iris.umd.edu/adass/proj/soc-cap.asp>.

Piven, Frances Fox, and Richard A. Cloward. 1977. *Poor People's Movements: Why They Succeed, How They Fail.* New York: Pantheon.

Portes, Alejandro, and Patricia Landolt, 1996. "Unsolved Mysteries: The Tocqueville Files II." *The American Prospect,* May 1, 1996–June 1. <http://www.prospect.org/print/V7/26/26-cnt2.html>

Putnam, Robert D. 1993. "The Prosperous Community Social Capital and Public Life." *The American Prospect,* March 21. <http://www.prospect.org/print/V4/13/putnam-r.html>.

Putnam, Robert D. 2000. *Bowling Alone: The Collapse and Revival of American Community.* New York: Simon and Schuster.

Requier-Desjardins, Denis. 1999. "On Some Contributions on the Definition and Relevance of Social Capital." <http://informel.c3ed.uvsq.fr/soccap1.htm>.

Russell, Dan. 2000. *Roots of a Social Justice Movement* (1970–75). <http://www.acorn.org/history-content.html>.

Ryan, William. 1976. *Blaming the Victim.* New York: Vintage.

Sirianni, Carmen, and Lewis Friedland. 2001. *Civic Innovation in America: Community Empowerment, Public Policy, and the Movement for Civic Renewal.* Berkeley: University of California Press.

Smock, Kristina. 1997. "Comprehensive Community Initiatives: A New Generation of Urban Revitalization Strategies." Paper presented on *COMM-ORG: The On-Line Conference on Community Organizing and Development.* <http://comm-org.utoledo.edu/papers.htm>.

Social Capital Interest group (SCIG). n.d. "Social Capital: A Position Paper." Michigan State University. <http://www.ssc.msu.edu/~internat/soccap/position.htm>.

Stoecker, Randy. 1994. *Defending Community: The Struggle For Alternative Redevelopment in Cedar-Riverside.* Philadelphia: Temple University Press.

Stoecker, Randy. 1997. "The CDC Model of Urban Redevelopment: A Critique and an Alternative." *Journal of Urban Affairs,* 12.3:237–52.

Stoecker, Randy. 1998. "Capital Against Community." In *Research in Community Sociology,* 8, ed. Dan Chekki. Greenwich, CT: JAI Press.

Stoecker, Randy. 2001. "Community Development and Community Organizing: Apples and Oranges? Chicken and Egg?" In *From ACT UP to the WTO: Urban Protest and Community Building in the Era of Globalization,* ed. Ron Hayduk and Ben Shepard. New York: Verso.

Swanstrom, Todd. 1993. "Beyond Economism: Urban Political Economy and the Postmodern Challenge." *Journal of Urban Affairs* 15:55–78.

Wylie, Jeanie. 1989. *Poletown: A Community Betrayed.* Urbana: University of Illinois Press.

Paradise Lost

Social Capital and the Emergence of a Homeowners Association in a Suburban Detroit Neighborhood

Robert Mark Silverman and Kelly L. Patterson

Social Capital in a New Place

This chapter analyzes the degree to which social capital influences organizational behavior in an urban neighborhood. Specifically, a case study focusing on the emergence of a homeowners association in a new residential subdivision in a suburb of Detroit, Michigan, is examined in order to determine the influence of social capital on organizational development. Moreover, this analysis sets out to evaluate existing sociological definitions of social capital and to further refine this concept. It is argued that by itself an analysis of social capital offers limited insights into the mechanisms that drive organization building. However, when viewed as one element embedded in a broader institutional and social context we find that the consideration of social capital expands our understanding of the intersection of organizational development, public participation, and political economy.

Before elaborating upon the manner in which social capital relates to the processes identified above, it is important to specify how this concept is defined in our analysis. The manner in which social capital is defined is critical, given the variety of ways that this concept has been applied in social sciences research. For instance, Foley and Edwards (1999) examined the existing literature concerning social capital and found that this concept is used in two distinct manners in the social sciences. In their dichotomy Foley and Edwards (1999) indicate that much of the work done by political scientists and economists concerning social capital focuses on societal relationships where the concept is defined as an expression of generalized norms and social trust. The most familiar example of this mode of reasoning is found in Putnam's (1993, 1995, 2000) research where social capital is treated as a generalized concept and applied in an expansive manner. In contrast Foley and Edwards (1999) indicate that much of the sociological research concerning this concept focuses on parochial relationships and emphasizes that social capital is heavily influenced by structural factors. An extensive body of sociological research has been developed which delineates the embedded nature of this concept. In large part, this perspective is reflected in the work of Bourdieu (1986) and Coleman (1988, 1990), and it is paralleled in Granovetter (1972, 1985) and Burt's (1992) discussions of social networks and embedded social relations.

More recently, sociologists have elaborated upon the definition of social capital, adding further specification to the embedded nature of this concept. For instance, Fernandez Kelly (1994, 1995) examined the role of neighborhood and social context in the shaping of social networks for African American and immigrant youth. Through this analysis, she finds evidence supporting a definition of social capital as a concept embedded in a specific social and spatial context. Similarly, Portes (1998) examines the use of this concept in the literature and concludes that social capital is best understood within a specific social and institutional context. Portes and Landolt (2000) draw extensions from this line of inquiry in their analysis of Latin American urbanism and migration where they conclude that social capital has limited application as a concept for analysis of social processes occurring beyond the parochial level. These issues are reemphasized by Silverman (2001) in a study of community-based organizations, where he finds social capital to be observable within a parochial context, though the concepts relevance for organizational behavior diminishes as organizations become more complex and formalized. This analysis leads Silverman (2001) to the development of a circumscribed definition of social capital, which is also adopted in this analysis. In this definition social capital is considered to be synonymous with what Velez-Ibanez (1983) refers to as a "bond of mutual trust." Accordingly, Silverman (2001) defines social capital as, "a bond of mutual trust emerging from shared values which are embedded in parochial networks." This definition is considered appropriate since it links social capital to an observable social context. As this definition applies to this case study, the manifestation of social capital can be observed in relation to the deliberations among residents, real estate developers, and representatives of local government concerning the formation of a homeowners association in a suburban neighborhood.

From this vantage point our understanding of social capital can be further refined, since a number of additional concepts found in the urban literature can be incorporated into the analysis. For instance, the urban and institutional context of this research site becomes important since it allows for the actions of public and private sector organizations to be considered in conjunction with an analysis of social capital. In many respects, this is an extension of Wacquant's (1998) analysis of social capital in the urban core which indicates that institutional actors have a substantial influence in shaping the structural conditions under which social capital is formed. Moreover, the focus of this research allows for social capital to be examined within the context of what Molotch (1976) identifies as an "urban growth machine." Particularly, the activities of two key actors in a growth machine, real estate developers and local government officials, are examined in relation to the scope of public participation in the development of a homeowners association and the degree to which social capital affects this organizational process.

As an extension of this inquiry, the values which social capital is based upon are examined within the context of Logan and Molotch's (1987) discussion of use values and exchange values. Consequently, this chapter argues that the contrast identified by Logan and Molotch (1987:2) between, "residents, who use places to satisfy essential needs of life, and entrepreneurs, who strive for financial return," in the form of economic exchange informs our analysis of social capital in the organizational development process. This contrast is apparent when comparing the values that entrenched residents of a neighborhood focus on with those referenced by members of urban growth machines when discussing the merits of emergent organizations such as the homeowners association examined here. In the context of this case study it is argued that social capital is activated among most residents through the identification of values based on aesthetic issues related to the manner in which they anticipate using their neighborhood on a daily basis. Because of their parochial nature, use values are considered to be of primary importance in the development of social capital among these residents. In contrast, social capital linked to exchange values is expected to dominate the dialogue of members of urban growth machines. This emphasis precludes the cultivation of a bond of mutual trust with residents who tend to focus on competing use values, subsequently hampering the organizational development process.

This perspective adds a cogent dimension to the analysis by incorporating an urban political economy perspective into the social capital debate. In essence, we examine the relationship between social capital based on values linked to communal aesthetics and social capital based on values tied to markets. The focus on residents and members of urban growth machines, as well as the emphasis on use and exchange values, is central to this analysis. Subsequently, it is argued that the embeddedness of social capital in parochial networks complicates the efforts of residents and the members of urban growth machines to develop new organizations since urban space is being defined differently by each group. Namely, the motivation to form organizations that enhance the residents' use of a neighborhood is potentially at odds with the efforts of members of urban growth machines to create organizations that enhance the exchange value of the same urban space.

This case study offers unique insights into the processes that influence organizational development at the parochial level for several additional reasons. First, the neighborhood under analysis is of interest because it epitomizes the popular image of a contemporary middle class neighborhood, while simultaneously possessing a diverse group of residents along the lines of occupation, race, age, and household structure. For instance, the neighborhood studied is a newly constructed community in a suburb approximately 26 miles from downtown Detroit and 10 miles from the Detroit Metropolitan Airport. The physical design of the neighborhood is consistent with planned unit developments (PUD) in other suburban communities containing single-family detached homes. Despite its outwardly homogeneous appearance, the neighborhood is socially diverse. Various occupational groups are represented in the neighborhood, which in part is a reflection of the metropolitan area's transition from its traditional industrial base to a more diversified service economy. This dynamic has produced a neighborhood where there is an even distribution of blue collar and white collar workers. The demographic characteristics of the households reflect this dynamic as well. For instance, approximately 60 percent of the homes are occupied by families with children, while the remaining 40 percent are occupied by young couples, empty nesters, or single adults. Similarly, the racial composition of the neighborhood is relatively mixed, with approximately 25 percent of the households African Americans, less than 2 percent Latino, and the remainder white.

In addition to these features the neighborhood itself is newly constructed, and subsequently its residents must address the need for the development of formal and informal social controls. However, the negotiation of community norms is not a simple internal process, but rather it is a process that involves interactions with larger institutions. In this case, the primary institutional actors were the real estate developer who was building the neighborhood and local government officials. Moreover, because the neighborhood is newly constructed, these institutional actors heavily influence the development of neighborhood social control. The extent of this influence becomes apparent when the role of these actors is considered in the context of the emergence of the neighborhood's homeowners association.

The focus on the emergence of a homeowners association adds an additional perspective to the analysis of organizational development at the parochial level since it fills a gap in the literature concerning this organizational type. Currently there is a body of research documenting the functions and rationales for homeowners associations. For instance, Dilger (1992) and Stabile (2000) discuss how these organizations have become institutionalized in communities across the United States. In his discussion of the proliferation of homeowners associations, Stabile (2000:222) argues that these organizations, "have met with approval by government at all levels, have been organized by government/business collaborations, and have passed the market test of acceptance by both producers (developers) and consumers (homeowners)." Others have examined the political and social implications of homeowners associations arguing that the devolution of responsibility for what has traditionally been considered public property and services to the neighborhood level has important implications for urban governance. For instance, McKenzie (1994) argues that homeowners associations facilitate the privatization of local government services and promote an image of citizenship that is circumscribed. In this context, citizenship is turned inward and becomes a parochial activity that is increasingly confined to the neighborhood level.

Some misgivings concerning the emergence of homeowners associations as organizations responsible for regulating the use of residential property, and for the provision of basic public services, such as landscaping, street cleaning, garbage collection, and infrastructure repair were highlighted by Garreau (1988). In essence, he argues that the formation of homeowners associations does not ensure that decision-making will be locally controlled or democratic. Rather, homeowners associations are considered to have a tendency to operate in an arcane manner and have the potential to create barriers along the lines of social class through the enforcement of elaborate rules that are written into covenants, conditions and restrictions (CC&Rs) of an organization's bylaws. Blakely and Snyder (1997:22) offer evidence to support these assertions and add that the formal structure of homeowners associations may actually result in reduced social interaction at the neighborhood level, since residents can turn to third parties to address violations of community norms, "rather than deal with each other in even the smallest disputes."

In the light of these observations, this case study attempts to examine how social capital and broader institutional forces shape this new organizational form. This inquiry focuses on the involvement of a real estate developers, local government officials, and residents in the establishment of a homeowners association. Subsequently, the goal of this analysis is twofold: to gain a better understanding of the degree to which each group imprints on the structure of these organizations, and to assess the manner in which institutional actors attempt to use social capital to promote their organizational goals.

Methods and Data

The findings reported here are based on qualitative methods. First, participant observation was used in order to understand the organizational development process from the perspective of residents. Using this method, data were gathered through observations made at four meetings that were held to plan and organize a homeowners association and through informal conversations with members of the groups involved in the study. In addition to participant observation various written documents were collected for analysis. These included correspondences, meeting minutes, electronic mail, and the proposed CC&Rs of the homeowners association being studied. Both researchers were engaged in the collection and analysis of data during the course of this study. Data were collected from July 2000 to January 2001. The research question grew out of a naturalistic process that unfolded in the neighborhood where the researchers resided, this situation created a high level of access to the research site.

Early in the research process the decision was made to conduct research surreptitiously. This decision was based on several considerations. First, the researchers lived in the neighborhood before the research question emerged. As a result the researchers were already accepted as residents and had established rapport with members of each group involved in this study. Because of their prior status as residents in the neighborhood, the introduction of a new role for the researchers would have jeopardized their access to aspects of the community that were central to the research question. Also, the status of the researchers as residents allowed them to participate in numerous informal conversations with members of each group involved in the study. In addition, the covert strategy adopted in this research was permissible since the researchers were stakeholders in the neighborhood being studied. As stakeholders, the researchers would remain in the neighborhood following the study's completion, which reduced the chances that research participants would be subjected to undue risks. Finally, from a methodological standpoint this research question afforded an opportunity for the parameters of covert participant observation research to be delineated within the context of a community study. This research question was particularly suitable to this mode of inquiry given its narrow scope and focus on a publicly observable process. Moreover, the initial decision to pursue a covert research strategy heightened the sensitivity of the researchers to issues concerning ethics, confidentiality, and empathy in the analysis. These factors contributed to a more dimensional portrait of the organizational development process, since the researchers were sensitized to their potential biases and multiple roles early in the analysis.

The diverse characteristics of the residents along the lines of occupation, race, age, and household structure also presented the researchers with unique methodological challenges. In an effort to increase the chances that all segments of the neighborhood were represented in the analysis a variety of data were collected during the research process. These data include field notes from observations and informal conversations with neighbors, letters distributed in the neighborhood by residents and the real estate developer, electronic-mail exchanged among residents and local government officials, and minutes from community meetings.

Democracy by Growth Machine

When assessing the degree to which real estate developers, government officials, and residents imprint on the structure of an emerging homeowners association it is important to recognize that institutional actors have greater access to this early stage of the organizational development process than residents. Typically, CC&Rs are drafted during the initial planning stages for a residential subdivision and incorporated into the deed for individual parcels of property (Dilger 1992; McKenzie 1994; Blakely and Snyder 1997; Stabile 2000). Although this is considered to be the normal process for creating homeowners associations, in practice developers sometimes propose CC&Rs after a portion of a neighborhood has been built and homes have been sold. When this occurs, the developer must negotiate with local government officials and residents in order for a homeowners association to be created. In essence, these were the circumstances surrounding the establishment of the homeowners association examined in this case study. In this instance, the developer decided to establish a homeowners association after approximately 30 percent of the homes in the subdivision had been sold. A few months after conveying his plan to form a homeowners association to a small number of residents, the developer distributed 20 pages of proposed CC&Rs to all of the residents in the neighborhood. When the CC&Rs were distributed residents were instructed to return a signed and notarized copy of the document to the developer along with a check for the association's dues. This action generated a high degree of concern among the residents of the neighborhood, which evolved into a series of meeting and exchanges between the residents, the developer, and local government officials.

Interestingly, in this case the developer and local government officials became allies in a manner that paralleled Molotch's (1976) concept of an urban growth machine. This alliance grew out of common interests that both parties shared in the development process. In essence, the developer sought to make financial gains by building and selling homes, while local government officials viewed housing development as a mechanism to enhance the local tax base. Moreover, the creation of a homeowners association and the devolution of responsibility for selected local services was in the interest of both parties, since the creation of a homeowners association would shift the financial responsibility for a number of local services from them to the residents of the neighborhood. The degree to which the developer and local government acted in unison to advocate for the creation of a homeowners association is illustrated when examining their efforts to control the scope of participation in the organizational development process and their efforts to frame the dialogue concerning the homeowners association.

Initially, the developer intended to limit the participation of residents in the homeowners association. This was formalized in the CC&Rs which stipulated that the developer would have sole discretion in appointing and removing members to the board of the homeowners association, while additional language stated that the CC&Rs could not be amended without the developer's consent. Efforts to limit participation extended beyond the language of the CC&Rs and were manifested in the actions of the developer and local government officials as residents attempted to form a dialogue concerning the establishment of a homeowners association. One of the most noticeable aspects of the developer's position concerning the homeowners association was his effort to limit the scope of dialogue and expedite the process. For instance, prior to each of the four meetings called to discuss the proposed homeowners association the developer would distribute letters to residents stating that negotiations concerning the homeowners association were coming to a close. For example, in a letter distributed prior to the third meeting the developer stated that "this will be the last opportunity to be involved in the covenants as the following week the final version will be presented to [the local government] for final review prior to recording." With the exception of these types of correspondences the developer had limited contact with residents as a group. Instead, the developer communicated with residents on an individual basis or through two individuals that he appointed as board members to the proposed homeowners association. In turn, these board members maintained a dialogue with the residents through community meetings, e-mail, and informal conversations. In additional, several rumors circulated in the neighborhood about the developer informally contacting a small number of residents and offering to exempt them from joining the homeowners association. Although these agreements were never documented, the rumors served to muddle the organizational development process and raise suspicion among the residents.

The actions of local government officials also circumscribed the scope of resident participation. For instance, some residents reported that they experienced difficulty obtaining information from local government concerning existing city ordinances, planning procedures, and the government's position on the need for a homeowners association. Other residents described how the local government required them to pay for government documents or for the use of a room in the municipal building where community meetings were held. Obliquely, these issues encumbered efforts to mobilize residents and maintain community participation. More directly, the curtailment of resident involvement also occurred in response to positions taken by the director of the local government's planning department. For instance, when one of the residents requested assistance directly from the planning director a response was sent using e-mail stating that the local government, "supplies water, sewer, and public safety protection, it does not supply legal opinions on matters outside its responsibility." Nevertheless, as the negotiations concerning the proposed homeowners association unfolded the planning director became one of the organization's strongest advocates.

In his efforts to encourage the residents to accept the proposed CC&Rs, the planning director highlighted the aesthetic and the financial benefits that the association would bring to the neighborhood. For example, in an e-mail sent to one of the residents the planning director stated that, "the purpose of these self-created regulations is to allow the developer/builder and then the homeowners to maintain a style or atmosphere specific to the community." In another instance, the planning director focused on the financial benefits of having a homeowners association. For instance, the planning director confronted one of the residents opposed to creating the association at a community meeting by suggesting that property values would decline in the community if a homeowners association was not created. In his interactions with residents most of the planning director's comments were underscored by the message that the local government had no intention of assuming responsibility for a number of public services in the neighborhood, and as a result the residents would ultimately be obligated to supply them on their own.

The positions of the developer and the planning director were reinforced by the board members who were appointed to the proposed homeowners association. Their support of the developer and planning director's position had two lasting effects on the organizational development process. First, since these residents were appointed by the developer, there was increased skepticism in the neighborhood about the openness of the process. Second, the strong partisan positions taken by the board members exacerbated internal divisions among the residents. As the leanings of the board members became more apparent their ability to act as advocates for the other residents was increasingly brought into question. For instance, in an e-mail correspondence with other homeowners one of the board members defended his position in the following manner:

> When [the developer] asked me to act as one of the Rep's, he said he was willing to compromise on anything that did not conflict with the [local government's] regulations. He is in a tough situation. He feels required—pushed by the [local government], I think—to establish some form of an association. He has put himself in a tough situation by foolishly not registering the CC&R's with the County BEFORE closing on any lots in this subdivision.

The efforts of the board members to be responsive to the concerns of the developer and local government compromised their ability to speak for the residents. Consequently, some residents felt that the board members were co-opted by the developer and the planning director. This diminished the legitimacy of the organizational development process in the eyes of some residents.

The cumulative effects of the positions and actions taken by the developer, the planning director, and the appointed board members was that resident participation subsided. In fact, meeting attendance declined rapidly as the positions of these key players began to dominate the dialogue. For instance, the first community meeting had over 30 residents present, or roughly one resident for each existing household. However, attendance dropped off noticeably as time passed, despite an increase in the number of occupied homes in the neighborhood. For instance, the second meeting had 15 residents in attendance, and the third and fourth had 12 or fewer. Moreover, attendance at meetings declined as the role of the developer and the planning director became more pronounced and residents opposed to the proposed homeowners association became disillusioned with the process. In the end, the original CC&Rs remained intact with the exception of a few minor changes that the developer allowed, and many of the residents stated that they would not join the newly created organization. In essence, the role of resident participation in the organizational development process was reduced to what Arnstein (1969) identifies as "tokenism" with a small group of residents being informed and consulted concerning the developer's plans for a homeowners association while the organizational development process was controlled by key players in the urban growth machine.

Homesteaders and Sojourners

Despite the efforts of the developer and the planning director to forge a consensus concerning the need for a homeowners association, at least one third of the residents remained opposed to the formation of this new organization while another third of the residents remained indifferent. For the most part, these two groups of residents withdrew from the planning process as the developer, the planning director, and the remaining residents' roles became more pronounced. As the organizational development process evolved it became apparent that the proponents of the homeowners association sought to mobilize support for their position by tapping into social capital based on two distinct sets of values. In one respect, there was an effort to appeal to a common interest in maintaining the neighborhoods aesthetics and a middle class lifestyle. In another respect, there was an attempt to gain support for the homeowners association based on mutual concerns about property values. In essence, both use and exchange values were being mobilized to gain approval of the homeowners association.

It is important to note that all of the residents shared these values to some degrees. However, the relative importance of use and exchange values varied from one resident to another, and this divergence in the emphasis on values divided the residents into two groups—homesteaders and sojourners. Residents who fit into the first group placed a greater emphasis on use values when considering the merits of the proposed homeowners association. The homesteaders expressed a desire to remain in the neighborhood for the long term, and their concerns focused on issues related to neighborhood upkeep, livability, and the cultivation of textured relationships. In contrast, the residents who fit into the group identified as sojourners placed a greater emphasis on exchange values as they articulated their position concerning the homeowners association. These residents focused on the immediate security of their financial investment in their homes, and saw the creation of a formal organization as a mechanism to protect that investment. In some cases, sojourners indicated that they intended to move away from the neighborhood after a few years and they wanted to see the homeowners association in place so the resale value of their homes would not be adversely affected. Even when such intentions were not expressed, sojourners concentrated on exchange values and expressed their preference for a formal contract that identified community standards.

The divergent interests of homesteaders and sojourners complicated efforts to garner support from all of the residents for the proposed homeowners association. This quagmire was rooted in the difficulties entailed in mobilizing social capital based on two distinct sets of values. For instance, it was relatively easy to convince sojourners to support the homeowners association, since their emphasis on exchange values coalesced with the developer's interest in generating profits from the sale of new homes and the local government's interest in enhancing the tax base. For some sojourners these shared values were reinforced by common professional ties, since some of the sojourners were employed in the real estate development industry. These common values and ties formed a bond of mutual trust among these individuals that promoted cooperation in the development of a homeowners association. In contrast, the homesteaders' emphasis on use values came into conflict with the developer, the planning director, and the sojourners' focus on exchange values. Value dissonance impeded the homesteaders' ability to mobilize social capital with the other individuals.

The lack of consensus concerning use values became apparent as homesteaders voiced their concerns about the lack of alternatives to the proposed homeowners association and the lack of representation on the association's board. For instance, one homesteader suggested an alternative to a homeowners association where residents would make informal arrangements to maintain green space in the neighborhood, but this option was never seriously considered when brought up in the community meetings. Similarly, on two separate occasions homesteaders requested that the local government assess the feasibility of creating a special assessment district or another alternative form of service delivery for the neighborhood, but these requests were not acted upon. Moreover, when homesteaders attending the first community meeting expressed concern about the a lack of elected representation on the board of the proposed homeowners association, a small group of sojourners dismissed the issue and changed the subject. Ironically, one of these sojourner was later appointed to the association's board by the developer. The clash between use and exchange values also emerged when homesteaders discussed the lack of mutual trust between themselves and other individuals involved in the organizational development process.

The breakdown of mutual trust between homesteaders and others involved in the dialogue concerning the homeowners association was a key to understanding why it was difficult for the neighborhood to reach a consensus. This issue became most apparent when examining the manner in which disagreements between homesteaders and the developer concerning use values resulted in a deterioration of social capital. The developer's decision to create a homeowners association unearthed the first signs that there was a lack of mutual trust in the neighborhood. For instance, a majority of the residents attending the first community meeting stated that they had been misled by the developer. One of the residents even decided to put a for sale sign in front of his home to protest the developer's proposed association, and he encouraged others to take similar action. The homesteaders had the most negative response to the announcement that there would be a homeowners association. In part, the situation was made worse due to the methods that the developer used to inform the resident about his decision to create an organization.

The first formal notification that residents received about the homeowners association took place following a barbecue that the developer invited residents to attend. The following is an excerpt of field notes from an informal conversation with two homesteaders about this incident:

> [The homesteaders] were mad about what [the developer] did because they felt that the barbecue was supposed to be a family event, but they later realized it was set up for business purposes. They were also mad because the people who worked for [the developer] were drinking alcohol, and because [the developer's assistant] called one of them a liar when he said he was told there was not going to be a homeowners association at the time they purchased their home. They were particularly upset because [the developer's assistant] seemed intoxicated at the time and questioned their honesty in front of their children. After this exchange, [the homesteaders] handed the CC&Rs back to [the developer's assistant] and left the barbecue.

This dispute was rooted in the contradiction that emerged since the developer's actions were incompatible with the residents' perceptions of the barbecue as an event organized to promote use values in the neighborhood. The developer's effort to mix business with pleasure offended some of the residents, and this undermined his ability to build mutual trust with them. Social capital was further weakened by the developer's next effort to notify residents about the homeowners association. In this instance a copy of the proposed CC&Rs was left anonymously on each resident's front porch along with a bill for association dues. The impersonal manner in which this notice was issued damaged social capital between the developer and many of the homesteaders.

The lack of trust between the developer and homesteaders was also linked to other incidents related to the quality of residents' homes and satisfaction with neighborhood conditions more generally. For example, residents who had negative experiences with the developer during the construction of their homes were less supportive of the proposed homeowners association. Likewise, residents who had grievances about the treatment of the neighborhood by the developer and his sub-contractors were less likely to support the association. For instance, homesteaders complained about construction traffic, the accumulation of trash, and the practice of leaving construction equipment in the neighborhood overnight. Diminished trust between the developer and homesteaders effectively blocked efforts to generate consensus for the proposed homeowners association. This was even the case among homesteaders who felt there was a need for an organization, but wanted to avoid further entanglement with the developer. This nuance is brought out in the following excerpt of field notes from an informal conversation with a homesteaders:

> [The homesteader] said he would like to see some rules in the neighborhood, and he was even willing to go along with other residents if a consensus was formed. His preference for neighborhood rules grew out

of some of the residents practices he did not like. For example, he pointed to one of his neighbor's homes where trash cans were left outside instead of being stored inside of the garage. He also said he did not like the fact that another neighbor parked a large panel truck from his business on the street. But, the homesteader did not see any point in having a homeowners association if all of the residents were not members, and he did not want the developer to control the organization.

The inability to form a consensus about neighborhood rules was complicated by the lack of mutual trust between the developer and the homesteaders. This impasse was widened by value dissonance between the homesteaders and the sojourners.

The emphasis that homesteaders placed on use values as opposed to the emphasis that sojourners placed on exchange values complicated efforts to generate support for the homeowners association. This division in the neighborhood is illustrated a series of e-mail exchanges between these two groups of residents concerning the quality of snow removal in the neighborhood. This dialogue began when a sojourner sent the following e-mail to a group of residents three days after a storm left over six inches of snow on the neighborhood's streets:

> I spoke to [the developer] this morning. [His company] just bought a new truck with a snow plow. He believes they will be in our division this afternoon with the plow to clean the roads. I realize this is in part [the developer's] responsibility. However, I also feel they are going the extra mile. . . . My hat's off to [the developer]!!

For this sojourner the developer's purchase of snow removal equipment and other actions linked to exchange values resulted in a positive assessment of his role in the neighborhood. However, the homesteaders evaluated the developer based on a different standard, the degree to which he enhanced the neighborhood aesthetically. For instance, one homesteader had the following reply to the message above:

> Well my "hat is NOT off to [the developer]!" It has been little more than 6 hours now since they have received a plow truck and my FRESHLY laid sod is now rolled up and I have tire tracks up my yard. Lord only knows what our yards will look like by Spring! And quite frankly, the only thing that I see that was plowed thoroughly is the drives that lead to the spec. homes! The streets are still a mess—along with my yard now.

Another homesteader recanted a similar experience with the developer, and indicated that it was never resolved to his satisfaction. Others wrote about unsafe driving conditions and getting stuck in the snow after the developer attempted to plow the streets. The sentiment of the home-steaders was epitomized in a brief e-mail that read, "the whole plow job and homeowners association is one big joke!!!!" In contrast, the sojourners' emphasis on exchange values reenforced their support for the homeowners association.

Conclusions

The divergent perspectives of homesteaders, sojourners, the develop-ers, and the planning director that are discussed in this case study are symbolic of a broader issue pertaining the role of social capital in the organizational development process. It is apparent that social capital affects organizations, particularly in the early stages of their develop-ment when values can be imprinted upon their formal structure and culture. However, the real question to be addressed involves which val-ues end up being transmitted from the parochial level to the organiza-tional level, and what broader institutional factors facilitate this process. In this case study, exchange values coalesced among sojourners, the developer, and the planning director to generate a bond of mutual trust that enabled these individuals to control the organizational develop-ment process. Of course, the presence of this social capital was only part of the story. The success of this organizational development effort was also a byproduct of the financial resources of the developer and the insti-tutional position of the planning director. In contrast, social capital based on use values that were shared by the homesteaders remained confined to the parochial level. Although it could be argued that in the case examined here the success of the urban growth machine was only partial, it should be noted that in the end one form of social capital pre-vailed as far as the organizational development process was concerned. As a result, social capital based on exchange values was mobilized to gain control of the process and shape the organizational structure of the proposed homeowners association. The ability to emphasize exchange values during the early stages of this organization's develop-ment meant that broader institutional patterns remained unaffected.

This finding exposes a fissure in the social capital debate, partic-ularly for those who describe social capital as a panacea for democratic institution building and grassroots mobilization. As described here, social capital is a small component of broader institutional processes. Without the infusion of values compatible with a participatory society at the organizational and institutional level, current experimentation with social capital may fall short of expectations. In essence, the "democratic disarray" that Putnam (1995:77) refers to may not be the result of an "erosion of social capital" at all. On the contrary, this disarray may be the product of the ascent of a form of social capital based on values that are incompatible with democracy itself.

References

Arnstein, Sherry R. 1969. "A Ladder of Citizen Participation." *Journal of the American Institute of Planners,* 35.4:216–224.
Bourdieu, Pierre. 1986. "The Forms of Capital." In *Handbook of Theory and Research for the Sociology of Education,* ed. John G. Richardson, 241–258. New York: Greenwood Press.
Blakely, Edward J., and Mary Gail Snyder. 1997. *Fortress America: Gated Communities in the United States.* Washington, DC: Brookings Institution Press.
Burt, R. 1992. *Structural Holes: The Social Structure of Competition.* Cambridge: Harvard University Press.
Coleman, James S. 1988. "Social Capital in the Creation of Human Capital." *American Journal of Sociology,* 94S:S95–S120.
Coleman, James S. 1990. *Foundations of Social Theory.* Cambridge: Harvard University Press.
Dilger, Robert Jay. 1992. *Neighborhood Politics: Residential Community Associations in American Governance.* New York: New York University Press.
Fernandez Kelly, M. Patricia. 1994. "Towanda's Triumph: Social and Cultural Capital in the Transition to Adulthood in the Urban Ghetto." *International Journal of Urban and Regional Research,* 18.1:88–111.
Fernandez Kelly, M. Patricia. 1995. "Social and Cultural Capital in the Urban Ghetto: Implications for the Economic Sociology of Immigration." In *The Economic Sociology of Immigration: Essays on Networks, Ethnicity, and Entrepreneurship,* ed. Alejandro Portes, 213–247. New York: Russell Sage Foundation.
Foley, Michael W., and Bob Edwards. 1999. "Is it Time to Disinvest in Social Capital?" *Journal of Public Policy,* 19.2:141–173.
Garreau, Joel. 1988. *Edge City: Life on the New Frontier.* New York: Anchor.
Granovetter, Mark S. 1972. "The Strength of Weak Ties." *American Journal of Sociology,* 78.6:1360–1380.
Granovetter, Mark S. 1985. "Economic Action and Social Structure: The Problem of Embeddedness." *American Journal of Sociology,* 91.3:481–510.
Logan, John R., and Harvey L. Molotch. 1987. *Urban Fortunes: The Political Economy of Place.* Berkeley: University of California Press.
McKenzie, Evan. 1994. *Privatopia: Homeowner Associations and the Rise of Residential Private Government.* New Haven, CT: Yale University Press.
Molotch, Harvey. 1976. "The City as a Growth Machine: Toward a Political Economy of Place." *American Journal of Sociology,* 82.2:309–332.
Portes, Alejandro. 1998. "Social Capital: Its Origins and Applications in Modern Sociology." *Annual Review of Sociology,* 24:1–24.

Portes, Alejandro, and Patricia Landolt. 2000. "Social Capital: Promise and Pitfall of its Role in Development." *Journal of Latin American Studies,* 32:529–547.

Putnam, Robert D. 1993. *Making Democracy Work: Civic Traditions in Modern Italy.* Princeton, NJ: Princeton University Press.

Putnam, Robert D. 1995. "Bowling Alone: America's Declining Social Capital." *Journal of Democracy,* 6.1:65–78.

Putnam, Robert D. 2000. *Bowling Alone: The Collapse and Revival of American Community.* New York: Simon and Schuster.

Silverman, Robert Mark. 2001. "CDCs and Charitable Organizations in the Urban South: Mobilizing Social Capital Based on Race and Religion for Neighborhood Revitalization." *Journal of Contemporary Ethnography,* 30.2:240–268.

Stabile, Donald L. 2000. *Community Associations: The Emergence and Acceptance of a Quiet Innovation in Housing.* Westport, CT: Greenwood Press.

Velez-Ibanez, Carlos G. 1983. *Bonds of Mutual Trust: The Cultural Systems of Rotating Credit Associations among Urban Mexicans and Chicanos.* New Brunswick, NJ: Rutgers University Press.

Wacquant, Loic J. D. 1998. "Negative Social Capital: State Breakdown and Social Destruction in America's Urban Core." *Netherlands Journal of Housing and the Built Environment,* 13.1:25–40.

6 Community Development Corporations and Social Capital

Lessons from the South Bronx

Brian Sahd

Introduction

Recently, much has been written on the concepts of Social Capital and Community Development Corporations (CDCs). Indeed, there appears to be an emerging group of researchers who discuss social capital and community development, defining both in similar terms, in order to examine specific issues relating to certain aspects of low-income communities or neighborhoods. My work in the South Bronx, as summarized later in this chapter, deals with a basic question: how do community development corporations (at least those representative of the South Bronx) impact the development of social capital? The first step in answering this question will be to flesh out these two concepts in order to consider their relevance for the South Bronx and beyond.

In this chapter, I contest some of the conventional wisdom surrounding CDCs and their impact in creating social capital. Several recent studies have suggested that CDCs are mechanisms that enable the creation of social capital by providing residents the means through which to determine the direction of urban growth. I suggest that this assessment is half true. While the present day CDCs have evolved into effective mechanisms through which planning and development can occur and services can be provided, they are not structured to be the avenues or conduits through which social capital is created for the neighborhood residents. More accurately, although these corporations can be seen as a third sector of the political economy of the city, taking a legitimate place along side the government and private sectors, they are not structured to engage residents. This was not the case when the predecessor of the first CDCs began their work in the 1970s. The principal characteristic of these early groups was their broad-based community involvement. The mature CDCs of today, far from being representative of resident interests, are characterized by market-type relationships.

What follows is not intended to reinvent the notions of social capital nor community development corporations. Instead it will utilize the work that has already been done in the conceptualization of these terms. What needs to be done is to peel away the layers of rhetoric and come to some understanding as to what constitutes social capital and what constitutes community development corporations. In the end we will have a clearer understanding of these two concepts and how they relate to each other.

Social Capital

Despite the attention being paid to the importance of the development of social capital by an increasing number of scholars and practitioners, its very widespread use has created its own polemics. Because social capital is being applied to a variety of issues, its theoretical relevance to the field is potentially diluted. It is for this reason that this chapter will begin with an attempt to deconstruct the concept of social capital, and rebuild it relying heavily on the elements outlined by Robert Putnam and Kenneth Temkin and William Rohe. This is undertaken to provide a framework through which to examine the role of CDCs in the formation of social capital over the past 30 years in the South Bronx.

It is important to note that there have been few attempts to empirically measure social capital and its impact on low-income neighborhoods. In fact, it is extremely difficult to quantify the elements attributed to social capital among individual residents and groups within communities. Indeed as Temkin and Rohe (1998) note, there is no empirical evidence to support whether social capital builds or stabilizes low-income communities.

Part of the problem is that even though the term has been widely utilized in social research, there is not one universally agreed-upon meaning of what constitutes social capital. Indeed, the more this concept has been studied and applied, the broader its meaning has become. Authors who have argued the concept, most notably Robert Putnam and Jane Jacobs, but more recently, Avis Vidal, Kenneth Temkin, William Rohe, Marilyn Gittell, and David Swindell, utilize the concept, in increasingly diverse ways, to examine a richly diverse set of processes. All of these authors (and those not mentioned who have recently become engaged in the discussion) have imposed their unique set of assumptions and theories on the concept.

Almost all definitions of social capital rely heavily on Robert Putnam's (1993) seminal study, *Making Democracy Work*. Putnam, although not the originator of the term or even the concept of social capital, is credited with bringing it into contemporary scholarship. Putnam attributes the development of the concept to L. J. Hanifan, a practical reformer in the Progressive Era who, in 1916, wrote about the importance of community involvement for the success of the educational system and attributed social capital with "those tangible substances [that] count for most in the daily lives of people: namely good will, fellowship, sympathy, and social intercourse. . . . The community as a whole will benefit by the cooperation of all its parts, while the individual will find in his association the advantages of the help, the sympathy and the fellowship of his neighbors" (Putnam 1993: 19). This definition forms the basis of the present day meaning of social capital.

According to Putnam (1995), social capital "refers to features of social organization such as networks, norms, and social trust that facilitate coordination and cooperation for mutual benefit." Similar to the notions of physical and human capital, social capital, accordingly, is generated from individual and communal productivity. The mechanisms used to generate this productivity, for Putnam, are trust and cooperation, and the more trust and cooperation is expanded within a community—the greater degree of the social capital—the better off are the residents. As Putnam (1995) explains this concept, "a well-connected individual in a poorly connected society is not as productive as a well-connected individual in a well-connected society. And even a poorly connected individual may derive some of the spillover benefits from living in a well-connected society."

Temkin and Rohe (1998) suggest that Putnam's concept indicates that the more social capital is created the more these networks of civic engagement nurture the norms of generalized reciprocity and encourage the emergence of social trust. Here *trust* is referred to as "bonding capital" and is defined by a feeling or a sense of mutual obligation to one another. Another concept, *cooperation or civic engagement,* is referred to as "bridging capital," the act of bringing together within a community people and groups that previously did not interact with or know of each other. Ross Gittell and Avis Vidal summarize the notion of social capital as presuming: "that the more people connect with each other, the more they will trust each other, and the better off they are individually and collectively, because there is a strong collective aspect to social capital: the social and economic system as a whole functions better because of the ties among actors that make it up" (Gittell and Vidal 1998:15).

Temkin and Rohe expand on the concept of social capital to include sociocultural milieu and institutional infrastructure. In their work, "Social Capital and Neighborhood Stability: An Empirical Investigation," these authors attempt to operationalize social capital in terms of Putnam's trust and cooperation components by including the creation of a sense of community where "residents feel a strong sense of community and are able to translate this feeling into effective collective action" (Temkin and Rohe 1998:71).

In their study, Temkin and Rohe attempt to demonstrate the positive effects social capital has on neighborhood stability. These authors, in fact, succeed in taking the concept of social capital out of the qualitative nature given to the concept by Putnam and infusing it with elements of an empirical nature in an attempt to quantify and measure social capital. For Temkin and Rohe social capital can be operationalized through a compiling of the elements of sociocultural milieu and institutional infrastructure in order to measure neighborhood change and or stability.

Sociocultural milieu involves strong neighborhood identity and contains community-building opportunities. A community with a strong sociocultural milieu is more prepared to combat threats, either from within or outside its borders. Conversely the the weaker the sociocultural milieu, the more likely a neighborhood will experience decline and decay.

Institutional infrastructure on the other hand, measures the level of formal organization evident within a neighborhood. As the authors explain a "successful neighborhood defense requires an effective pre-existing neighborhood group or a number of residents who can come together and form a group in the face of a potential threat" (Temkin and Rohe 1998:70). The authors continue, "the neighborhood must be able to leverage a strong sense of place into a collective movement that is able to form alliances with actors outside the community and influence decisions that affect the neighborhood's character over time" (Temkin and Rohe 1998:70). Some authors have used this interpretation to make the case that community development corporations are the prime mechanism to create and sustain social capital within a neighborhood. Social capital then is a resource that can be acquired and used by individual residents, groups, or collections of groups to achieve community-building outcomes. In a recent article, Marilyn Gittell, Isolda Ortega-Bustamante and Tracy Steffy (2000) discuss social capital in their examination as it relates to women-led community development organizations. These authors begin from the vantage point that social capital is created where there is strong citizen participation, increased civic engagement, and neighborhoods that are in the midst of emerging as revitalized and stabilized places to live. CDCs, according to the authors, are the "primary vehicle for development in low-income neighborhoods," and the basis for the creation of social capital (Gittell et al. 2000).

However, when examining social capital as it is actualized by community development corporations, it becomes apparent that what is missing when the discussion moves from the theoretical realm and is applied to actual events is the absence of resident involvement in the development of neighborhoods. What has occurred in the South Bronx, and in most other cities in which CDCs have evolved over the past 30 years, is the maturation of these neighborhood institutions away from providing avenues for residents or resident groups engagement to more top-down and market-type relationships. That is, residents are involved less in the participatory functions of their neighborhoods.

For the present discussion, social capital will be defined as the interaction among and between individuals residents as well as community-based organizations (including community development corporations) in an effort to development trust, cooperation and civic engagement so as to, as Gittel et al. (2000) states, "contribute to the vitality of a community's civic capacity." The question left to answer, then, is whether CDCs, as they have evolved into a new institutional infrastructure within a maturing sociocultural milieu, create social capital and in turn enhance, or are mechanisms for, neighborhood stability? Through the examination of South Bronx CDCs this discussion will attempt to provide substantive information regarding the manner in which this interaction between and among the individual residents and the CDCs takes place in order to "increase the capacity of communities and their ability to address community problems and enhance the democratic process" (Gittell et al. 1998).

I suggest that the CDCs of today are not structured to "create" social capital nor able to meet the criteria to be effective social capital generating organizations. Indeed, they cannot. CDCs, by the definition that has evolved, are not representative of the community they serve. Furthermore, they are not participatory organizations, instead being operated as businesses with a board of directors (rarely inclusive of residents from the target neighborhood), a large professional staff, budgets in the tens of millions of dollars, and a wide range of administrative as well as programmatic activities. In fact, their main resource for growth and expansion come from the fees they charge their tenants, the government fees they receive for providing services and, in growing instances, the profits that are generated by for-profit subsidiaries. This was not always so, particularly since CDCs have their evolutionary roots in social capital generating activities.

Community Development Corporations

The concept of community development corporations evolved over a period of 10 to 15 years, with roots going as far back to the early housing/tenant movements that seemingly erupted on the scene in the early 1960s and was enhanced by the implementation of federal programs such as Community Action and Model Cities. It was during the 1960s and 1970s, when the country experienced unprecedented political, social, and civil unrest, that residents had their best opportunity to directly integrate themselves in planning and development issues. And for a time, as the case of the South Bronx demonstrates, residents were in control of what was planned and developed in their neighborhoods. Residents, who collectively formed such South Bronx groups as the People's Development Corporation (PDC), South East Bronx Community Organization (SEBCO), the Mid Bronx Desperados (MBD) and the Banana Kelly Community Improvement Association, began to redevelop, initially at least, the area without much outside interference or assistance.

As the 1970s ended and the 1980s began, the democratic perspectives and attitudes of these groups became increasingly difficult to maintain. One reason for this was shifting federal policies and programs in the community development field. In less than six years federal funding for community development projects was cut in half, going from $2.6 billion in 1979 to $1.1 billion in 1986. With less money these nascent organizations had to explore new ways to make ends meet. They developed new rules and entered into new partnerships with local government agencies as well as private corporations and foundations. What is more, their successes in rebuilding the South Bronx drew the attentions of these government agencies, private corporations and foundations, and, perhaps more importantly, real estate developers. This latter group began to refocus its attention and subsequently its interest in the South Bronx. In order to survive, the community groups that originated as democratic collectives, in the tradition of the early tenant groups and fortified by the CAA and Model Cities experiences, soon evolved into business-like corporations—the Community Development Corporations—engaging in market-type relationships that competed with the private sector and thus became a part of the "network." The resident groups that did not adapt with the changing decade, like the PDC, did not survive.

As will be discussed community development corporations, particularly those in the South Bronx are now organized and function similar to for-profit entities. The CDC model has manifested itself in such a way as to make participation by residents virtually impossible, by excluding residents from the decision-making process of the organization. Today's CDCs view residents as clients, much like hospitals or other service providers see their constituents as clients. This model, of course, has emerged as the opposite of how CDCs were first developed, as collective efforts of residents that were led by a coalition of residents working together to improve the living conditions of the neighborhood.

What has eventually evolved, for the most part, are community development corporations that are integrated into the "system" and been given legitimacy by the public and private sectors in which they operate. In fact, CDCs are now considered the "third sector" in urban development, having been given this legitimacy by government agencies and private institutions that work and operate in developing low-income urban areas. Furthermore, resident involvement in planning and development, especially in low-income neighborhoods, is now measured by the activities of their community development corporations. Not only have residents lost out on an engagement mechanism to have control over the planning and developing their own neighborhoods, but they are also being ignored by the public sector established to protect their interests. Certainly, then, instead of creating social capital by strengthening the bonds between the residents and their communities, CDCs are weakening these bonds and making it harder and harder for residents to build the trust and the networks that are so important in the development of social capital. Writing in the mid 1980s, Neal Peirce and Carol Steinbach saw this emerging trend. Speaking of the 1980s CDCs the authors suggest that "Community development organizations today are becoming increasingly sophisticated, drawing support from a growing number of state and local government and from an ever-widening universe of private foundations and corporations," (Pierce and Steinbach 1987:8) and getting away from their grassroots origins. Instead of CDCs being run by members of the neighborhood, the authors go on to describe the evolving staff and directors as "savvy and well-schooled in deal making, many have worked in the private sector or in government." If social capital is as Robert Lang and Steven Hornburg (1998:8) have described, "the link between people and place," then the CDC is seen by many as the glue that holds this link together.

The definitions that have emerged to describe CDCs have codified this relationship. Community Development Corporations, according to Nye and Glickman are:

> Non-profit, community-based organizations that work in geographically defined areas or neighborhoods with a high concentration of low-income residents. CDCs are community controlled and pursue a comprehensive vision of community change to revitalize economic, physical and social conditions to benefit local residents. CDCs pursue multiple strategies for change, mobilize public and private resources for development and build community alliances. (Nye and Glickman 2000: 163)

Similarly, Avis Vidal (1995) defines CDCs as "nonprofit, community-based organizations whose mission is to make the low- and moderate-income communities in which they work better places to live. . . . CDCs are typically founded by and grounded in the communities they serve, with residents and other neighborhood stakeholders constituting the majority of the governing board." Likewise, Pierre Clavel, Jessica Pitt and Jordan Yin (1997) define CDCs as "Non-profit voluntary associations . . . [that are] citizen-run, neighborhood-based."[1] And according to Peirce and Steinbach resident control of CDCs is one of the major and unqualified success of the field.

On the other hand, Piven and Cloward (1977), although writing in the late 1970s, well before the emergence of the concept of community development corporations, suggested that organizing residents in a formal manner (such is the case with CDCs) leads to "co-optation and a reduction of their voice to be heard." More recent scholars remain skeptical of the CDC. Many have argued that CDCs have become "a part of the problem by becoming too technical and too large and by abandoning their previous function of advocating and organizing" (Clavel et al. 1997).

Sara Stoutland (1999:194) in her chapter, "CDCs: Mission, Strategy and Accomplishments," suggests that the popular characteristics of a CDC include several elements:

> A concern about all aspects of community life, while seeking to address a comprehensive set of needs.

A belief that residents have the most knowledge of what needs to be done in their own neighborhood and that the CDC should be in a position to control the resident through active engagement.

Seek to choose activities that reinforce one another and produce mutually beneficial effects.

Pierce and Steinbach (1987:12) seem to have picked up on this emerging dichotomy: the more sophisticated a CDC becomes the more its development threatens to weaken social capital-creating instinct. As the authors argue, many CDCs are obliged to become so focused and project-oriented that the community residents become less and less important and "such traditional CDC goals such as developing minority leaders or empowering the poor residents" are going by the wayside.

Just as social capital has been overused to the extent that a common definition is difficult to state, so, too, has the concept of the CDC been over-extended. Clearly CDCs can and do attempt to improve the living conditions of the low-income neighborhood in which they are established. On the other hand, CDCs have had a difficult time creating a viable community while maintaining true to their grassroots, resident involvement traditions. As will be discussed in the next section, many CDCs are not resident-led and do not even allow for resident involvement or engagement mechanisms. As we examine the development of four South Bronx CDCs it is important to keep the dual aspect of CDCs in mind.

South Bronx CDCs

By any measure, the changes that occurred in the South Bronx during the past 40 years have been dramatic. From the late 1940s through the late 1960s, this particular area of New York City experienced transformation and slow decline. By the early 1970s, however, this gradual transformation mutated into rapid degeneration. By the time the fires began to consume the housing stock in the southern end of the borough between 1973 and 1975, the South Bronx was a near wasteland.

Much has been written about the South Bronx during this chaotic period; more has been filmed and turned into Hollywood fodder. And what baseball fan watching the 1977 World Series will ever forget the startling pictures, along with Howard Cosell's commentary, of the fires that were burning the Bronx?

The late 1960s and early 1970s were dramatic years for the country as a whole, and for the South Bronx in particular. Nationally and internationally the South Bronx became a symbol of urban destruction and decay—an area increasingly perceived by many as being without any hope of ever recovering. In a relatively short period of time the South Bronx became synonymous with all the ills that were affecting cities across the country and the world. Roberta Gratz (1994:90), in her book, *The Living City*, cogently states what most believed about the area: "The South Bronx is this country's most awesome symbol of urban decay and despair. It epitomizes the plight of the nation's cities, and dramatizes the failure of government policies." This vision of the South Bronx was not particular to the United States. The area became an international metaphor for urban decay. In France there is a saying "C'est quoi, ce Bronx"? Literally it means, "What is this, the Bronx"? Figuratively it means "What a dump!"

The historical processes that left the South Bronx, as well as other urban areas across the country, in turmoil and chaos are complex. Certainly, in a few short years during the 1960s and 1970s the South Bronx went from being a comfortable middle-class, blue-collar neighborhood to a devastated and dangerous place to live. But looking at these years provides only a piece of the story. One needs to look to the preceding years to get a total picture. At no other time in the nation's history did circumstances converge in such a way as to undermine and erode the fabric of an urban area to such a dramatic degree in such a short period of time. The changes that occurred in the South Bronx are many and can be traced to the aftermath of World War II. Employment sector changes, economic shifts, resident flight, erosion of tax bases, government policies that alternated between involvement and abandonment, decline in real estate values, the civil rights movement, Vietnam War protests, federal housing moratoria, and economic crises all heavily impacted urban America in general and the South Bronx in particular. The confluence of circumstances reflected in these events left the South Bronx with 650,000 fewer jobs in the 10 years between 1965 and 1975. One half of this loss came in the manufacturing sector at the time the largest employment sector in the South Bronx.

With the jobs leaving, the mostly white workers soon followed. White flight, which began as a trickle in the late 1950s, was all but completed by the late 1960s. The fleeing residents took other things with them, primarily the businesses, the real estate values and the tax base. In the 15 years from 1962 to 1978 the area lost almost three-quarters of its population—nearly 90 percent of its white population—and one-half of its housing stock.

There were demographic changes as well. New residents, mainly African Americans and Latinos (principally Puerto Ricans) moved to the

South Bronx in large numbers, not a significant occurrence in and of itself since the South Bronx periodically experienced shifting populations. What was different about this latest in-migration was the fact that people were coming into the area without the prospect of employment.

The federal government's attempts to address this emerging decline in the social and economic situation—the War on Poverty, Community Action, and Model Cities—while valiant ventures, at best did little more than place the proverbial finger in the dyke. And when the civil rights marches, the Vietnam War protests, and the student riots reached their apex in the late 1960s, governments at all levels seemed helpless.

This confluence of circumstances had no historical precedent and hit low-income, urban areas, the South Bronx in particular, very hard. By the mid-1970s this neighborhood of New York City was devastated, depleted, and seemingly out of the consciousness of government and private institutions.

However, the same circumstances that had devastated the South Bronx also managed to create an environment for hope. Even through the War on Poverty, the Community Action Agencies, and Model Cities were "too-little-too-late" programmatic ventures, they did manage to institutionalize resident involvement. And as a result, residents used whatever they could from these government programs to address and mitigate their worsening living conditions.

The trajectory of resident involvement in the affairs of their neighborhood can also be traced to the social conscience awakening of the 1960s. This certainly was a period of great upheaval, but it was also a period of great enthusiasm and empowerment. The counter culture nature of the 1960s and its effects on the residents engaged in their own urban struggles and grassroots organizing is widely recognized: the climate provided the impetus for the involvement of residents in the planning and development of low-income, mainly minority neighborhoods. The 1960s were a time when individuals challenged the distribution of power within, and the order and structure of, the system. Residents demanded access to the political process as well as inclusion in the decision-making apparatus of the process. Marilyn Gittell (1980:30), in her book *Limits to Citizen Participation*, summarizes the sentiment of the time, "Poor and working-class populations were seeking an entrée into the system at the same time that they were trying to change the distribution of power within the system. The pressure for access was a priority, participation became the byword."

During the worst of the devastation and tumult that occurred in the area, throughout the late 1960s and for much of the 1970s, South

Bronx residents began a movement to reclaim what was being lost to abandonment and arson. Early CDC-type groups, such as the People's Development Corporation (PDC) began a movement to restore the South Bronx one building at a time. The method PDC used was an example of how social capital can be created by linking people to their place: it enjoined the individual to use his or her own time and energy to construct their own home. Utilizing government work programs and vacant and/or abandoned buildings, the PDC was able to offer residents a job at the same time they were rehabbing their own homes. This sweat-equity, urban homesteading concept made a big splash and received much media attention as well as government financing. By the late 1970s, four or five years after being organized and with only one rehabbed building to its credit, the PDC was flush with federal money and its leader, Ramon Rueda, was a media star and a much in-demand speaker on resident involvement issues. Sweat-equity and urban homesteading, although the most grassroots movement to come out of the 1970s, was not the model that eventually dominated the "third sector."

Concomitant with the efforts of the PDC, several other organizations were establishing themselves in the community development arena. Prominent among these was the Mid-Bronx Desperados (MBD), the South East Bronx Community Organization (SEBCO) and the Banana Kelly Community Improvement Association. All three eventually rejected the more grassroots structure of sweat-equity and self-help and emerged by the early 1980s as community development corporations, becoming critical actors in the rebuilding of the South Bronx.

It was in the changed environment of the late 1960s and early 1970s that South Bronx residents began to take matters into their own hands. Beginning in the late 1960s and continuing through the early 1980s, residents organized themselves into groups to save their neighborhoods. Without money, operational planning, experience, or political connections, these groups relied solely on their persistent determination. Tom Robbins (1996), an early participant in these grassroots groups, wrote that these community groups were, "born as little more than rag-tag bands of outraged citizens warriors, armed only with strong vocal cords and good intentions."

The rag-tag groups of residents who started a movement to reclaim the South Bronx one building at a time eventually became responsible for the direction in which community involvement and social capital creation would take place. But back then they were the social capital. Leaders of this movement developed a trust among neighborhood residents through their efforts, their determination to stay and work to improve a deteriorating neighborhood. These early community groups began the process of network building, cooperation, and civic engagement between their nascent organization and the wider community.

Moreover, the organizations that were founded in the early 1970s became the mechanism through which urban planning and development would reshape the neighborhoods of the South Bronx. Finally, these same organizations established an institutional basis within their individual communities through which outside public and private institutions could become engaged.

Social Capital Creation by Early Community Development Corporations

PEOPLES DEVELOPMENT CORPORATION

The neighborhood in which the PDC arose was in as bad a physical condition as any neighborhood in the South Bronx. By 1974, the year PDC was established, Morrisania was listed as having close to 16,000 dwelling units, with over half vacant or abandoned. Out of the roughly 8,000 units not abandoned, only 20 percent (1,600) were considered sound and livable. By 1979, 95 percent of all dwelling units in Morrisania were either owned by the city or well on their way through property tax foreclosure.[2]

Skillfully motivating one hundred local residents, the PDC, comprised of 12 individual members and led by the charismatic Ramon Rueda, took over a building on Washington Avenue. After "liberating the keys from the security guard in the building,"[3] PDC members began a two-week period of squatting. Within a short period of time the PDC brokered a deal with the NYC Housing Authority that involved the release of the building in return for its rehabilitation and for providing the squatters (who had been living in deteriorating buildings in the neighborhood) the first opportunity to rent the apartments. According to Rueda, the use of this grassroots support made the difference. Before the PDC became involved in the project, the city was unwilling to rehab the building. With PDC involvement it took only several weeks to accomplish what political leaders in Morrisania had been unable to get the city to do through ordinary political channels: finish reconstruction and provide a certificate of occupancy.

After this success, PDC turned its attention to another vacant building a few doors down the street located at 1186 Washington Avenue. This five-story building became the group's major achievement.

What the PDC did next had a lasting impact on community involvement and the creation of social capital far outlasting their own organization. PDC combined the physical resource of the vacant building, the physical resources of the residents—their labor, and the poverty conditions of the people of the South Bronx into the area's first sweat-equity programs.

Using the techniques learned during their first squatting experience, the PDC took over 1186 Washington Avenue with no outside resources except those of its members. Using only their own skills and resources, the homesteaders, laboring in the evenings and on weekends, worked diligently to create a livable place for themselves in a neighborhood that they could call their own. At the same time, the PDC took an active role in the neighborhood and started to focus on cleaning the area surrounding 1186 Washington Avenue. The members took what was once a garbage-strewn and abandoned lot and created Unity Park, a place where residents could enjoy a bit of green in an otherwise burned-out and deteriorating community. The PDC held block parties and street fairs to generate awareness and interest in its cause. Because of the early social capital work being performed by the PDC, the organizations developed friendly relations and remained, according to Katz, on "good terms with its neighbors" (Katz 1983:12). Starting out small, becoming involved in one or two buildings at a time, was a modest endeavor and not likely to create a great deal of attention.

In the summer of 1975 the group was able to secure outside funding for their organization for the first time. Although the federal summer youth employment funds were small, even by 1975 standards, they had a huge impact on the PDC and the community involvement movement as a whole. With federal funds, the PDC was able to recruit a new crop of homesteaders, convincing the new members that the PDC would be able to provide them not only with jobs, new skills and a new apartment (all powerful incentives in their own right), but also, as Katz writes, "it was a rare opportunity to get some dignity through the creation of the housing, and enjoy doing it at the same time" (Katz 1983:12). By all accounts the structure of the PDC and the way in which the members interacted were different than any other community group that had ever existed. Rueda believed that the PDC was breaking the mold and recalled that the organization was not like the rest of the "poverty pimps providing services in the area." Rueda and the other members of the organization built an organization with a commitment to democratic control from inside the group. As activists who were involved in the antiwar movement, and national and welfare rights struggles, the founding members of the PDC knew the benefits of collective action and active participation.

Sweat-equity allowed these resident-workers to become owners of their apartments without making the ordinary payments required to buy into a cooperative. It took the resident-workers over two years to complete the renovations—a minor miracle, when almost everyone else in the city was indifferent to the conditions of the South Bronx. According to Rueda, "these new apartments are more than apartments. They are the base for a much larger goal to fill the empty lives of thousands of youths with a sense of collective purpose, to give them jobs, training, hope and confidence in their ability to change the world for the better" (Fried 1977: A1). When attempting to explain the reasons why the PDC was able to accomplish what it did, Rueda stated, "emerging from the indignities of street life and unemployment, the pride and promise of self-organized, steady work cannot be underestimated" (Katz 1983:13).

MID BRONX DESPERADOS

While the PDC was building an organization on sweat equity, self-help and democratic control (all in an attempt to build social capital within South Bronx communities) other organizations were creating new forums in which resident could become involved in community development. The Mid Bronx Desperados, the South East Bronx Community Organization, and Banana Kelly Community Improvement Association were neighborhood groups that emerged at approximately the same time as the PDC. These groups, headed respectively by Genevieve S. Brooks, the Rev. Louis Giganti, and Harry DeRienzo worked to reclaim and reshape their neighborhoods.

In 1974 Brooks was running the Seabury Day Care Center. A resident of the South Bronx since 1954, she lived through its deterioration and devastation. As a Southerner the idea of community involvement was not foreign to Brooks. "Being a Southerner, when a lot of [government] programs were not available to us, we grew up not depending on [the government]. We lived on a farm and we knew that if we were going to make it we had to do it ourselves and not depend on anyone else. We had to work."[4] As Brooks soon found out living on a farm in the South is vastly different from living in the poor neighborhoods of the South Bronx. In the 1960s Brooks participated in the Town Hall meetings held during the Lindsay Administration. In order to vent her frustrations and anger at what was happening to the neighborhood, Brooks attended these meeting, bringing with her several other residents from her neighborhoods. These meetings, according to Brooks, were "the only means that allowed us a voice. We attended these meeting in groups in order for us to have our say in what was happening in our community."[5]

It was Brooks' increased involvement in her community, specifically the Morrisania and Clairmont sections of the South Bronx, that led her and several other residents to establish the Seabury Day Care Center. After several years managing the day care center, Brooks expanded the scope of her attention and organized other neighborhood groups in an effort to "halt the tide of dis-investment and deterioration in the neighborhood." As Brooks recalls, the only way Seabury was going to have an impact on the community was to partner with other neighborhood groups, pulling together collective resources and address the neighborhoods problems in a concentrated manner. This was another early example of creating social capital by linking people to their locality.

In late 1974, after a series of meetings involving six organization and groups from the community, the Mid Bronx Desperados (MBD) was established. MBD was an all volunteer coalition of resident groups determined to "respond to the overwhelming incidence of arson in the area and to halt and reverse the massive tide of devastation occurring in the community."[6] Along with the Seabury Day Care Center the coalition members included 1555 Seabury Tenant's Association, The Bronx Boys and Girls Club, Tried Stone Baptist Church and St. John's Chrysostom. Brooks, at the urging of the other groups, was chosen as the first president of this new coalition.

Similar to PDC's experience, MBD faced despair and disappointments early on and had a difficult time keeping the disparate groups together. Over the next few years MBD remained an all-volunteer organization, with Brooks as the only paid staff member and free office space provided by the Seabury Day Care Center. It would be six years before MBD finally experienced substantive results. In 1980 the group acquired its first wholly operated and controlled project, a 143 unit, three-building, urban homestead site in the Crotona Park area.

To keep the partnership operating in the early days, Brooks took MBD down a different path from the one traveled by the PDC. Instead of concentrating her efforts on homesteading and sweat equity, with residents renovating and then owning their own units, Brooks took the advice of fellow organizer/developer Fr. Louis Giganti. Fr. Giganti introduced Brooks to Fred Ruben, a Long Island real estate developer. This emerging partnership between MBD and the real estate industry marks a turning point in CDC development, one that represents the beginning of a movement away from resident engagement.

Ruben owned several buildings in the area, which had, by the early 1970s, become deteriorated and almost abandoned. In 1975–76 Brooks partnered with Ruben and Ruben's sometime partner Jerome Chatsky, of the PRC construction company to develop 174 units of housing in five buildings on Boston Road. The project became known as MBD-1. Ruben provided the Section 8 designation to the buildings, Chatsky was in charge of the reconstruction of the units and MBD responsible for getting the necessary approvals from the city as well as tenant selection and placement. The agreement stipulated that MBD would ultimately become the controlling and managing agent for the buildings. For its part MBD received a third of the tax shelter funds for the properties totaling approximately $100,000.[7]

The next year 1979, MBD went out on its own. With money from the Boston Road project, MBD was able to secure additional money to redevelop the 143 units of housing in Crotona Park. Using city urban homesteading funds, MBD not only rehabilitated these 143 units, but was also able to begin development of an industrial park on the site. By the early 1980s MBD had established themselves as a neighborhood institution. According to Brooks:

> After years of heartache and struggle we were finally able to open our own offices. During our first five or six years we were an all-volunteer organization, operating in the Seabury Day Care Center . . . and . . . it was hard keeping the organization together. It would take us six years before getting our own projects; it was not quick. But after we did a few projects we began getting recognized. We began working with other organizations and foundations that wanted their money to go to an organization that would be around for the long haul.[8]

By 1980 MBD was an established organization in charge of managing five buildings with over 300 units and receiving the tax shelter funds. This was far more than what PDC was able to do in the same five or six year period. After the first building on Washington Avenue, PDC was having a difficult time securing the necessary financial funding for its additional seven buildings. It would not be until after the famous visit by President Jimmy Carter to the South Bronx in 1977 that the PDC acquired the funding to continue its work. Furthermore, whereas the PDC was struggling to redevelop its buildings through sweat equity and self-help, allowing the residents to participate in the decision making process or planning and redevelopment, MBD was moving toward becoming a developer and landlord, managing rental housing units for fees, something that Fr. Louis Giganti and SEBCO had been doing since the mid-1970s.

SOUTH EAST BRONX COMMUNITY ORGANIZATION

Fr. Louis Giganti was a young Catholic priest stationed at St. Athanasius Church in the Hunts Point section of the South Bronx since the early 1960s. Like Brooks, Fr. Giganti also had firsthand knowledge of the changing environment. He was stationed in the South Bronx in 1962 because, in his words, he was Italian and spoke Spanish. Hunts Point was a changing neighborhood. The Jewish residents were moving out, while Latinos (mainly Puerto Ricans) were moving in. The Catholic Church wanted to bring in a priest to attend to the needs of this changing population.

For the first few years Fr. Giganti immersed himself in the religious activities of his growing parish. The neighborhood was changing so rapidly, however, that by 1964 the priests could no longer ignore the social and economic problems that were beginning to plague the members of their parish. According to Fr. Giganti, "We were only concerned with religious activities and gearing our people towards a better Christian life. But people were suffering terribly from other things."[9]

Fr. Giganti and a small team of volunteers from his parish canvassed the entire Hunts Point neighborhood including Simpson and Fox Streets, two of the most deteriorated, distressed, crime- and drug-ridden streets in the South Bronx.

> We did a whole program to get the residents of Simpson and Fox streets involved. There were a total of 42 buildings, with 4,000 of the worst tenement apartments in the city. We went all over. We went into card games, where all black men were hanging out, to convert them, to engage them. We tried to raise the collective consciousness. We had parties, brought neighbors together. And once people got to know their neighbors and share experiences with them, we got them excited.[10]

From this, Fr. Giganti moved on to start the Simpson Street Neighborhood Organization in 1965 to combat the growing deteriorating environment in his neighborhood. By 1968, Fr. Giganti and the Simpson Street Neighborhood Organization were becoming known in the area as advocates and organizers. In late 1968 Fr. Giganti had established the Longwood Management Company with a $47,000 grant he received through the Model Cities program. Fr. Giganti used this grant to rehab his first building on Simpson Street.[11]

To achieve a wider impact Fr. Giganti convinced other neighborhood organizations and institutions to form the South East Bronx Community Organization (SEBCO) later that same year. Initially this 13-member organization was comprised of businesses, churches and neighborhood organizations including Simpson Street Development Corporation, St. John's Church, Casita Maria, the Longwood Management Company, Sesda, American Bank Note, the Third Baptist Church, and St. Athanasius.[12] Fr. Giganti headed this new organization. Citing strength from numbers, Fr. Giganti reasoned that if one organization (Longwood) could secure financial support to rehab one building, there was no telling how much financing and many buildings 13 organizations would be able to secure. As Fr. Giganti remembers, the idea behind this "coalition of organizations was to be the developer of the neighborhood." Using his experience at Longwood, Fr. Giganti believed that he "could receive federal grants, Model Cities and Section 8 hosing vouchers to rebuilding the entire neighborhood."[13]

And it might have worked, except for the 1968 Nixon housing moratorium. Nixon's action effectively pulled the financial rug out from under nascent SEBCO. Fr. Giganti began to have doubts that the coalition would survive. He recalled that "between 1968 and 1972, SEBCO did very little . . . because of the Nixon moratorium. I was not even sure SEBCO would succeed. It was a very rough time for us." SEBCO almost did not survive this period. According to Fr. Giganti, "when nothing was being done at that time, [member] groups started to drop out. [At the end] only six original groups remained."[14]

It took five years of planning, but finally in 1975 Giganti and the remaining member organizations of SEBCO, which at the time included Simpson Street Development Corporation, St. John's Church, Casita Maria, and the Longwood Management Company, got involved in their first project. Aldus Green was a 100-unit building on Aldus Street and owned by a private real estate developer. The developer Hy Kraus approached Fr. Giganti with an offer; he would make SEBCO a partner in the development of the building, if Fr. Giganti assisted in getting resident support for the redevelopment plans. As part of his involvement with Kraus, Fr. Giganti managed to acquire 360 units of Section 236 housing (financial subsidies to build moderate-income units), but the problem for Fr. Giganti was that even though SEBCO had the financing, it did not have the buildings.

Fred Ruben had buildings. Ruben owned several buildings on Simpson Street. Fr. Giganti contacted Ruben with a proposition. If Ruben would supply the buildings and bring in a contractor, SEBCO would develop the buildings. Similar to the MBD deal, this was a three-way partnership between SEBCO, Ruben and Chatsky, the general contractor. Each of the three received one-third of the $750,000 in public financing when the project was completed. With its $250,000 share SEBCO open its first office on 163rd Street. By 1980 SEBCO was managing over 2,000 units in eight building complexes.

It is easy to see how Fr. Giganti and SEBCO influenced MBD and the emerging community development organizations. Fr. Giganti brought together elements from the public and private sectors and community groups. His organization, as well as the growing number of other CDCs, was evolving into a business-like development corporation that viewed residents as tenants rather than partners in rebuilding the community.

BANANA KELLY IMPROVEMENT ASSOCIATION

The most dramatic example of a CDC that began by attempting to create social capital, but eventually led to almost destroying a neighborhood is the Banana Kelly Improvement Association. By all accounts, Kelly Street, located in the southeastern section of the South Bronx, was a prime contender for Roger Starr's (1985) "Plan Shrinkage" strategy. Of the dozens of buildings that lined Kelly Street, only three were fully occupied, with scattered residents living in a few others. In 1977 the city decided to demolish several of the abandoned buildings.

Frank Potts, a homeowner on Kelly Street, feared that the demolition of the buildings would have devastating effects on the entire neighborhood (and of course on his properties in particular). Harry DeRienzo, a social worker at Casa Maria, a local settlement house, who knew Potts' son, Leon, from pick-up basketball games, heard that Kelly Street was in danger of total abandonment. What grew out of this casual friendship begun on the basketball court became on of the most celebrated community-based organizations in the nation. As Gratz relates:

> It was difficult to think of the block and its environs, a virtual stockpile of vacant buildings and rubble, as anything but hopeless. A group of neighborhood residents knew better . . . They understood real hopelessness. They had lived with it in one form or another for many years. In their eyes, neither Kelly Street nor the three buildings scheduled for demolition were beyond redemption. They rallied to rescue the three vacant buildings . . . argued with government bureaucrats and pleaded for the right to renovate the buildings themselves for their own use. They adopted a motto, "Don't Move, Improve" and organized the Banana Kelly Improvement Association. (Gratz 1994:110)

DeRienzo and Leon Potts felt that they could make a difference. After speaking with leaders of other organized resident groups in the area, including Rueda at PDC and Fr. Giganti at SEBCO, DeRienzo and Potts decided that they would establish a similar group to help stabilize their neighborhood. They decided to establish Banana Kelly around a grass-roots, democratically structured framework. Thirty or so other neighborhood residents and area organizations joined DeRienzo and Potts to form this new neighborhood organization. The goal was to assume ownership of the abandoned buildings and renovate them. According to DeRienzo, "In August 1977, 30 area residents 'liberated' one city-owned and two privately owned properties. They were claimed for the people of the neighborhood and would be renovated through 'sweat equity'" (Cohen and DeRienzo 1988:17). Banana Kelly acted as general contractor and developer and through its residents provided the "sweat" necessary to reconstruct cooperative housing. Using a seemingly unlimited resource[15]—neighborhood residents looking for a job and a better place to live—Banana Kelly, like the PDC, traded labor for ownership.

By the time Banana Kelly was formed, although not officially established, in late 1977 the social capital enhancing idea of self-help and sweat-equity had been legitimized by the PDC. Although, as DeRienzo soon found out, this type of urban development was not easy to maintain. Of the original 30 members, only five remained active within Banana Kelly as 1978 came to a close. The others, according to DeRienzo, took a "wait and see" attitude, deciding that it was better to watch than to become involved.[16]

DeRienzo, Potts and the rest of the resident members of Banana Kelly knew that, in order to legitimize themselves for those within and outside the neighborhood, they needed to accomplish something tangible; something that the rest of the neighborhood could see. That something came in the form of an empty lot, one of the thousands across the South Bronx. As Leon Potts recalled:

> It's hard to keep people involved when you don't even know if you can keep your promise, so anything to show we were still moving was a plan. We had sixteen- and nineteen-year-old dropouts to whom we offered hope of eventual skill/training, but we never knew if and when that program funding would come through. During the demolition period, we figured if we could just get them used to working hard everyday, we would have done some good. Most participants believed it would still be a developer who would do the job. They had lived their lives with someone always doing it for them. Many of their parents were on welfare. The system told them that someone else always does it for them. (Gratz 1994:120)

"We needed to get something going that was visible," recalled DeRienzo, "a short-term project that would draw in a nucleus of people and establish a track record."[17]

While trying to establish Banana Kelly, securing the necessary funding sources to purchase and rehab the three abandoned buildings on the block, DeRienzo, Potts and the other resident members set their sights on an empty lot behind Kelly Street to be redeveloped as a garden.[18] Resident members of Banana Kelly cleared the lot. Block parties and other events were held to raise awareness and money, vegetables and flowers were planted and a barbecue pit was built in order to have summer neighborhood cook-outs. As Leon Potts related "The important thing was to get people involved, give them something they could see and keep spirits up—all our spirits up" (Gratz 1994:119).

During 1978 and 1979 Banana Kelly was hard at work trying to secure the necessary funds to support the organization. The members decided to be aggressive. DeRienzo and Potts met with both Rueda and Fr. Giganti; each by-now seasoned community activist was invaluable to the nascent Banana Kelly. Fr. Giganti helped DeRienzo gain access to city housing agencies. Indeed, SEBCO and Banana Kelly would eventually work together to renovate a 60-unit building on Kelly Street. Banana Kelly's sweat-equity crew worked as laborers on the building and SEBCO would share in the developer's profits.[19] But it was from Rueda and the PDC that Banana Kelly received the most inspiration. Rueda taught DeRienzo about CETA and its importance to sweat equity. Rueda provided guidance and insight into the workings of city government. As DeRienzo stated, "Ramon was our inspiration, He was always there for us. He took me by the hand and showed me how to act."[20]

From the advice given by these two charismatic resident leaders DeRienzo and the rest of the Banana Kelly's resident-members soon began to work the system to meet their needs. To address a neighborhood rat problem Banana Kelly asked the city's Bureau of Pest Control for assistance in removing the debris from the interiors of the three targeted buildings. They turned to the National Guard to assist with clearing another vacant lot so that a park could be built. They obtained excess cement donated from construction companies to pave what would become basketball and paddleball courts as well as walkways and sidewalks (Gratz 1994:119–120).

It took two years, but by the time Banana Kelly managed to receive financing and title to the three buildings in late 1979, DeRienzo, Potts and the other resident leaders that stayed established the organization as a premier institution within the neighborhood. Two years later, in 1981, 21 families moved into the three newly renovated Kelly Street buildings. The total cost of renovation and rehab was $540,000 ($26,000 per unit, which was almost half the $45,000 for Section 8 developer-sponsored rehab). The organization also managed 186 city-owned units, had 20 buildings in the renovation pipeline and administered a budget of over a $4 million. This was a euphoric time for the organization. But it was also on the verge of reaching a crossroad.

With limited government resources coupled with private contracts and support these early community development groups led the drive to rebuild the South Bronx's decrepit and deteriorating housing stock. PDC, MBD, Banana Kelly and SEBCO were very different organizations, but they had several common elements. For one they were neighborhood-based organizations that, in the words of Steven Katz, took matters into their own hands and questioned the right of "downtown banks and bureaucracies to control other people's lives." For the first time, the residents had a chance to affect a situation of genuine control and mutual responsibility (Katz 1983). For another, these organizations started small, piecing together a web of government monies and private support to first gain control of one or two buildings on a block, then branching out to more buildings and more blocks. Ignoring conventional wisdom, these early groups took control of vacant buildings—rehabbed them—and assumed eventual ownership. Finally, these organizations placed heavy emphasis on linking the residents to their neighborhood; creating social ties, trust and networks to achieve the common goal of reclaiming and rebuilding the neighborhood.

These were not the only neighborhood-based organizations in the nation's poorest communities that took matters into their own hands to create organizations in which residents could have some control over their living situation. In the mid-1970s and early 1980s, however, these four groups were on the front lines of creating a movement that had a tremendous impact on the devastated South Bronx and on the way in which residents could become involved in the rebuilding of their neighborhoods. These early community groups created urban oases amid ruin and destruction. Part developers, part job trainers, part contractors, part managers, these groups were able to weave together disparate public programs and increasing private monies to establish what eventually became a standard in community-based planning and development—the Community Development Corporation.

While it is true that PDC, MBD, Banana Kelly and SEBCO spearheaded the early community involvement movement in the South

Bronx, the manner in which this movement was to be defined was not set in stone. Utilizing competing concepts of resident involvement, PDC's and Banana Kelly's sweat equity and urban homesteading and MBD/SEBCO's community development organizing, this emerging sector fought for the minds and souls not of the residents of the South Bronx, but of the public and private sectors.[21] This was not a knock-down, drag-out fight, however, but one that was pursued individually and slowly over a period of time. Early on it looked as though the PDC's sweat equity and urban homesteading with its democratic underpinnings would be the dominant form to attempt to build and create social capital. However, by the early part of the 1980s, it was clear that the community development corporation, with its market-driven approach, would prevail.

To understand the shifting pathways of social capital development within the CDC context, it is again necessary to put the field in a broader framework and discuss conditions that were occurring on the national and local scene, both in terms of government policies and spending as well as in terms of the emerging influence of the private sector. The election of Ronald Reagan as president had a tremendous impact on resident groups that were working to rebuild the South Bronx. Reagan's economic policies and budgetary spending, stemming from his belief that the federal government was too heavily involved in the affairs of the States and from his efforts to cut federal spending for social programs and taxes, changed the environment in which these community groups worked.

But politics in Washington was not alone in changing the climate in which CDCs operated. In an attempt to begin to curb the deteriorating housing stock, New York City Council passed Local Law 45,[22] which shortened the time necessary to foreclose on a building. Still weak from the fiscal crisis and near bankruptcy in the mid-1970s,[23] the city, as a result of this law, turned out to be administratively unprepared for its emerging landlord responsibilities. The fact was that by 1982, just four years after the law took effect, the city had become the largest property owner and landlord in New York, presiding over 35,000 occupied apartments in over 8,000 buildings, with another 5,000 vacant buildings with 12,000 apartments.[24]

Local Law 45 was only the beginning. Programs and policies to rid the city of its management duties were being implemented in quick succession. The newly renamed and reshaped Department of Housing Preservation and Development (HPD), had responsibilities for managing this growing real estate, instituted several programs including the

Community Management Program, 7A, Tenant Interim Lease and Management in Partnership. These were just a few of the many attempts HPD and its Division of Alternative Management (DAMP) used to disinvest itself from the foreclosed property, each with its own formula for transferring the newly acquired property in private hands.

Furthermore, the changing environment at both the national and local levels heavily affected community groups such as the PDC, Banana Kelly, SEBCO and MBD and the manner in which resident involvement evolved during the decade. By 1983, PDC effectively collapsed as an organization, while SEBCO and MBD were just beginning to flourish. And in what may be the most telling example of how resident involvement was changing, the Banana Kelly Improvement Association,[25] which was based on the PDC model of cooperative participation of each member in the decision-making process, adapted to the changing environment by transforming itself into a community development corporation model pioneered by SEBCO and MBD—one that was less democratically run and resident-engaging to more business-like, market-focused and hierarchically controlled.

By 1982 throughout the city there were close to 850 buildings with 16,000 apartments involved in various HPD programs. Because of the rising legitimacy of MBD, SEBCO and Banana Kelly, these groups were among the organizations on the receiving end of these "vesting" programs. Over the course of the decade the city "vested" hundreds of buildings throughout the South Bronx. In the Melrose and Morrisania sections alone (two of the poorest sections in the city) almost 180 buildings with over 3,500 units were under various city programs by 1989. To handle these newly acquired and distressed properties and the thousands of low-income residents who lived there, community groups such as SEBCO, MBD and Banana Kelly began to expand both administratively and programmatically. They started to increase their staff to include professional developers and management personnel. They also broadened the provision of social services. As the 1980s wore on, a pattern began to emerge: these groups began to function as businesses where the bottom line was paramount: more buildings, more financing, and more rehabilitation. They even came to be referred to as corporations— Community Development Corporations—no longer run and operated by residents, but instead hierarchical organization that diverged from the representative nature in which they developed. As DeRienzo noted in 1988, as the professionalization of the community groups grew they "became more developer than organizer, and in the process their constituency became their clients" (Cohen and DeRienzo 1988:19).

The Fall of the PDC and the rise of CDCs

The early 1980s was also a time when things began to fall apart for the residents who were involved in the PDC. Despite the national attention and the improved financial conditions, signs of conflict began to emerge. In 1978, almost overnight, the PDC went from a struggling resident organization involving 40 people with a limited budget from small grants, unemployment checks, and summer youth employment programs to a multimillion dollar organization employing over two hundred residents. Looking back, Rueda knew that this success was a double-edged sword:

> My objective was to take people off the streets and help them to turn their life around. I wanted to teach them how to fish, not feed them fish. Was I successful at this, yes. Was I successful at instituting an organization, no. I did not believe in the system. I was not willing to let PDC become a part of the system. The neighborhood had all the ingredients in making a difference. We were receiving funding from some external sources and we were beginning to be successful at spreading the work we were doing.[26]

After the Carter visit, it seemed that everyone wanted to visit and see for himself or herself what was going on in the South Bronx. Rueda was becoming a much in-demand speaker at hearings, conferences, and other meetings. The organization, dismissed as irrelevant by New York City government officials a short while before, was now at the forefront of the housing redevelopment movement (Gratz 1994:110).

But the newfound attention (and the finances that came with it) had an unintended effect. According to Gratz the organization crumbled under the weight of too much money too soon, too much internal disarray, and too much outside attention. Katz was more pragmatic; he suggests that no grassroots organization could have withstood the kind of uncontrolled growth that PDC witnessed. "[The PDC] management had no experience working as a team; there was little trust between workers and management; the operation was badly under capitalized, especially in terms of covering administrative overhead and cash flow needs; it did not have good relations with its vendors and vertical lines of authority had never been implemented" (Katz 1983:19).

By early 1980 PDC members were no longer working in the democratic environment that the organization once had. Rueda had left the organization. Homesteaders were turning into laborers; working for wages and sweat equity became something one had to do to get a

CETA job. "Pulling sweat" for the PDC no longer meant a commitment to an individual apartment, to the organization, nor to the neighborhood (Katz 1983:20).

The social capital concepts of self-help, sweat equity and urban homesteading began to lose the luster that they had during the height of PDC's popularity. Even with the success of Banana Kelly in the late 1970s and early 1980s, these resident-inspired, democratically formed groups in which residents were involved in the decision-making mechanism, were becoming rare. Outside forces were pulling apart these organizations. The federal government was cutting funds and diverting others. The City was receiving thousands of distressed and abandoned buildings at an alarming rate. Because there was no infrastructure in place to manage these buildings; most of them were either sold into private hands or were demolished. Some, however, were sold or given to not-for-profits to manage. These not-for-profit community groups themselves needed to develop an infrastructure capable of managing and operating dozens of buildings with thousands of residents. They had to make the necessary repairs to the buildings and either manage them or allow the residents to become their owners and managers. At the time, the city was looking to put back into the tax-paying column as many buildings as possible, as quickly as possible. As it turned out, organizations capable of taking many buildings off city rolls and returning them to tax paying property status had the best chances of survival.

SEBCO, Banana Kelly, and MBD

Near the end of the 1970s Fr. Giganti realized that SEBCO,[27] the organization he founded along with St. John's Catholic Church, the settlement house Casita Maria (where DeRienzo began his career), and the Simpson Street Development Association, would be better off developing properties alone, without private partners. Fr. Giganti was not satisfied just developing a few buildings along Fox and Simpson Streets; he wanted to redo the entire Hunts Point neighborhood. He remembers feeling like "kids putting our fingers in holes of a dike to stop the leaks, there were too many and the dike finally broke."[28] In the early 1980s SEBCO was getting funds from both the private and public sectors. HUD provided the organization with an $800,000 to rebuild a garden. The Local Initiatives Support Corporation (LISC) and the Ford Foundation gave it a grant to start SEBCO Securities, which eventually became a $23 million program. The City gave it the necessary Section 236 funds to develop and manage 360 moderate-income apartments.

Today Fr. Giganti believes that the reason SEBCO is so successful in rebuilding the Hunts Point neighborhood was that he alone had secured the political power base to do so: "We would never have done anything, if we did what Banana Kelly and Rueda [at the PDC] did."[29] Using federal and city rehabilitation funds, Section 8 and the sale of tax shelters to investors SEBCO was able to rehabilitate more than 2,000 apartments in the Hunts Point Section of the South Bronx.[30]

Ed Logue, the director of the City's South Bronx Development Corporation in the early 1980s, praised Fr. Giganti and his development prowess. "This [SEBCO's accomplishments] is the most successful critical mass of neighborhood rebuilding in the whole City. I have a stock line about Giganti. I always say that I wish I could clone him" (Jonnes 1986:379). Logue was not the only one who saw Fr. Giganti as a savior and a model to be emulated. Others agreed.

In the fall of 1980 the Ford Foundation established the Local Initiatives Support Corporation (LISC) with an initial $10 million grant to serve as an umbrella development agency for community development corporations in distressed neighborhoods.[31] With the $10 million, LISC began to provide the emerging community development organizations (CDCs) with loans, grant and technical assistance. Anita Miller, a program officer at the Ford Foundation who joined LISC in the 1980s and headed the Comprehensive Community Revitalization Program (CCRP) until 1999, echoed Logue's sentiment. "SEBCO showed that it was possible to rebuild a neighborhood with scale" (Gratz 1994:117). By 1985, the first four years of its existence, LISC directed over $60 million into the South Bronx alone in the forms of low-interest loans, loan guarantees, grants and technical assistance (Jonnes 1986: 378). This money went mainly to neighborhood groups like SEBCO, MBD and Banana Kelly, groups that Miller suggested "were known quantities that could produce in scale." Miller recalls that:

> At the time the general feeling was that the problems were so large . . . LISC was coming from the private sector to work with these small organizations. We were looking for the revival of the South Bronx. We were intrigued by the growth of these neighborhood groups, the Clergy coalitions who organized tenants, and forced landlords to make repairs to deteriorating buildings. When we decided to fund these organization, at a time when it was not very politically wise to do so. We wanted to rebuild on a large scale. The CDCs had a larger mission to rebuild their neighborhood. Giganti was very important. He was the first of these CDC's to begin to pull together scale.[32]

According to Miller, MBD also became a good partner. "We came to the rescue of the local groups when they ran into legitimate problems. We helped them to dream and then carry out their dreams"(Jonnes 1986:378). Miller helped MBD pieced together a menu of tax shelters, public funding allocations and private money (from LISC, which targeted nearly $60 million to South Bronx development groups alone and from the Community Reinvestment Act of 1977, which by 1981 earmarked nearly $15 million in loans eventually made its way to community organization in the South Bronx). MBD, in fact, turned out to be the major beneficiary of Carter's visit to Charlotte Street. It was the organization that worked with Ed Logue to build the suburban type subdivision, redeveloping the entire block with hundreds of apartments that it managed.

Using LISC and Enterprise funds, CDCs have developed 3,000 units of rehabbed housing over a twelve-year period beginning in 1985. These new projects, all currently managed and operated by the CDCs, house a substantial number of families drawn from New York City's homeless, doubled-up and/or low-income populations.

However, some things remain clear; the PDC, the vanguard of the democratic resident movement in the South Bronx of the 1970s slowly died. Taking its place were the emerging community development corporations such as MBD, SEBCO and Banana Kelly that had abandoned cooperative decision-making for a business-like structure. These groups transformed themselves from resident-created organizations into development agencies somewhat disconnected from the residents. Once touted as grassroots organizations composed of a collection of resident groups and concerned individuals, the community organizations were becoming managers, landlords and developers; the same institutional mechanism that some of them fought against in the 1970s.

Today, MBD, Banana Kelly and SEBCO are no longer resident-led grassroots organizations. They have made the transition to Community Development Corporations. They became a part of the industry standard. They became landlords and managers to dozens of buildings and tens of thousands of residents. They became entrepreneurs of sorts, developing and running commercial businesses. To survive they had to learn how to compete within a new environment. Gratz saw this in the mid 1980s.

Sadly, it seems that in New York and other cities the neighborhood movement has come full circle. Banana Kelly [adopted from the PDC] style groups were modestly celebrated for doing what no one else dared do and in places no one else thought worthwhile at a time of slow private development activity. Community efforts reseeded the Bronx and other sites of urban decay. Change was accomplished, but its lessons are predominantly ignored. A new initiative is now taking root in these reseeded areas. Cities are going into the real-estate business and will select a new set of players. (Gratz 1994:137)

Looking back, however, Brooks harbors a sense of remorse for this turn of events. "I don't see organizations and programs benefiting our people," she said:

> For us it was more of a mission. Tenants came first. Tenants today need to learn that MBD is not going to be around forever. They need to take charge of their lives. Back in the day, everyone [the residents] had a share in the organization; we were in touch with all the tenants. We were there to work with the people not to direct them. To include them in the decision making process through interviews I did with them. It kept us grounded. It is not like it is today. No longer would a group of residents go to town meetings and fight for rights. The staff of MBD gets paid to do this for them. I hoped that we would have gone out of business by now.[33]

Fr. Giganti sees this change differently: "I knew that self-help would be a short-lived program. And that it had no future. I knew this by living it. The concept was good, but giving something to those who had nothing—mostly young kids—feeding them, keeping them off the streets, keeping them alive . . . how much can you do . . . a few buildings at a time? We didn't have enough young people to make that much of a difference."[34]

Conclusion

The historical analysis of South Bronx CDCs is a study of how social capital was created, but only for a short while. To begin, neighborhood groups and residents organized themselves in a democratic manner. Second, these groups were able to maintain the engagement of residents (and neighborhood groups) through their activities in planning, designing and redeveloping their respective neighborhoods. Third, these groups were able to develop a strong socio-culture milieu, that is, they were able to recreate a strong sense of place within the neighborhood, while increasing its political, economic and social identity. Finally, these groups formed a mechanism in which to build their institutional capacity, the level of formal organizational activities within the community.

The question remains as to whether or not social capital is being created by the community development corporations of today? This is a much different question than whether or not CDCs *can* create social capital. The answer to the first question has been, at best, overstated. Many of the current authors taking up this debate definitively suggest that indeed CDCs are creating social capital; that CDCs are redeveloping buildings, that residents are participating in a democratic (or at least in a representative) manner, that local accountability is being promoted and that local control over the neighborhood is being accomplished (Gittell and Vidal 1998; Kochinsky 1998; Temkin and Rohe 1998).

The preceding analysis, however, suggests that despite decades of efforts to stimulate the creation of social capital, residents today have very little influence in, and virtually no control over, the planning and development of their neighborhoods. Residents, then, far from being linked to their place, are being separated from the place in which they live.

Given past (and current) political rhetoric and scholarly research, it seems strange that this is the case. History does show that social capital can be created by CDC-type organizations. The housing movement of the early 1960s, for the first time on a coordinated scale, gave residents the ability to organize, mobilize, and make changes in their environment. Later, with the federal government programs of the mid- to late 1960s, including Community Action and Model Cities (themselves influenced in part by the early tenant movement) mechanisms for this engagement were codified into law.

The trajectory of market-driven planning and development would have continued unimpeded through the 1970s had it not been for a confluence of circumstances that eventually led to an almost complete destruction of inner-city neighborhoods. The restructuring of the national and international economy, the civil rights movement, the Vietnam War, real estate and economic downturns, urban white flight, and an explosion of crime and drugs contributed to the devastation and destruction of urban areas. The South Bronx exemplified this changing environment and became the poster child for everything that was wrong with urban America.

In spite of these adverse conditions (or perhaps because of them) a silver lining emerged. The environment that nearly destroyed the South Bronx also allowed residents the opportunity to do what they never could have before—create social capital by taking charge and control of planning and redeveloping their own neighborhood. Members of the South Bronx community started small, collaborative community efforts. And despite the enormity of the task, these groups were able to initiate startling change. By the end of the 1970s and into the early 1980s the People's Development Corporation, Banana Kelly Improvement Association, Mid Bronx Desperados and the South East Bronx Community Organization were on their way to rebuilding the South Bronx spatially, socially, and economically.

In hindsight, the 1970s was a unique decade, an aberration, in the history of planning and development. At no other time before or since have residents secured the power and influence to affect planning and development in the neighborhoods of the South Bronx. Yet, this is exactly what appeared to have happened in the 1970s. The private and public sectors, which were simply no longer interested in the South Bronx, effectively isolated the area from the rest of the city. Whether consciously recognizing this or simply reaping the benefits of this lack of attention, the community groups that formed during this era, the PDC, Banana Kelly, SEBCO and MBD among them, were able to bring about substantive change. Harry DeRienzo described this situation with 20/20 hindsight. He stated that in the 1970s a vacuum was created when both the public and private sectors left the area. This vacuum subsequently was

> filled by residents [who were involved in] self-help, sweat-equity. No one was paying attention to us. There was this attitude of "it's your job, you do it." We got our strength from functioning in this vacuum, not from the backing of government, private sector or the banks. In the mid-1980s, when the city got back into the bond market [spending million on housing] the vacuum collapsed and we had to again compete with the private sector.[35]

With not-before-seen freedom made possible through the vacuum created by disinterested government and private sectors, community groups such as the PDC, Banana Kelly, MBD and SEBCO began to redevelop their neighborhoods out of sheer desperation.

As it turned out, the capacity of residents to affect change was fragile and fleeting, almost superficial. One of the most obvious lessons to be learned from this historical analysis is that neighborhoods, even ones as devastated and abandoned as the South Bronx during the 1970s, are tied to the larger social, economic and political forces within the borough, city, state and nation. The vacuum in which these residents were able to control was soon filled. The autonomy afforded these groups by both the public and private sectors was short-lived. The social capital that was being created so freely eventually ceased. By the mid-

1980s the community groups, in order to survive, turned away from ones built on relationships among residents to ones characterized by market-type relationships.

Many forces were responsible for this shift. The 1980s brought a sea change in political, social and economic conditions. The federal government acted swiftly in withdrawing from the urban arena. Reagan dramatically cut support for cities, leaving market forces to dictate what was developed. Moreover, the national economy was heading toward a deep recession. New York City's government, which desperately attempted to address the deteriorating conditions of its inner-city neighborhoods, was in such weakened financial condition that it was nearly powerless to do much in the way of filling the gaps. Seeing opportunity, both private not-for-profit and for-profit institutions vied for power and position in these distressed areas.

And groups such as the PDC, SEBCO, MBD and Banana Kelly faced new competitions that had not existed in the 1970s. With these new challenges still evolving, these groups were forced to either transform into business-like corporations (thus abandoning their attempt to link residents to their neighborhoods) or disband altogether. Most choose the former and structured their organizations into hierarchical community development corporations able to prosper within the new political and economic realities. The residents, who were once the main forces behind the organizations, now became the organizations' clients.

In their book, *Urban Problems and Community Development,* Ferguson and Dickens (1999:42) argue that there are five categories of capital: physical, financial, intellectual (and here I would add human), political and social. These five assets, according to the authors, are created or enhanced through community development and become the assets that "provide the capacity" for growth (Ferguson and Dickens 1999:42). If the evolution of the CDC is seen within the prism of these five assets, it is clear that social capital is only one out of five elements that could be enhanced or augmented within a neighborhood. From this standpoint, the CDCs look good. Clearly they create physical, economic, intellectual, and even political capital through their housing and commercial developments. Where the CDC comes up short is in creating or enhancing social capital.

But perhaps it is too much to ask of CDCs to provide a holistic framework within which all five assets are created. Maybe it is enough that they do what they presently do. CDCs have been instrumental in transforming the inner city on a grand scale. Tens of thousands of low-income residents are living in newly renovated housing units. Tens of thousands more have been able to enhance their economic status through newly created access to social services, job training, and other programs that are taken for granted in higher-income neighborhoods. CDCs are experts at outreach, education, organization, and mobilization of residents. There appears little doubt that CDCs are committed to their mission of improving the lives and living conditions of the low-income communities.

The reality of present day community involvement, at least for the South Bronx, is that community development corporations have become entrenched systemic mechanisms, ones not likely to be supplanted any time soon. What is also indisputable is the fact that in the light of what social capital has come to represent, an asset in which collective action, democratic engagement, and citizen participation is critical, CDCs are not creating social capital. Decisions are made at the top, with little or no input from the residents/clients.

The definition of what a CDC is and what it can accomplish must be brought in line with current realities. In order for CDCs to create social capital they must begin by encouraging the linkages among the residents, whom they were established to serve, so that significant networks of communication, collective action, and mutual aid can be fostered and maintained.

Notes

1. Clavel et al.: 435–437.
2. For more detailed information, see Katz 1983.
3. Ramon Rueda, Interview, July 17, 1998.
4. Genevieve Brooks, Interview, July 17, 1998.
5. Ibid.
6. Ralph Porter, Interview, July 23, 1998.
7. Keep in mind that in the mid-1970s New York City was experiencing a major fiscal crisis, the effects of which were clearly felt in the South Bronx.
8. Brooks interview, July 1998.
9. Fr. Louis Giganti, Interview, November 30, 1998.
10. Ibid.
11. This grant may not have been acquired solely on the influence of Fr. Giganti. The redevelopment of his first building on Simpson Street coincided with the city's own redevelopment plan for Simpson and Fox Streets.
12. Fr. Giganti, Interview, March 11, 1999.
13. Ibid.
14. Ibid.
15. Most of the self-help, sweat equity housing participants were underemployed or unemployed, living on subsistence incomes.
16. DeRienzo interview, April 1999.

17. DeRienzo interview, May 1, 1998.

18. Community Action and Model Cities had poured hundreds of millions of dollars into the South Bronx (Model Cities alone spent some $300 million). Despite the good intentions and some lasting positive influences of these poverty programs, the South Bronx experienced major devastation throughout the 1970s. In hindsight, it is clear that one of the long-term consequences of Model Cities was that entire neighborhoods were surgically disrupted in order to make way for development projects that never materialized. This "planner's blight," as the condition became known, and the fires that followed, left the South Bronx with thousands of empty, rubble strewn lots—covering an estimated 500 acres—scattered among viable residential buildings. It was on one of these empty lots that Banana Kelly would create the South Bronx's first community garden.

19. I received two divergent accounts of this collaboration. According to Fr. Giganti this was a partnership to "show Banana Kelly and Harry the ropes." For DeRienzo, it was a hard lesson to learn. He remembers that Banana Kelly received little if any money from this collaboration project.

20. DeRienzo interview, April 1999.

21. It should not be overstated that these groups were effecting a great deal of change. The attention that the PDC, MBD, SEBCO and the other development groups were getting at the time was relative. Neither public officials nor the public was really paying much attention to the South Bronx in the mid-1970s. At the time the area was burning, Roger Starr, then the director of New York City Planning, could not have made this point clearer when he proposed his "Planned Shrinkage" concept in the early months of 1976 for the South Bronx.

22. Passed in 1977, Local Law 45 had a quick impact on residential real estate in low-income neighborhoods. The South Bronx would not feel its full impact until the mid-1980s.

23. As alluded to in the previous chapter, New York City experienced a severe economic and fiscal crisis that severely constrained local government authority when the city was placed in receivership by the state, which forced the city to reduce its spending in return for refinancing of its debts. See, among others, John Mollenkopf, *A Phoenix in the Ashes* (Princeton, NJ: Princeton University Press, 1992).

24. Bonnie Brower, "Missing the Mark: Subsidizing Housing for the Privileged, Displacing the Poor" (Association of Neighborhood and Housing Development and the Housing Justice Campaign, 1989, 23). These buildings, of course, are not included in the New York City public housing inventory.

25. Although Banana Kelly was formed in 1977, its impact on the South Bronx community-involvement movement, for this discussion, is relevant to the 1980s.

26. Rueda interview.

27. While it is too simplistic to consider SEBCO as a present day example of resident-led community involvement, it did have its roots in this type of involvement when it formed in 1968. By the mid-1970s, however (around the time Fr. Giganti ran and won a seat on the New York City Council), SEBCO became an organization solely controlled by Fr. Giganti.

28. Fr. Giganti interview, November 30, 1998.

29. Ibid.

30. Section 8 was the federally funded rent subsidy under which a resident was mandated to pay 30 percent of his/her rent and the federal government

would pay the rest. When Fr. Giganti combined Section 8 with the sale of tax shelters SEBCO would gain enormous financial benefits.

31. The mission of LISC is to spur the growth and impact of local CDCs by providing grants, loans, equity capitol and technical assistance to help them undertake housing and economic development projects in their own communities. The mission of the Enterprise Foundation, which joined LISC in this effort in New York City, is to assist not-for-profits to produce housing for low-and moderate-income residents.

32. Anita Miller, Interview, July 13, 1998.

33. Brooks interview, July 1998.

34. Fr. Giganti interview, December 1998.

35. DeRienzo interview, May 1st, 1998.

References

Clavel, Pierre, Jessica Pitt, and Jordan Yin. 1997. "The Community Option in Urban Policy." *Urban Affairs Review,* 32.4:435–458.

Cohen, Harriet, and Harry DeRienzo. 1988. *City Limits,* March:19.

Ferguson, Ronald F., and William T. Dickens, eds. 1999. *Urban Problems and Community Development.* Washington, DC: Brookings Institution Press.

Fried, Joseph. 1977. "Loan From City and 'Sweat Equity' Create an Oasis." *New York Times,* December 21:A1

Gittell, Marilyn. 1980. *Limits to Citizen Participation.* New York: Sage.

Gittell, Marilyn, Kathe Newman, Janice Bockmeyer, and Robert Lindsay. 1998. "Expanding Civic Opportunity: urban Empowerment Zones." *Urban Affairs Review,* 33.4:530–559.

Gittell, Marilyn, Isolda Ortega-Bustamante, and Tracy Steffy. 2000. "Social Capital and Social Change: Women's Community Activism." *Urban Affairs Review,* 36.2:123–147.

Gittell, Ross, and Avis C. Vidal. 1998. *Community Organizing: Building Social Capital as a Development Strategy.* Thousand Oaks, CA: Sage.

Gratz, Roberta Brandes. 1994. *The Living City: How America's Cities Are Being Revitalized by Thinking Small in a Big Way.* 2nd ed. Washington, DC: Preservation Press.

Jonnes, Jill. 1986. *We're Still Here.* Boston: Atlantic Monthly Press.

Katz, Steve. 1983. "The Faded Dream." *City Limits,* April:11.

Kochinsky, Julia. 1998. "Challenging the Third Sector Housing Approach: Impact of Federal Policies (1980–1996)." *Journal of Urban Affairs,* 20.2:117–135.

Lang Robert E., and Steven P. Hornburg. 1998. "What Is Social Capital and Why Is It Important?" *Housing Policy Debate* 9.1:1–16.

Nye, Nancy, and Norman J. Glickman. 2000. "Working Together: Building Capacity for Community Development." *Housing Policy Debate,* 11.1:163–198.

Peirce, Neal R., and Carol F. Steinbach. 1987. *Corrective Capitalism: The Rise of America's Community Development Corporations.* New York: Ford Foundation.

Piven, Frances Fox, and Richard A. Cloward. 1977. *Poor Peoples Movements: Why They Succeed, How They Fail.* New York: Pantheon Press.

Putnam, Robert D. 1993. *Making Democracy Work: Civic Traditions in Modern Italy.*
    Princeton, NJ: Princeton University Press.
Putnam, Robert D. 1995. "Bowling Alone: America's Declining Social Capital."
    Journal of Democracy, 6.1:65–78.
Robbins, Tim. 1996. *City Limits,* 21.9:19.
Starr, Roger. 1985. *The Rise and Fall of New York City.* New York: Basic.
Stoutland, Sara E. 1999. "Community Development Corporations: Mission,
    Strategy, and Accomplishments." In *Urban Problems and Community
    Development,* ed. Ronald F. Ferguson and William T. Dickens, 193–240.
    Washington, DC: Brookings Institution Press.
Temkin, Kenneth, and Rohe, William. 1998. "Social Capital and Neighborhood
    Stability: An Empirical Investigation." *Housing Policy Debate,* 9:1:61–88.
Vidal, Avis C. 1995. "Reintegrating Disadvantaged Communities into the Fabric
    of Urban Life." *Housing Policy Debate,* 6.1:169–230.

3

The Effects of Race, Gender, and Religion

Community Development Corporations (CDCs) in the Deep South

The Interaction of Social Capital, Community Context, and Organizational Networks

Robert Mark Silverman

Social Capital as an Embedded Concept

Recent scholarship concerning community-based organizations has focused on evaluating organizational performance and assessing the feasibility of grassroots approaches to neighborhood revitalization. In much of this research the analysis of individual organizations has been divorced from the local community context in which such entities are embedded. Although this trend is prominent with respect to several organizational types, it is especially apparent in the current scholarship concerning community development corporations (CDCs). The purpose of this chapter is to expand the analysis of these organizations by considering the effect that local context has on inter-organizational relations. In particular, this research examines the manner in which structural factors influence the behavior of CDCs and the organizational networks they access. This research is based on a critical case study focusing on such organizations in a single city in the Deep South, Jackson, Mississippi. The directors of these organizations were interviewed and field research was conducted in order to identify factors influencing the development of inter-organizational networks.

Of principal interest to this research is the degree to which structural conditions affect the mobilization of social capital, particularly as these factors apply to CDCs. This focus critically examines one stream of existing scholarship which has identified social capital as an essential component of community-based neighborhood revitalization efforts (Putnam 1993, 1995; Portney and Berry 1997; Wilson 1997; Dionne 1998; Gittell and Vidal 1998; Wallis 1998; Wallis, Crocker and Schechter 1998; Woolcock 1998; Dasgupta and Serageldin 1999; Putnam 2000). In this body of work, the positive effects of dense pools of social capital on community building are emphasized. In contrast to earlier work, this research highlights the interaction among three factors: resource scarcity, community structure, and the mobilization of social capital. Through this analysis, the conceptual framing of social capital is refined, and a better understanding of the manner in which social capital affects organizations at the community level is obtained. It is argued that the interaction of these factors causes organizations to access distinct forms of social capital, and this influences the activities they pursue and the collaborative partnerships organizations create.

As a result, this chapter suggests that social capital has boundaries. It is not applied in a generic form and it does not produce uniform results across social settings. Rather, social capital is linked to the social and organizational context in which it is embedded, and it is not easily transferred to another. Furthermore, this chapter suggests that all forms of social capital are not necessarily compatible with one and other, or interchangeable. Instead, it is argued that most forms of social capital operate autonomously and, subsequently, the prospects of basing collaborative activities on the synthesis of various forms of social capital are limited. Although these issues are pronounced here, each is discernable in the existing literature concerning social capital. As a result, this chapter highlights a dimension of social capital which has been overlooked in prior scholarship.

This chapter also adds clarity to an existing disciplinary split among scholars concerning the conceptualization of social capital. Foley and Edwards (1999:141) discuss this divergence and point out that social capital is primarily viewed as a "normative variable" by political scientists and economists, while sociologists and applied social scientists see social capital as a structural phenomenon. One of the clearest articulations of the normative interpretation of social capital is found in Putnam's (1993, 1995, 2000) work. In essence, Putnam has generated a broad definition of social capital, describing it as the product of social relations composed of networks, norms, reciprocity, and trustworthiness that affects society in a positive or negative manner by facilitating coordination and cooperation. Although this definition frames social capital as a generalized concept akin to civic virtue, it leaves some of the more critical questions concerning the role of social capital in community development unaddressed. Particularly, questions that seek to examine the relationship between social capital and organizational context are not well developed. Consequently, this body of scholarship has framed social capital as the synthesis of values and civic involvement, but the institutional context in which values are nurtured has been left out of the social capital literature. In contrast, the sociological perspective offers a remedy to this dilemma by considering social capital in concert with factors embedded in local context.

The emphasis on context-specific forms of social capital is a core theme in the sociological literature. For instance, Bourdieu (1986:249) stipulates that social capital is the aggregate of relationships that "exist only in the practical state, in material and or symbolic exchanges which help to maintain them." Similarly, Coleman (1988, 1990) emphasizes that social capital is embodied in personal relations tied to social structure. In fact, Coleman (1990:318–321) specifies that social capital is created and maintained within social structures characterized by closure, stability, and a discernible ideological rationale for social exchange. More recent studies have expanded these core themes in the sociological literature by examining the manifestation of social capital in relation to spacial dynamics and neighborhood characteristics (Fernandez Kelly 1994, 1995; Sampson, Morenoff and Earls 1999). Nevertheless, a tangible definition of social capital remains elusive in the sociological literature, despite a clear delineation of the sources of social capital and the structural parameters in which it is found. In the absence of a concrete definition of social capital the concept fluctuates between being characterized as an "aggregate" of relationships, a "process" that gives individuals access to material goods, or the "ability" to secure resources (Bourdieu 1986; Portes 1998; Schneider 1999; Portes and Landolt 2000). The irony of this predicament is that the building blocks of social capital are well developed within the sociological literature, while the essential nature of social capital remains enigmatic.

For instance, there is agreement across disciplinary boundaries that shared values are integral to the formation and maintenance of social capital. It is also well established that social capital involves the mobilization of these values through networks linked to kinship, ethnicity, occupation, class, neighborhood, and other ascribed characteristics in a manner that is flexible and responsive to local context. Similarly, at least in the sociological literature, there is agreement that Granovetter's (1985) discussion of embeddedness is directly applicable to the relationship between mobilizing shared values within existing networks and the formation and maintenance of social capital. Essentially, the embeddedness of shared values within existing social structures creates the closure necessary for sustained social interactions, while simultaneously allowing for variation in the types of social capital that are produced in different settings. Notwithstanding the relative consensus regarding the conceptual foundations on which social capital rests, the parameters of social capital itself remain unspecified. However, the foundation from which social capital emerges—shared values embedded in what Granovetter (1985:490) describes as "concrete personal relations or structures (or 'networks')"—infers that social capital is synonymous with what Velez-Ibanez (1983) identifies as a bond of mutual trust.

Defining social capital as a bond of mutual trust emerging from shared values which are embedded in parochial networks highlights the degree to which social capital has boundaries. The presence of such boundaries has two noteworthy ramifications. First, they ground social capital in an observable context. Second, boundaries make it possible for social capital to assume many forms, since it is the product of a range of possible values that are embedded in varied settings. There is a clear distinction between this definition and others that describe social capital as the product of generalized trust or an expression of civic virtue. The advantage of conceptualizing social capital as a phenomenon embedded in finite social settings is that this definition creates opportunities to identify instances where it emerges. Specifying the parameters of social capital ensures that the concept is not reified as it is in other scholarly writings. Rather, social capital is identified as one element in the community development process that interacts with other forms of capital. The embeddedness argument facilitates a better understanding of the relative importance of social capital in the internal operation of organizations, and it also offers insights concerning the role of social capital in the development and maintenance of inter-organizational networks.

The embeddedness argument suggests that the durability of social capital decreases as personal relations become less regularized. As a result, the role of social capital is more pronounced in the internal operation of an organization than it is in inter-organizational networks. For instance, shared values or parochial interests embedded within an organization allow for closure and the emergence of a bond of mutual trust. This is the essence of Granovetter's (1972) discussion of relationship built using strong ties. As a result, social capital based on strong ties is expected to flourish in relatively small, homogeneous organizations where these relationships exist. This differs from inter-organizational networks, which are formed using what Granovetter (1972) identifies as weak ties. In such networks concrete personal relations are less intense. Consequently, the development and maintenance of social capital across organizations is dependent upon the degree to which closure can be achieved around a discernable set of shared values. In essence, the scope of inter-organizational networks must be circumscribed when such ties are formed in order to promote a bond of mutual trust. Once closure around shared values is achieved, these values are institutionalized so that a newly formed inter-organizational network is sustainable.

This chapter develops this line of inquiry by examining the influence of shared values on CDCs and their effects on organizational activities and collaborative behavior. This research direction is an extension of recent work which explores the role of organizational mission, structure and other factors on CDCs (Bratt 1997; Clavel, Pitt and Yin 1997; Stoeker 1997a; Stoeker 1997b; Yin 1998; Cowan, Rohe and Baku 1999; Gittell and Wilder 1999). Given this orientation, this chapter examines the degree to which a relationship exists between the values held in an organization and the programs and partnerships produced. Such an analysis expands our knowledge of the influence of social capital on organizational interactions, and it assists in the development of more general theory concerning the role of social capital in organizational behavior. The results from this study are of additional interest in the light of earlier research which suggests that value dissonance across organizations is common, causing the emergence of social capital to appear to be a localized phenomenon (Suttles 1972; Putnam 1993; Thomas and Blake 1996; Chang 1997; Greeley 1997; Portney and Berry 1997; Wood 1997; Foley and Edwards 1999). For instance, previous research indicates that factors such as a commitment to pluralism, a preference for democratic institutions, racial and ethnic ties, loyalty to parochial groups, neighborhood attachment, and common religious structures independently influence the development of social capital. In fact, no study has identified a form of social capital that operates independent of the given context in which it is found. As a result, one can conclude that any given form of social capital is community specific.

CDCs and Race

To test the embeddedness of social capital in local community context, this study focuses on CDCs in Jackson, Mississippi. This setting is unique for two reasons. First, all of the CDCs in Jackson are located in African American communities, and each has a black executive director and staff.

Second, these organizations are unique since they are embedded in neighborhoods impacted by patterned disinvestment, institutional racism, and historic segregation. These aspects of Jackson's CDCs are discussed in subsequent sections in greater detail. It is hypothesized that CDCs in Jackson respond to these condition by retreating into the black community and concentrating on the cultivation of social capital and inter-organizational ties with other local black institutions. In effect, this case study tests the degree to which organizations focus on mobilizing specific forms of social capital, exclusive of others, when embedded in a local context characterized by acute resources constraints, spacial isolation and racial segregation. In addition to testing this general hypothesis, the importance of this argument is that it links social capital to structural explanation for some aspects of organizational behavior.

This is a critical extension of existing research on these organizations for two reasons. First, it expands the discussion of the role of local context in the development and maintenance of networks between community-based organizations and other entities. Second, it initiates this discussion by highlighting structural constraints that affect black CDCs, a type of organization focused upon in the pioneering CDC literature. A return to this focus is important because it revives themes related to structural inequalities in society that this organizational form was designed to address.

This focus is evident in early scholarship on CDCs which described these organizations as relatively insurgent organizations in the black community which emphasized social change and community empowerment (Tabb 1970; Perry 1972; Fish 1973). According to this literature CDCs were intended to play a pivotal role in leveling racial hierarchies in urban communities and expanding grassroots control in black neighborhoods. What is most instructive about the literature examining the early development of CDCs is the emphasis on the black community and the role of race in organizational development. It is argued that CDCs came about because of structural inequality in society, a lack of institutional remedies to address deprivation in urban black neighborhoods, and limited access to mainstream institutions due to racial discrimination. In essence, this literature advocated for the mobilization of race-based social capital as a strategy in response to structural inequality and racial barriers to development in urban black neighborhoods.

Despite growing interest in mobilizing social capital for community development, this emphasis in the CDC literature was short lived. Upon examination, the preponderance of existing CDC literature minimizes this dimension of the history and operation of these organizations. Although there is greater variation among CDCs, and many have taken on new roles since their inception, there is no reason to conclude that the diversification of themes in research pertaining to these organizations reflects a reduction in structural inequality or an abandonment of mobilizing race-based social capital as a strategy among many black organizations. Despite this situation there still appears to be an unwillingness among scholars to revisit issues of structural inequality as they relate to race and community control in the CDC debate.

Instead of revisiting these issues researchers have moved toward a more functional description of CDCs. Often, a rosy picture is drawn and these organizations are depicted as entities that build local capacity and promote community-based planning (Perry 1987; Twelvetrees 1989; Robinson 1996; Clavel, Pitt and Yin 1997; Stoutland 1999). In this reformulation, the study of CDC development has been sanitized. Typically, historical accounts of these organizations begin with a brief discussion early the CDCs formed in the 1960s to promote comprehensive community building efforts in black neighborhoods. This discussion is followed by an account of how these organizations became more specialized functionally during the 1970s primarily to address housing issues. Finally, the discussion concludes with an examination of how contemporary CDCs became more diversified and fragmented programmatically, focusing on a variety of development and social service needs in urban areas. The growing emphasis on form, function, and programmatic idiosyncracies in this stream of the research has displaced much of the earlier focus on structural constraints and organizational goals. Regardless of which period of CDC development one examines, current scholarly writing about these organizations has increasingly described their role in a generic and relatively race neutral manner. Although this line of inquiry can sometimes lead one to conclude that the emergence of CDCs has transformed local institutional relations and begun to alter prevailing social patterns and structural relationships, the extent to which these changes have occurred has seldom been the focus of research. Instead, the primary focus of this body of research has been on technical and managerial issues specific to the structure and mechanics of programs pursued by CDCs. Moreover, the literature has described the evolution of a relatively conservative and mainstream approach to community development among these organizations, and characterized this development as a sign of their maturation. In essence, a shift has occurred in the CDC literature which has resulted in relatively little inquiry focusing on the role these organization can play in addressing structural inequality in the communities where they are found.

This trend in the study of CDCs has produced a picture of these organizations very different than the pioneering scholarship which emphasized issues of race, empowerment, and the reordering of social relations. Nonetheless, the question of when, and to what degree, CDCs were transformed remains opened. In part, the bias in the literature is a reflection of the unrepresentative sample of organizations studies. Although the growth and proliferation of CDCs has taken place over three decades, existing scholarship has focused on only a few, large, well institutionalized organizations with long track records. A substantial amount of the research is skewed toward these organizations, leaving a number of questions unaddressed about how hundreds of smaller, less established CDCs operate in modern urban communities. The seriousness of this dilemma is intensified since these organizations are relatively new to many communities in the United States and not always incorporated into what Yin (1998) has identified as a community development industry system. In fact, it is increasingly recognized that CDCs are found in a variety of settings across the country and each is in a different stage of development (Bratt 1997; Keating 1997; Stoecker 1997a; Stoecker 1997b; Vidal 1997). Yet, the debate concerning this variation is grossly underdeveloped. For instance, the existing literature suggests that CDCs vary in size, tenure, and mission; however, the manner in which local context shaped the parameters in which these organizations operate, particularly in reference to race relations in a community, is absent from most analysis. The current research on CDCs leaves many questions concerning the role of local community context, racial inequality, and grassroots control in new organizations unanswered. In essence, the contemporary dialogue either: depicts CDCs as democratically oriented organizations that create linkages between local communities and a more diverse cross section of society, describes these organizations as vehicles for grassroots mobilizations and social integration abstractly, or simply ignores issues related to local community context entirely. As a result, too little is know about too many CDCs.

This chapter revives the structural component of the CDC debate. In particular, it explores the links among the historical context of a community, perceptions of racial attitudes at the community level, and the scope of inter-organizational networks. The findings of this chapter indicate that these factors shape the parameters for decision-making among directors of CDCs and they influence the scope of inter-organizational relations. Although this critical case study focuses on a single type of organization, black CDCs, and the structural context that promotes the mobilization of race-based social capital, it also indicates that further analysis of the interaction of structural conditions on CDC behavior is warranted in other community settings.

Methods

The data for this chapter comes from a series of formal interviews with CDC directors in Jackson, Mississippi. These interviews were conducted during October 1998 and November 1998. When contacted for interviews, informants were asked to be part of an academic study of CDCs and inter-organizational relations. During the interviews informants were asked a series of open-ended questions about the organization and operation of the CDCs they directed and the factors that influenced decisions to collaborate with other organizations. The questions were drawn from an interview guide that was prepared in advance. The interview guide consisted of 13 items and 19 probes. This research instrument focused on a core set of questions which related to the theoretical issues under examination. In particular, the research instrument focused on identifying the organizational networks CDCs participated in and the factors that influenced an executive director's decision to collaborate with other organizations. Each interview was administered at the given informant's CDC during normal operating hours.

The nature of this study demanded that the research instruments be concise and flexible. It was anticipated that informants would only be available for short periods of time, since they were involved in the operation of a CDC. As a result, the interview was designed to be administered in one hour. Of course, in some instances interviews exceeded one hour, but the placement of questions and themes in the text of the interview guide allowed for the acceleration of interviews if informants became anxious to resume their work. The emphasis on remaining unobtrusive helped facilitate rapport with informants since they were reassured that the interview would not interfere with their daily routine.

Given the small population under examination, a number of methodological steps were taken to insure that the entire population of CDCs in Jackson was identified. Two lists of community-based organizations were referenced for this study. One was a list of neighborhood organizations registered with the City of Jackson. The other was a list of community-based organizations compiled by the Mississippi Urban Research Center at Jackson State University. In addition, individuals active in Jackson's non-profit community were consulted to ensure that all CDCs were identified. The comprehensiveness of the list of CDCs in the population was also verified by means of snowball sampling throughout the research process (Jorgensen 1989). In total, a population of seven CDCs was identified in Jackson. The executive director of each CDC was approached for an interview. All of them agreed to be interviewed. This was advantageous, since interviewing the entire population reduced several concerns related to reliability that are often associated with studies of small populations (Glaser and Strauss 1967). In addition to the primary data gathered through in-depth interviews and field observations, secondary data was collected to develop a more detailed picture of the community studied. The source of this data was the 1990 Census of Population and Housing Summary Tape File 3A (U.S. Department of Commerce 1990).

Jackson as a Critical Case

This study focuses on CDCs in Jackson, Mississippi. This city has many features that make it a critical case study of the effects of local community context on black CDCs. For instance, it is a majority-minority city with a history of segregation, institutional discrimination and other racial barriers that impact the perceptions of organizational actors. In many respects, the effects of historic patterns of racism in the Deep South are illustrated well in Jackson. Even in the modern era these patterns have been clearly manifested in this setting. In fact, racial strife has been visible in Jackson for decades. It surfaced during the civil rights movement in cases such as the assassination of Medger Evers, and it continues to be evinced in contemporary debates over the desegregation of historically black colleges and universities (HBCU) and banning the confederate flag which are trumpeted in the local media and from the State Capital near downtown. Of course, race relations are not static, they have evolved in the city in response to both demographic and political change. However, these developments have been incremental in nature, and changing racial dynamics have not prevented underlying social inequalities from being rearticulated in this environment. Given this local context, the growth of progressive grassroots institutions has occurred slowly in the city. Moreover, Jackson only recently began to experience the development of many community-based organizations.

For instance, CDCs are relatively new institutions in Jackson. In fact, the oldest organization was chartered in 1991. The recent emergence of CDCs presents a unique research opportunity since a number of organizations can be examined in the early stages of their development without having the analysis muddied by variability in tenure.

Furthermore, these relatively new organizations are highly visible at the local level, in part, because Jackson, the largest municipality in Mississippi, is relatively small by national standards. In 1990 the city had a population of 196,594 (U.S. Department of Commerce 1990). This is important because CDCs have opportunities to interface and exchange in Jackson regardless of whether they take advantage of them. In short, the size of the city fosters a social environment where everyone knows everyone in the CDC community.

The number and variety of CDCs in Jackson is beneficial to this research for other reasons as well. Despite their recent emergence, there are currently seven CDCs in the city and each varies in terms of constraints, capacity, and mission. For instance, the organizations in Jackson have staff ranging in size from a single person to 14 individuals. Specifically, three CDCs have fewer than four staff members, three have four to seven staff members, and one has more than eight staff members. The CDCs also have various levels and sources of funding. These sources include Community Development Block Grant (CDBG) monies, state and federal grants for projects and programs, funds from foundations, and Low-Income Housing Tax Credits (LIHTC). Although funding levels vary widely, CDBG monies and funds for federal projects and programs have been the most prevalent sources of support for the CDCs in Jackson with other funding opportunities being pursued more recently. Additionally, each of the CDCs has an organizational mission that emphasizes slightly different activities such as: housing, business development, social service delivery, job placement, and advocacy. As a result, this research site allows for the study of new organizations without sacrificing the ability to examine various degrees of institutional complexity.

It is also important to make note of some of the demographic characteristics of the CDCs and their directors, since these factors add context to this study's findings and give one a more comprehensive understanding of the local environment in which these CDCs are embedded. For example, most of the CDCs are administered by men. The population of CDCs in Jackson has five male directors and two female directors. Moreover, four of the CDC directors had administrative experience in the non-profit sector prior to holding their current positions and three had worked in another CDC at an earlier point in time. Of the remaining CDC directors, two had held positions in the banking industry, and one was in a leadership position in a neighborhood organization before becoming the director of a CDC. Finally, one of the more important characteristics of the CDCs and their directors relates to race. All of the CDCs have strong ties to the black community. Each CDC serves a community that is almost exclusively black, and each CDC has ties to at least one significant black institution in the metropolitan area. Additionally, all of the CDC directors are black, all of the CDC staff members are black, and each of the CDCs has a governing board that is majority black.

These features are of greater interest when the general political climate in which Jackson's CDCs are embedded is taken into consideration. The city's CDCs operate in a unique environment since all of the major local political institutions they regularly interact with are controlled by African Americans. For instance, the Mayor of Jackson, four of the seven city council members, the director of the city planning department, the director of the redevelopment authority, the chief of police, and the fire chief are all black. Additionally, major non-profits and businesses active in the neighborhoods where CDCs are located, such as the Jackson Metro Housing Partnership, the local office of the Fannie Mae Corporation and the local chapter of the United Way have black directors. In fact, Jackson's CDCs operate in the shadow of a substantial black urban regime and they fill a supporting and subordinate role to political interests in the black community. Of course, the presence of a black urban regime does not automatically translate into material advantages for local black communities. As Reed (1988) indicates, black urban regimes are typically handicapped by the historic legacy and structural constraints characteristic of the older core cities that they inherit. The black urban regime in Jackson faces many of these constraints as well. In short, this research setting offers a unique vantage point from which to examine CDCs, particularly when a final dimension, the overall demographic makeup of Jackson, is taken into consideration.

The city's racial composition is the final area of interest mentioned because it emphasizes the degree to which Jackson is a racially polarized city. Jackson is not a multicultural city. The demographic transformation that many American cities went through in the 1980s and 1990s never materialized in Jackson. The city's population is principally composed of blacks and whites, with a virtually invisible population of new immigrants and other minority groups. In 1990 blacks represented 55.7 percent of the city's population and whites represented 43.6 percent of the city's population (U.S. Department of Commerce 1990). Although *de jure* legal segregation ended in Jackson following the civil rights movement, socially and institutionally the city remains segregated in noticeable ways. For instance, in 1990, 82 percent of the Census tracts in Jackson had populations that were either

Table 7.1. Demographic of MSA, City, and CDC Neighborhoods

Variable	Jackson MSA	City of Jackson	CDC Neighborhoods[1]
Population	395,396	196,594	26,631
Percentage Black	41.24	55.74	94.86
Percentage White	58.1	43.61	4.93
Median Household Income 1989	$26,365	$23,270	$11,639
Percent of Households Receiving Public Assistance	10.58	10.83	24.80
Median Housing Value	$59,300	$53,600	34,970

Source. U.S. Department of Commerce, Bureau of the Census. 1990. *1990 Census of Population and Housing Summary Tape File 3A.* Washington DC: Data User Services Division.
[1] The CDC Neighborhoods include twenty-seven Census block groups that were located within the boundaries of the CDCs identified in Jackson, Mississippi.

in excess of 80 percent black or over 80 percent white (U.S. Department of Commerce 1990). Moreover, in 1990, only 2.5 percent of the city's Census tracts had black or white populations ranging between 45 and 55 percent (U.S. Department of Commerce 1990). In short, there were very few Census tracts with a racial mix similar to the city as a whole. This issue becomes more acute when the demographic make-up of neighborhoods within the boundaries of Jackson's CDCs is contrasted with the city and surrounding metropolitan area (see Table 7.1).

Table 7.1 highlights several contrasts between the neighborhoods that CDCs focus upon and the city as a whole. Some dimensions of Table 7.1 merit further discussion. First, the data indicate that Jackson's CDCs were all located in black neighborhoods. Moreover, the demographic features of these neighborhoods paralleled many of those that Wilson (1987) identified in his analysis of the intensification of black poverty on the South Side of Chicago. Wilson argued that this outcome was driven by disinvestment, middle-class flight to the suburbs, the decentralization of industry, and deindustrialization. Some of the same structural processes that contributed to the destabilization of black neighborhoods in Chicago also unfolded in Jackson during the postwar period, and these processes were reenforced by racial dynamics in this setting. Subsequently, by the time CDCs emerged in Jackson, structural constraints and historic patterns of development had already combined to limit the range of available community development options. Although conditions were not identical to those of the past, structural inequality and perceptions of racial antagonism remained salient. As a result, CDCs mobilized race-based social capital to pursue community development. The manner in which perceptions of structural constraints and race relations influenced the adoption of this strategy became clear during interview with CDC directors.

Black Social Capital

All of the directors of CDCs described how their organizations identified and mobilized race-based social capital for community development. This response to structural constraints manifested itself in a variety of ways in each of the organizations. Factors linked to local community context affected how these organizations defined the community they served, how they made decisions related to staff and governing board development, and how they cultivated inter-organizational networks. Race-based social capital was mobilized across each of these areas in order to adapt to the environment in which CDCs were embedded.

One of the most fundamental areas in which the relationship between structural constraints and the mobilization of race-based social capital became apparent was the manner in which CDCs defined the communities they served. The definition of the local community was in large part the product of residential segregation and disinvestment in Jackson. These demographic and spacial patterns prompted the CDC directors to view the communities their organizations served as poor, socially disorganized, economically depressed, isolated and black. Residential segregation affected the communities served by CDCs in Jackson in a similar manner to inner-city neighborhoods in the cities described by Massey and Denton (1993). When individual CDC directors discussed the community that their organization focused upon, their definition incorporated many of the structural constraints that produced and maintained residential segregation and concentrated poverty. In addition, the definition of the community incorporated group and geographic boundaries in a manner similar to that described by Suttles (1972). This definition of the community amalgamated an area's distinct racial identity with institutionally defined spacial boundaries. As a result, each CDC defined the community it focused upon as a black inner-city neighborhood with distinct boundaries, however this definition also recognized the structural forces that produced that community.

Defining the community in this manner influenced the internal development of each of the CDCs and the organizational networks they mobilized. For instance, decisions concerning staff and governing board development were made with reference to the this definition of the community. As one CDC director described, where staffing issues are concerned, "you should always make an effort to get folks from the community." This would ensure that staff were familiar with the local context in which the community was embedded and sensitive to the experiences and perceptions of local residents. Given the demographic composition of the community this also ensured that all of the staff members in CDCs were black. In essence, the definition of community features had a strong influence on the mobilization of race-based social capital where staffing decisions were concerned. However, the decision to hire black staff members was not just driven by population demographics; black staff members were also thought to bring additional access to local networks to CDCs. The common experience that members of the community shared was considered to be an asset to these organization, and it was also considered a buffer against co-optation. This issue became more pronounced when CDC directors discussed the rationale for maintaining majority black governing boards for their organizations.

The importance of community representation on an organization's governing board was emphasized by all of the CDC directors. For instance, one director pointed out that the first goal in constructing a governing board is to recruit people who, "live or work in the community, either the residents or business owners in the community, those are your key stakeholders." In part, the identification of local stakeholders was an important issue due to the grassroots orientation of the organizations. However, the need for community representation and control was also linked to the desire of CDC directors to defend their organizations from external threats and co-optation. This issue became particularly pronounced because many potential external governing board members from outside the community were representatives of institutions that had contributed to structural inequalities in the communities where CDCs had been formed. Therefore, a core group of community members needed to form a majority on an organization's governing board before outsiders were asked to join. This allowed for a degree of closure around race-based social capital to emerge. Once this majority was in place additional board members were added who brought resources and racial balance to the body. For instance, one CDC director explained that additional board members "might help you raise dollars" and at the same time said "that's where you're gonna get diversity."

The emphasis on promoting community control through staff and governing board membership is reflected in other studies of CDCs, for instance Robinson (1996) identifies this as a general concern among CDC directors. However, in Jackson's CDC environment local community context dictates that organizational control be demonstrated through a visible black majority. Because of historical and continuing patterns of racism in the community, actual representation becomes necessary. It allows organizations to gain legitimacy and trust in the communities where they are located, and it also promotes inter-organizational networks that are essential to a CDC's survival. In large part, such networking occurs with other institutions in the black community. For example, each of the CDC directors indicated that his/her organization regularly networked with at least one local black institution. These ties existed between: CDCs and local HBCUs, the local black bank, local chapters of national black organizations, local black community-based organizations, black fraternal societies, black professional organizations, and the black press. The presence of numerous sustained networks among black CDCs and black organizations was a clear demonstration of the mobilization of race-based social capital for community development ends. It also illustrates how inter-organizational networks are sustained and institutionalized through closure around a specific form of social capital. The importance of this strategy is punctuated when the context of these organizational relationships is contrasted with interactions between black CDCs and organizations outside of the local black community.

To some degree CDCs interacted with organizations outside of the local black community. For example, five of the CDCs had received funding from sources such as: the federal government, the State of Mississippi, the City of Jackson, and a variety of local and national foundations and organizations in the private sector. Nonetheless, there was a qualitative difference in the nature of the relationships between CDCs and organizations with their origins inside of the black community as opposed to the relationships between CDCs and non-African American controlled organizations. In contrast to black organizations, CDC directors characterized interactions with groups from outside the black community as bureaucratic and fleeting in nature. Typically, a CDC would approach a non-African American organization for funding or because that outside organization administered a particular program the CDC wanted to access. These interactions were highly formalized and lacked the development of sustained personal contacts between a given CDC's director and a representative of an outside organization. On the other hand, CDC directors described relations between their organizations and others in the black community as more stable and enduring.

Unlike interactions with non-African American organizations, these organizational ties were sustained, textured, and regularized. In these types of relationships CDC directors had greater access to key decision makers, interactions were more likely to be based on informal contacts, and the directors were more likely to approach these organizations since they were controlled by blacks who were perceived to have a heightened level of sensitivity and concern for issues that CDCs focused upon in black communities.

The relationships between CDCs and other black institutions were depicted as multifaceted and based on shared values and mutual trust. It is notable that the actual genesis of each of the CDCs in Jackson can be traced to a sustained relationship with one or more local black organization. In contrast, interactions between CDCs and organizations outside of the black community came later, entailed fewer contacts, and were formalized and bureaucratic. Often, interactions that occurred with outside organizations were brokered through other black institutions or through a key black contacts in an outside organization. The presence of another black organization or a black contact in an outside organization was considered to be a safeguard against exploitation and co-optation. This was particularly important in situations where the director of a CDC had concerns about an outside organization's motivation for establishing a relationship. For example, CDC directors were cautious when dealing with commercial banks, given the history of discriminatory lending practices in the black community. As one CDC director pointed out, "the banks will participate because of CRA, the Community Reinvestment Act, that's their inspiration." The misgivings that CDC directors had about working with banks and other institutions that have contributed to structural inequality in black communities were somewhat eased when networks were cultivated with other black organizations that shared their concerns. For instance, the CDC director cited above maintained a membership in the National Association of Urban Bankers, which is a group of black bankers. This affiliation supplied the director with access to information about trends in private sector finance and key black contacts in the banking industry.

In the same manner that structural constraints and perceived racial barriers affected how black CDCs defined the communities that they focused on, thus influencing decisions concerning staff and governing board development, structural constraints and perceived racial barriers also impacted the types of inter-organizational networks that were cultivated. One CDC director discussed this issue as it related to the need for a black perspective throughout the community development process:

In many situations though, race is an issue, because empathy, empathizing, just understanding the person, sometimes there's a breakdown in communication because of that. It creates some barriers that are difficult to cross at times. Even though racism may not be present, just the mere fact that different experiences, different environmental influences are present, makes a difference in the ability to communicate sometimes. When you're talking about dealing with an organization we're partnering with, simply because of some cultural differences, sometimes they make it difficult to understand why situations are as they are, or understand the person. It's just a simple fact that these differences do impact.

As this comment indicates, perceptions of race, which are shaped by history and local community context, have important implications for inter-organization relations. Because of acute patterns of discrimination and structural inequality in this local context a need for the mobilization of race-based social capital emerged in Jackson.

Erasing the Color Line

In large part, the ability of a CDC to mobilize inter-organizational network is a function of the structure and local context in which it is embedded. For this reason, the organizational behavior of black CDCs in Jackson may differs from community-based organizations in other settings. As this chapter has argued, race-based social capital was mobilized in Jackson in response to racial barriers and other structural constraints that characterized this local community context. The implication of this adaptation is that there are few strategies that facilitate networking, aside from those linked to race-based social capital, available to CDCs in this setting. Unfortunately, this predicament may not supply CDCs with enough information to sustain community-building efforts in the long term. This issue came to the forefront when one CDC director reflected upon the possible implications of relying exclusively on race-based networks for community development:

> Well, I guess in one way it's kind of beneficial because you have kind of a homogeneous group. But on the other hand, you have a group of people who do not get the benefit of working with a wider and a more diverse group of folks. Even getting to know the different issues that different people would bring to the table. You know, you think of the times not too distant ago when corporations perhaps would not have any African Americans, for instance, around the table, and that was a perspective that was missing. And then, when people begin to come to the table a little bit more, it was like, "Ah, there's something that we've not thought about."

In many respects the mobilization of race-based social capital is a strategy of last resort for black CDCs. It is indicative of the limited range of opportunities available to network with organizations outside of the black community, and it speaks to the need for aggressive efforts to expand institutional access to individuals and communities that are disadvantaged by structural inequality in society.

At the very least, the presence of the types of structural constraints that make the mobilization of race-based social capital necessary underscores the need for remedies that promote affirmative action policies in institutions that have contributed to the reproduction of structural inequality historically. For instance, Squires and O'Connor (2001) argue that the employment of African Americans in key positions of the lending industry should be a critical component of strategies to address mortgage discrimination and disinvestment in minority communities. This is because it is believed that these individuals can function as gatekeepers to minorities seeking credit, and expand the scope of institutional resources and networks available to minority communities. These remedies should be a component of an expanded community reinvestment strategy. In addition to such remedies there is a need to develop new networks within the existing community development industry system that allow CDCs to establish bridges to larger institutions along the lines described in the literature dealing with intermediary organizations (Clavel et al. 1997; Gittell and Vidal 1998). In other words, African Americans and other under-represented groups need greater access to resources, positions, and decision-making in large public and private sector institutions in society. Additionally, these institutions need to respond simultaneously by creating stronger intermediary organizations to deliver technical assistance to community-based organizations. Without a focused effort to promote affirmative action, reinvestment in urban neighborhoods, and the cultivation of new networks among core institutions in society, it is likely that mobilizing race-based social capital within a narrow range of local organizations will remain the only viable strategy for CDCs in settings similar to the one discussed in this chapter.

References

Bourdieu, Pierre. 1986. "The Forms of Capital." In *Handbook of Theory and Research for the Sociology of Education*, ed. John G. Richardson, 241–258. New York: Greenwood Press.

Bratt, Rachael. 1997. "CDCs: Contributions Outweigh Contradictions, a Reply to Randy Stoecker." *Journal of Urban Affairs*, 19.1:23–28.

Chang, Hedy Nai-Lin. 1997. "Democracy, Diversity, and Social Capital." *National Civic Review,* 86.2:141–147.

Clavel, Pierre, Jessica Pitt, and Jordan Yin. 1997. "The Community Option in Urban Policy." *Urban Affairs Review,* 32.4:435–458.

Coleman, James S. 1988. "Social Capital in the Creation of Human Capital." *American Journal of Sociology,* 94S:S95–S120.

Coleman, James S. 1990. *Foundations of Social Theory.* Cambridge: Harvard University Press.

Cowan, Spencer M., William Rohe, and Esmail Baku. 1999. "Factors Influencing the Performance of Community Development Corporations." *Journal of Urban Affairs,* 21.3:325–340.

Dasgupta, Partha and Ismail Serageldin, eds. 1999. *Social Capital: A Multifaceted Perspective.* Washington, DC: World Bank.

Dionne, E. J. Jr., ed. 1998. *Community Works: The Revival of Civil Society in America,* Washington, DC: Brookings Institution Press.

Fernandez Kelly, M. Patricia. 1994. "Towanda's Triumph: Social and Cultural Capital in the Transition to Adulthood in the Urban Ghetto." *International Journal of Urban and Regional Research,* 18.1:88–111.

Fernandez Kelly, M. Patricia. 1995. "Social and Cultural Capital in the Urban Ghetto: Implications for the Economic Sociology of Immigration." In *The Economic Sociology of Immigration: Essays on Networks, Ethnicity, and Entrepreneurship,* ed. Alejandro Portes, 213–247. New York: Russell Sage Foundation.

Foley, Michael W., and Bob Edwards. 1999. "Is it Time to Disinvest in Social Capital?" *Journal of Public Policy,* 19.2:141–173.

Fish, John Hall. 1973. *Black Power/White Control: The Struggle of the Woodlawn Organization in Chicago.* Princeton, NJ: Princeton University Press.

Gittell, Ross, and Avis Vidal. 1998. *Community Organizing, Building Social Capital as a Development Strategy.* Newbury Park: Sage.

Gittell, Ross, and Margaret Wilder. 1999. "Community Development Corporations: Critical Factors that Improve Success." *Journal of Urban Affairs,* 21.3:341–362.

Glaser, Barney G., and Anselm L. Strauss. 1967. *The Discovery of Grounded Theory: Strategies for Qualitative Research.* New York: Aldine De Gruyter.

Granovetter, Mark S. 1972. "The Strength of Weak Ties." *American Journal of Sociology,* 78.6:1360–1380.

Granovetter, Mark S. 1985. "Economic Action and Social Structure: The Problem of Embeddedness." *American Journal of Sociology,* 91.3:481–510.

Greeley, Andrew. 1997. "Coleman Revisited, Religious Structures as a Source of Social Capital." *American Behavioral Scientist,* 40.5:587–594.

Jorgensen, Danny L. 1989. *Participant Observation: A Methodology for Human Studies.* Newbury Park: Sage.

Keating, W. Dennis. 1997. "The CDC Model of Urban Development: A Reply to Randy Stoecker." *Journal of Urban Affairs,* 19.1:29–33.

Massey, Douglas S., and Nancy A. Denton. 1993. *American Apartheid: Segregation and the Making of the Underclass.* Cambridge: Harvard University Press.

Perry, Stewart E. 1972. "Black Institutions, Black Separatism, and Ghetto Economic Development." *Human Organization,* 31.3:271–278.

Perry, Stewart E. 1987. *Communities on the Way: Rebuilding Local Economies in the United States and Canada.* Albany: State University of New York Press.

Portney, Kent E., and Jeffrey M. Berry. 1997. "Mobilizing Minority Communities: Social Capital and Participation in Urban Neighborhoods." *American Behavioral Scientist,* 40.5:632–644.

Portes, Alejandro. 1998. "Social Capital: Its Origins and Applications in Modern Sociology." *Annual Review of Sociology,* 24:1–24.

Portes, Alejandro, and Patricia Landolt. 2000. "Social Capital: Promise and Pitfall of its Role in Development." *Journal of Latin American Studies,* 32:529–547.

Putnam, Robert D. 1993. *Making Democracy Work: Civic Traditions in Modern Italy.* Princeton, NJ: Princeton University Press.

Putnam, Robert D. 1995. "Bowling Alone: America's Declining Social Capital." *Journal of Democracy,* 6.1:65–78.

Putnam, Robert D. 2000. *Bowling Alone: The Collapse and Revival of American Community.* New York: Simon and Schuster.

Reed, Adolph. 1988. "The Black Urban Regime: Structural Origins & Constraints." In *Power Community and the City: Comparative Urban Community Research,* vol. 1, ed. Michael Peter Smith, 138–189. New Brunswick, NJ: Transaction.

Robinson, Tony. 1996. "Inner-City Inovator: The Non-profit Community Development Corporation." *Urban Studies,* 33.9:1647–1670.

Sampson, Robert J., Jeffrey D. Morenoff, and Felton Earls. 1999. "Beyond Social Capital: Spacial Dynamics of Collective Efficacy for Children." *American Sociological Review,* 64:633–660.

Schneider, Jo Anne. 1999. "Trusting that of God in Everyone: Three Examples of Quaker-Based Social Service in Disadvantaged Communities." *Nonprofit and Voluntary Sector Quarterly,* 28.3:269–295.

Squires, Gregory D., and Sally O'Connor. 2001. *Color and Money: Politics and Prospects for Community Reinvestment in Urban America.* Albany: State University of New York Press.

Stoecker, Randy. 1997a. "The CDC Model of Urban Redevelopment: A Critique and an Alternative." *Journal of Urban Affairs,* 19.1:1–22.

Stoecker, Randy. 1997b. "Should We . . . Could We . . . Change the CDC Model?, a Rejoinder." *Journal of Urban Affairs,* 19.1:35–44.

Stoutland, Sara E. 1999. "Community Development Corporations: Mission, Strategy, and Accomplishments." In *Urban Problems and Community Development,* ed. Ronald F. Ferguson and William T. Dickens, 193–240. Washington, DC: Brookings Institution Press.

Suttles, Gerald D. 1972. *The Social Construction of Communities.* Chicago: University of Chicago Press.

Tabb, William K. 1970. *The Political Economy of the Black Ghetto.* New York: Norton.

Thomas, June Manning, and Reynard N. Blake, Jr. 1996. "Faith-Based Community Development and African-American Neighborhoods." In *Revitalizing Urban Neighborhoods,* ed. W. Dennis Keating, Norman Krumholz, and Philip Star, 131–143. Lawrence: University Press of Kansas.

Twelvetrees, Alan. 1989. *Organizing for Neighborhood Development: A Comparative Study of Community Development Corporations and Citizen Power Organizations.* Brookfield, VT: Avebury.

U.S. Department of Commerce, Bureau of the Census. 1990. *1990 Census of Population and Housing Summary Tape File 3A.* Washington DC: Data User Services Division.

Velez-Ibanez, Carlos G. 1983. *Bonds of Mutual Trust: The Cultural Systems of Rotating Credit Associations Among Urban Mexicans and Chicanos.* New Brunswick, NJ: Rutgers University Press.

Vidal, Avis C. 1997. "Can Community Development Re-Invent Itself?: The Challenge of Strengthening Neighborhoods in the 21st Century." *Journal of the American Planning Association,* 63.4:429–438.

Wallis, Allan. 1998. "Social Capital and Community Building: Part Two." *National Civic Review,* 87.4:317–336.

Wallis, Allan, Jarle P. Crocker, and Bill Schechter. 1998. "Social Capital and Community Building: Part One." *National Civic Review,* 87.3:253–271.

Wilson, Patricia. 1997. "Building Social Capital: A Learning Agenda for the Twenty-First Century." *Urban Studies,* 34.5/6:745–760.

Wilson, William Julius. 1987. *The Truly Disadvantaged: The Inner City, the Underclass, and Public Policy.* Chicago: University of Chicago Press.

Wood, Richard L. 1997. "Social Capital and Political Culture: God Meets Politics in the Inner-City." *American Behavioral Scientist,* 40.5: 595–605.

Woolcock, Michael. 1998. "Social Capital and Economic Development: Toward a Theoretical Synthesis and Policy Framework." *Theory and Society,* 27:151–208.

Yin, Jordan S. 1998. "The Community Development Industry System: A Case Study of Politics and Institutions in Cleveland, 1967–1997." *Journal of Urban Affairs,* 20.2:137–157.

Social Capital and African American Church Leadership

Sherri Leronda Wallace

Introduction

Scholars argue that the process of federal devolution, beginning with the Reagan/Bush administrations, has launched debates for renewed interest in urban redevelopment from the local community perspective. Under the aegis of the Clinton/Gore administration, this process executed through "comprehensive" strategic planning activities relied heavily on participation by local/secular and increasingly faith-based community economic development organizations to represent and articulate community needs and priorities (Gittell and Wilder 1999; Ramsay 1998), which laid the foundation for the new Bush/Cheney administration's White House Office of Faith-Based and Community Initiatives, designed to facilitate "compassion in action." The primary goal of such participation is to broaden the networks of collaborative partnerships of sacred and secular organizations for urban revitalization projects, as well as create new opportunities for investment in declining or stagnant communities. Numerous scholars across the disciplines agree that sustained community development and growth is the result of higher rates of (1) economic growth based on the amount of public/private financial investments and/or funding deposited in a neighborhood for businesses, houses, commercial buildings, and infrastructure over a concentrated period of time; (2) efficient government which emanates from political capital, which is the capacity to collectively define clearly one's interests, and develop an organized strategy to achieve those interests (Turner 1999); and (3) civic engagement and participation. Although scholars agree in the respective literatures on the basic meanings, elements, and contexts for economic and political capital, the discussions and conclusions germinating in contemporary scholarship on the definition of social capital "remain somewhat ambiguous" (Silverman 2001:241). Silverman (2001:241–246) suggests also that the exact manner in which social capital functions is not well understood, given contributing factors such as "the commitment to pluralism, a preference for democratic institutions, racial and ethnic ties, loyalty to parochial groups, neighborhood attachment, and common religious structures, [which] independently influence the development of social capital" at the local level.

The purpose of this work is to define social capital in the context of faith-based community economic development and African American church leadership. I present a primary case study based on face-to-face interviews—conducted between June 1998 and June 1999—and secondary/supplementary data with a small sample of ministers and leaders in an African American community in a post-industrial city, which focuses on the types of initiatives pursued and used by a transplanted civil rights activist/pastor, whose prominence influenced local community revitalization in the absence of a well-known established faith-based community development corporation, and led to national church-based, collective economic advancement strategies through the formation of broader networks and collaborative activities. My overall approach entails not so much a shift as a widening of the social capital debates to incorporate and understand the impact and uniqueness of African American church leaders in civic engagement and community affairs because much of the faith-based community economic development activity is being undertaken by mostly "large, elite [African American] churches which usually have well-educated, activist, and economically astute pastors" (Lincoln and Mamiya 1990:258) who more often than not, work independently of their faith-based organizations to affect community change. Having conducted past examinations of different community economic development strategies, I now take a narrow look at local faith-based leadership and its influence on social capital mobilization. I argue that social capital in the local context, especially in the African American community, is best understood when the unique role of church leaders, a particular/peculiar historical phenomenon, is taken into account. Rather than a definitive study of two fields clearly in nascent stages of inquiry, this work seeks to heighten awareness and interests for further discussion and research exploration on social capital as it functions through African American Church Leadership.

What Is Social Capital?

Social capital has a long intellectual history in the field of social science. Broadly defined in the field of sociology, social capital is defined as "a bond of mutual trust emerging from shared values that are embedded in parochial networks," which recognizes its degree of variation both within and across varied settings/boundaries (Silverman 2000:244). Similarly within the field of planning, social capital is viewed as "the organized voice of the community, which can be measured by civic infrastructure derived through activities such as community organizing, citizen participation and community-based decision making" (Turner 1999:16). It is based on a community development strategy, which "consists of [bonding or bridging] networks and norms that enable participants to act together effectively to pursue shared objectives" (Gittell and Vidal 1998:15). For political scientist Robert Putnam, who revived the term in the 1990s, social capital refers to the product of social relations composed of the "features of social life—networks, norms and trust—that enable participants to act together more effectively to pursue shared objectives, individually and collectively" (Putnam 1995: 664–65). The "core idea of social capital theory is that *social networks have value* [emphasis mine]. Just as a screwdriver (physical capital) or a college education (human capital) can increase productivity (both individual and collective), so, too, social contacts affect the productivity of individuals and groups" (Putnam 1995:19). In other words, "whereas physical capital refers to physical objects and human capital refers to properties of individuals, social capital refers to connections among individuals" (Putnam 2000:19). In social capital we begin with face-to-face interactions, then we progress to exchanges, which may grow into obligations, and ideally end up with trust—the individual's belief that the benefactors of one's reciprocal networks will act on one's behalf and not against them (Cnaan et al. 1998:8). When this structure is in place, civic associations can be formed resulting in strong social ties and civic participation in which, most often, these social ties are perceived as an asset, but can in some instances become a liability from an economic development perspective (Woolcock and Narayan 2000:226).

Emanating from the early twentieth-century writings of Lyda J. Hanifan, then a state supervisor of rural schools in West Virginia, social capital was used to stress the importance of community involvement in public schools to build both individual and collective "tangible substances" such as: good will, fellowship, sympathy, and social intercourse, accumulating social capital, "which may immediately satisfy . . . social needs and which may bear a social potentiality sufficient to substantial improvement of living conditions [benefiting] the whole community" (Hanifan 1916:130 as quoted in Putnam 2000:19). Putnam (2000:19–20) and Woolcock and Narayan (2000:229) continue to trace the use of the term and found that the same concept was independently rediscovered in the works of various scholars in the 1950s by Canadian sociologists to characterize the club memberships of *arriviste* suburbanites; in the 1960s by an exchange theorist and urban scholar Jane Jacobs to laud neighborliness in the modern metropolis; in the 1970s by American economist Glenn Loury to analyze the social legacy of slavery; and in the 1980s by French social theorist Pierre Bourdieu and by German economist Ekkehart Schlicht to underline the social and economic resources embodied in social networks. It was the seminal work highlighting the social context of education by American sociologist James S. Coleman, "who put the term firmly and finally on the intellectual agenda in the late 1980s, using it (as Hanifan had originally done)" (Putnam 2000:20). Coleman (1990:302 as quoted in Cnaan et al. 1998:7–8) suggests that social capital "is not a single entity, but a variety of different entities having two characteristics in common [which] consist of some aspect of a social structure, and . . . facilitate certain actions of individuals who are within the structure." It refers to the level of networks, both informal and formal in a given locality, and indicates the ways and extent to which people relate to and are engaged with others through informal social interactions, organized groups such as civic associations and churches, as well as through professional relationships (Cnaan et al. 1998:7–8).

In the late 1990s, the social capital context is extended by American political scientist Marion Orr (1999) to address the complexities of networks embedded in African American education in the local Baltimore public school system. Orr (1999:13) constricts the term to "Black Social Capital," which is the "ability to work together to achieve social ends, based on past experiences and attachments, with minimal reliance on direct payments or coercion." These past experiences and attachments might include "community networks, organizations, common bonds, loyalty, and trust and confidence, but it is conceptually and analytically distinct from cooperation" (Orr 1999:13). The term is further broadened, in this millennium, to include the role of women in community development work, who most often perceive their role "collectively" as "social change agents" over and above their individual career aspirations or considerations (Gittell, Ortega-Bustamante and Steffy 2000:134). Recently, Woolcock and Narayan (2000) traced the evolution of social capital research as it pertains to economic development across the disciplines, identifying four distinct approaches with their implications for development theory—communitarian, networks, institutional, and synergy—that characterize the norms and networks that enable people to act collectively. Basically, since Putnam's identification of the role of social capital in regional governance and economic development in Italy (1993) and his later suggestion of its importance on civic participation and institutional performance in the United States (1995), it has provided the "inspiration for most current work, which has since coalesced around studies in nine primary fields: families and youth behavior; schooling and education; community life (virtual and civic); work and organizations; democracy and governance; collective action; public health and environment; crime and violence; and economic development" (quote from Woolcock and Narayan 2000:229; Gittell and Vidal 1998:14).

Social Capital: Meanings and Contexts in the African American Sacred Community

Throughout African American history, leaders of the Black Church have struggled with the issue of whether or not to become involved in various strands of civic engagement leading to broad social action/movements. Should the Black Church actively participate in attempts to change American temperament toward a more favorable balance for the politically, socially, and economically disadvantaged and disillusioned? If so, how can a particular local church be most effective given its economic, political, and social resources? As Brazier (1969) observed, for example, one church group might be more effective by working internally on its own attitudes toward racial issues and other racial groups rather than becoming actively involved in building collective and collaborative partnerships in a social movement. However, another church group might be ready to become directly involved in collective marches, mass protests, and local/national voter registration drives and other activities necessary to bring about change. Given that churches vary by size and resources, the levels of civic engagement and activism will affect the formation of social capital in their respective involvement. Thus, the partnerships and tools necessary for building social capital in increasingly socially excluded and marginal racial communities will have to address this wide array of development. In this context, Orr's (1999:13) use of the term, which implies the "ability to work together to achieve social ends, based on past experiences and attachments, with minimal reliance on direct payments or coercion" most accurately applies with respect to African American community economic development initiatives.

Putnam's (2000) extensive research on faith communities found that close to half of all associational memberships in all of America are church related, and the same is true for personal philanthropy and volunteerism. As an "important incubator of civic skills, civic norms, community interests, and civic recruitment," churches, in general, facilitate activism in men, and especially in women (see Cnaan et al. 1998:11; Reese and Shields 1998), who "learn to give speeches, run meetings, manage disagreements, and bear administrative responsibility. They also befriend others who are in turn likely to recruit them into other forms of community activity. [Thus], churchgoers are substantially more likely to be involved in secular organizations, to vote and participate politically in other ways, and to have deeper informal social connections" (2000:66). Although Putnam asserts that religious sentiment in America generally seems to have become less tied to religious institutions and more toward highly individualized religious psychology (2000:74), he acknowledges that African American churches continue to be especially prominent in recent efforts to revitalize inner-city communities, thereby building social capital for marginalized community residents.

Throughout American history, the Black Church continues to be the oldest, most resilient, and only autonomous social institution in the African American community. As scholars of the Black Church have argued in the past, African Americans regardless of social strata tend to be more religiously vigilant than other Americans because the Afrocentric religious tradition distinctively encourages mixing religion and community affairs. Lincoln posits that the Black Church is the role model for contemporary community economic development. It evolved from an era of bondage where there was no freedom, no legal redress, no health protection, no social services to buffer the needs for counseling, child welfare, housing, employment, or financial assistance for enslaved Africans (Lincoln in Reed 1994). Before, during, and after emancipation, politically disenfranchised and economically destitute African citizens looked to the Black church for both spiritual and human nurturing (Billingsley 1999; Calhoun-Brown 1996, 2000; Mukenge 1983; Lincoln in Reed 1994; Malone 1994; DuBois 1903). For it was the Black Church which "defied the hostilities that forbade it to be born, overcame the repression that sought to destroy it, and survived to become the seedbed and the mother of the African-American culture" (Lincoln in Reed 1994:2; Washington 1996; Malone 1994; Wilmore 1990).

African American churches also are particularly central to social capital and civic engagement (Putnam 2000:68). Both during and after the civil rights struggle, the church functioned as "institutional center" by providing the movement with "an organized mass base; a leadership of clergymen largely economically independent of the larger white society and skilled in the art of managing people and resources; an institutionalized financial base through which protest was financed; and meeting places where the masses planned tactics and strategies and collectively committed themselves to the struggle" (Morris 1984:4). Thus, the Black Church knows the power of civic engagement by experience, for its existence in the political economy grew out of unmet needs that included not only spiritual, but also physical, social, psychological, and economic demands (Lincoln and Mamiya 1990; Frazier 1963). Because the Black Church was the only institution available to African Americans, it was virtually a collective and comprehensive system (Nelsen and Nelsen 1975). Black churches gave "spiritual refuge and reassurance," but they also spawned the first black banks, burial societies, insurance companies, schools, and homes of the aged as support services to spiritual needs of their people (Lincoln in Reed, 1994:2; Lincoln 1984, 1974). Orr (1999) argued in his study on the early Baltimore community that black churches, "once established . . . quickly became the social, political, economic, educational, and even cultural centers" of the African American community. In fact, the earliest efforts at "economic self-help, education, and political organization" involved "activities of many of these churches to foster a sense of racial unity, becoming the 'cradles of black consciousness and organizations' and 'affording a vehicle for collective action for the congregations and the population at large'" (Orr 1999:24), which laid the foundation for contemporary faith-based community economic development groups and activities.

Broadly speaking, most faith-based community economic development groups today are engaged in traditional areas of housing development, but have recently expanded activities to include health services, crime prevention, education, job creation through workforce/entrepreneurial training, economic development through small business incubators, cooperatives and commercial franchises, consulting support and technical assistance on loan programs, and/or establishing credit unions/financial institutions (Cisneros 1996:14; Ramsay 1998:610; Reese and Shields 1998). Most of these activities have been executed through faith-based community development corporations (CDCs), which devise and implement their own approaches, according to their agency missions, opportunities, and resources (Cisneros 1996:14) and are limited to certain types of congregations under certain conditions (Reese and Shields 1998). For faith-based organizations in African American communities, the range of activities concentrates more narrowly on religious orientation (Ramsay 1998; Thomas and Blake 1996), historical/cultural values (Walsh 1999; Franklin 1984) and the specific needs of local congregants/residents within the community. Owens (2000:9) categorized most Black Church-Associated Community Development Corporations' revitalization efforts as those activities involved in the manifesting of the spiritual mission based on Christian social gospel; building financial independence for congregations; becoming producers, developers and administrators of community programs; and being a force of collective political empowerment to public and private institutions on behalf of the community. Owens (2000) argues that Black Church-Associated CDCs are geared toward sustained community development "producing goods and services that better the conditions of [African Americans], individually and collectively." Recognizing that building economic, social, and political capital is a complex integrated process in a world which barred integration into the economic and social institutions in the larger society, African Americans historically looked to visionary leaders, working independently yet collectively, who could best articulated a message of "Hope," which embodied principles of social justice and collective economic advancement.

In addition to offering existing buildings, administrative infrastructure, and visionary leadership with supportive volunteers, many African American church leaders are proving to be more efficient than their peers in government and/or secular social programs given their broad networks of exchange, based on cooperation/obligations and trust. Tradition situates local African American church leaders more favorably than their political/business peers. When a local/national crisis occurs, it is the African American church leaders who are called upon to provide the moral vocabulary for the conditioning realities characterizing inner cities (Campolo 2000:139), advise politicians and to lend credibility to public action, or simply to be part of the solution (Cnaan et al. 1998:5; Ramsay 1998). It is these "conditioning realities" that extends the mission of today's African American church leaders to become leading actors/institutions in recent efforts to rebuild urban and low-income communities, to combat phenomena including teenage pregnancy, the drug economy that has led to the disproportionate incarceration of African American youth, perpetual welfare mothers, homelessness, AIDS, and unemployment, to name few. Given the level of trust placed upon them, African American church leaders are more aptly suited to take a broader beyond-the-sanctuary approach to mobilizing social capital and transforming the lives of their communities (Reed 1994:14).

African American Church Leaders:
Unique Social Capital Agents

William Edward Burghardt (W. E. B.) DuBois promoted collective economic advancement based almost exclusively on principles of Black self-determination. Articulating the "dual consciousness" of the African American in a "world, which yields him no true self-consciousness, but only lets him see himself through the revelation of the other world," DuBois asserted:

> [I]t is a peculiar sensation, this double-consciousness, this sense of always looking at one's self through the eyes of others, of measuring one's soul by the tape of a world that looks on in amused contempt and pity. One ever feels his two-ness,—an American, a Negro; two souls, two thoughts, two unreconciled strivings; two warring ideals in one dark body, whose dogged strength alone keeps it from being torn asunder. (DuBois 1953:3)

Although DuBois supported integrationist strategies and objectives, which were not values generally shared by the African American masses who believed it promoted white supremacy, his articulation of the America's historical "moral dilemma" greatly influenced the economic/social activities and cultural awareness found the involvement of Black church leaders in community development initiatives (Franklin 1984:193). It was DuBois who recognized the intrinsic role of religion in the center of African American society. The "religion of the slave" viewed Christianity as a religion of the oppressed and downtrodden of society. Exposure to the biblical stories of oppression, persecution, and enslavement of the Hebrews, "God's Chosen People in the Old Testament," caused many African Americans to identify with Jews and to consider themselves "God's Chosen People in America" (Franklin 1984:193; Wilmore 1982). Three things characterized this particular/peculiar religion—"the Preacher, the Music and the Frenzy" with the Preacher being the "most unique personality developed by the Negro on American soil" (DuBois 1953:190). Given the social and economic freedom to speak out against social injustices, African American preachers became the community leaders/visionaries utilizing their "power of the pulpit" to organize effective civil rights and economic justice movements culminating in the passage of the Civil Rights Act of 1964 and the Voting Rights Act of 1965, which substantially ended the codification of racism in the United States (Calhoun-Brown 2000:169). After civil rights, faith-based community economic development struggles in African American communities began to focus on "comprehensive social empowerment," a view articulated by Martin Luther King, Jr. (1967). King was a visionary African American preacher, who believed comprehensive social-economic-political empowerment, acquired via civic engagement/activism, was an essential part of the struggle to achieve human equality, civic virtue, and the "right relationship with God" (Walker 1991:24). Thus, through active religious affiliation and participation in the Black Church, African American leaders and community residents have been able to acquire the skills to build human and social capital, while at the same time collectively organizing to amass economic and political capital for their respective communities and national policy agendas.

Many nationally prominent protest-oriented pastors today are adherents to King's view (1967), which is shown in their personal ministries, ensuing direction, and nature of the African American church involvement in contemporary faith-based initiatives. In highlighting the success of progressive post–civil rights African American church leaders across the nation, there are a few that stand out as pacesetters and role models in community revitalization projects (Billingsley 1999; Reese and Shields 1998; Malone 1994; Reed 1994). Although full discussion of these various African American church leaders and their projects is beyond the scope of this work, it is important to note that these leaders, like King, hold fast to the principles of social justice by mobilizing collectively, through partnerships and collaborative efforts, to alleviate poverty and social exclusion toward more integration into the mainstream for all citizens. These norms and values motivate not only religious leaders, but also most faith-based organizations. Emanating from the biblical commandment, primarily based on the gospel of Matthew in the New Testament, which directs believers to feed the hungry, help the stranger/needy, clothe the naked/poor, save/rehabilitate the prisoner, and care for/visit the sick; black churches, in general, serve as the "port of entry for newcomers" by providing the civic space for the disconnected and disillusioned in inner cities (Walsh 1999). African American church leaders, therefore, often function as the "paramedics of society," where the government and other secular institutions fail (Walsh 1999).

In this vein, one can see importance of social prestige (Cnaan et al. 1998) and loyalty (Silverman 2001) to religious structure/organization as factors affecting social capital in the local context. As Woolcock and Narayan (2000) argue, the basic idea of social capital is that an individual's "family, friends, and associates constitute an important asset, [which] can be called on in a crisis, enjoyed for its own sake, and leveraged for material gain." When one is bankrupt of these social ties or a diverse stock of social networks and civic associations, as are so many of the nation's poor and disenfranchised, then one cannot actively benefit from the exchange of information and resources leading to secure employment and decent housing. Given that African American church leaders are often and traditionally sought after for their social prestige, social/moral values, moral vocabulary, and political/economic persuasion, they are viewed as naturally possessing more human and social capital than other African American leaders and can thus effectively function as the voice of the despondent in championing resources, amenities, and opportunities necessary for community economic development (Cnaan et al. 1998). One such African American church leader is the focus of this study because of his unique social capital as a protest-oriented transplant in upstate New York.

A Case Study of African American Ministerial Influence on Social Capital Mobilization

The locus of the social capital base in the African American communities and faith-based community economic development activities traditionally revolve around the leadership of the clergyman. The factor of social prestige (Cnaan et. al. 1998) attached to the local clergy, who are largely economically independent of the larger white society, elevates their political and social position in the exchange networks, which is a major asset individually and collectively for economically destitute and disconnected African American communities. Individually, clergy leaders who benefit from a large and diverse network can utilize the exchange as a resource that can apply to furthering the goals of their own church ministries; but collectively, they can use the exchange as a source of valuable information and entrepreneurial contacts with other clergy/congregants in a position to assist, contribute or volunteer to work together to achieve social ends for the broader community. When individuals in local communities are bankrupt of these social ties, they most often look to the local clergy and church as the source of information and resources, trusting that s/he can assist them with their needs/problems out of feelings of obligation toward humankind. Given the level of trust placed in African American church leaders and their perceived absence of class bias toward the poor in general, and women in particular, these leaders are the usually the first sought in the times of crisis, sometimes even before the family and/or other social service agencies, which is how they most significantly influence the socialization process in their respective communities (Calhoun-Brown 1996:937). This influence allows them to effectively function as the singular and celebrated voice of their congregants/communities in mobilizing resources, acquiring local amenities, and garnering opportunities necessary for better quality of life.

The main focus of this exploratory analysis is to present a primary case study, which focuses on the types of initiatives pursued and used by a transplanted civil rights activist/pastor, whose prominence influenced local community revitalization in the absence of a well-known, established, faith-based community development corporation, and led to national, church-based, collective economic advancement strategies through the formation of broader networks and collaborative activities. The goal is to present a model, which can be used to heighten interests for further discussion and stimulate broader research efforts exploring dimensions of social capital as it functions in a local context, particularly African American communities. My question is, what defines African American ministerial influence on social capital mobilization as it is advanced through local faith-based community economic development activities? The data is derived from a series of face-to-face interviews conducted between June 1998 and June 1999 with a prominent African American clergyman, the late Rev. Dr. Bennett W. Smith, Sr.,[1] and other additional ministers/leaders who work with him on collaborative activities/projects. I sought to answer how this particular minister, as a "prophet of protest" transplanted in Buffalo, was able to move into the local political area and effectively influence the local policy agenda garnering community economic development activities for his church/community. The case study analysis proceeds by (1) identifying the types of community economic development pursued by local African American churches in general, (2) characterizing the leadership approach/model used by Smith to mobilize social capital, and (3) highlighting some implications regarding social capital theory.

Types of African American Church Community Economic Development Activities in Buffalo, New York

Like most faith-based community economic development groups, African American churches engaged in these activities in upstate New York began through the traditional area of housing development. The face-to-face interviews with local ministers revealed that only a small number of the African American churches have expanded their individual developmental activities to include other major projects, like those mentioned above, such as: private schools, health services, workforce/entrepreneurial training, small business incubators, and/or establishing credit unions/financial institutions. Collectively, African American church leaders in this study had established one inner-city commercial plaza, but there was no evidence of individual cooperatives, commercial franchises, or consulting support and technical assistance on loan programs. These same small number of churches executed their individual major developmental activities, especially those which utilized government funds, through required church-based community development corporations (CDCs), whereby the pastor of the church serves, in most cases, as board president. This gives the pastor the authority to devise and implement their visions according to their religious orientation and cultural values, as well as church missions. In this vein African American churches in Buffalo function much the same way as other African American churches in similar environments nationwide.

The late Rev. Dr. Bennett W. Smith, Sr., senior pastor of the largest and wealthiest African American church in the city of Buffalo, St. John Baptist Church, came in the early 1970s to build the African American community socially, politically, and economically. As the first African American church in the city awarded a government-sponsored public housing contract by the Department of Housing and Urban Development, the congregation sought a pastor with a reputation of strong leadership skills, charisma, prestige, and business expertise to negotiate with political officials and facilitate the completion of the 150-unit complex, called McCarley Gardens. At the time, St. John was the only Black church in the city involved in housing development initiatives. The other major development initiative, in which Smith was involved, was the Ellicott Community Redevelopment coalition of 13 Black churches, which led to the Town Gardens Housing and Commercial Plaza on the East side. Spearheaded by a southern-born son of a sharecropper, the late Rev. A. Charles Ware, this $7 million dollar project was developed with the vision of serving as a "mecca" for one-stop shopping and job creation for area residents. Today, the plaza is still a viable inner-city shopping center serving as the vinculum of under-utilized and under-represented small businesses.

With respect to individual African American, church-based, community development corporation housing development initiatives, St. John for a long while was the only individual African American congregation with the financial resources in any sizeable allocation to sponsor low- and moderate-income (LMI) housing for families. After McCarley Gardens was erected for LMI residents, Smith moved toward the development of a 150-unit housing complex for senior citizens, St. John Towers. However by the early 1980s, other local African American congregations were using their social networks to move into housing development. Capitalizing on a political confrontation between Smith and the mayor, J. Griffin, whom the vocal Smith had accused of being racist and whom he refused to endorse during the 1977 campaign, Smith recalls that as a form of political payback, the city gave a 90-unit contract to the only African American minister who supported the mayor's campaign. This 90-unit was Friendship Manor sponsored by Friendship Baptist Church. Other housing development projects were the 50-unit God's City sponsored by the former Mt. Ararat Baptist Church (now New Mt. Ararat Temple of Prayer), and more recently the Ellicott Towers and First Shiloh Senior Citizen's complex, both sponsored by the First Shiloh Baptist Church as partnerships with the city's municipal housing development agency. Other black churches with smaller senior citizen housing developments are Pilgrim Baptist and Gethsemane Baptist churches. Only a few Black congregations are actively engaged in single-family housing via actual construction and rehabilitation efforts for LMI families in various parts of Buffalo's impoverished Fruitbelt neighborhood. These churches include Mt. Ararat Temple of Prayer, Greater Refuge Temple of Christ Church, and Gethsemane Baptist Church.

Even though several African American churches sponsor individual credit unions, it appears that the St. John Credit Union is the only church credit union that has programmatically applied its financial resources to economic development or neighborhood revitalization in the broader African American community with the development of a major Family Life Center, under construction. The only other church with a community-based Family Life Center is Greater Refuge Temple of Christ Church. In the areas of education and political involvement in civil rights/integrationist issues, many of the African American ministers argued that Bennett W. Smith, Sr., almost single-handedly paved the way for Black church involvement in educational initiatives citywide. Expanded and broad-based private educational opportunities for local African Americans came as a by-product result of Smith aggressively protesting against the discriminatory practices of major companies in the Operation PUSH "Selective Patronage" campaigns. Although the national African American-oriented political organization, Operation PUSH, had 15 national programs that promoted African American entrepreneurship, placed disenfranchised racial veterans in jobs, aided and counseled addicts, and assisted in legal problems for economically poor racial communities, its most renown program was the campaign for academic excellence, "Project EXCEL," underscored with the self-esteem statement "I AM SOMEBODY."

Rev. Smith aggressively advocated and won the installation of "Project EXCEL" in Buffalo's local public school system by arguing, "Blacks must now stop 'cursing the darkness and light a candle.' We must excel in the institutions of education in this country, so as to be able to effect change for the benefit of Black people" (Smith 1978:A16). A full discussion of the political and economic failures of the national project EXCEL program is beyond the scope of this present work; however, one can surmise that the EXCEL campaign became the catalyst for the St. John Christian Academy, a private church-based state-chartered school, founded by Smith in the mid 1980s. A strong advocate of "Afrocentric" cultural values for upward social mobility, Smith instituted several other related programs held on St. John Baptist church premises, such as government-funded programs like the HUD job training site designation for welfare-to-work participants, and "Project Gift" for the mentally and physically challenged children, among others. This opened the door for local churches to establish and/or partner with Smith and each other for more formal education and job training programs with public and private agencies/institutions.

Two additional Black churches have private elementary charter schools, Greater Refuge Temple Christian Academy of the Greater Refuge Temple of Christ Church and Cornerstone Academy of True Bethel Baptist Church. First Shiloh Baptist church is the only Black church with an accredited chartered high school, First Shiloh Christian Academy, and city-funded Summer Fun Program and After School Enrichment Program for selective tutoring programs. One church, Bethel AME, is the oldest Black institution in the city of Buffalo as well as the first to establish the comprehensive Bethel Head Start program in Western New York. Greater Faith Bible Tabernacle and Friendship Baptist Church have their own Head Start program as well. The New Mt. Ararat Temple of Prayer, under the pastorate of Elder D. Brown, is in the process of establishing a local Institute of Fine Arts to support its Arts Museum as well as to conduct an inner city orchestra and drama school for youth. This same congregation actively partners with a neighboring non-denominational faith-based organization, Urban Christian Ministries, which has a very strong youth development program component.

Given all of the moderate, yet progressive activity of these local churches, few are involved in support services or broader community economic development initiatives individually, but collectively they comprise a diverse network of resources and opportunities with their peer congregations. One new local initiative bringing together a consortium of large and smaller churches initiated by a local minister, the "Genesis Project," is aimed at family preservation and empowerment for local African American families. Still in the early stage of development, it is intended to be a one-stop family support center for area families to gain information and training in dealing with problems of today. Other coalitions of Black churches, the Interdenominational Religious Consortium (IRC) made up of about fifty Black churches of various sizes, and the Ministerial Rehabilitation Initiative, a partnership with the City of Buffalo Community Development Agency, are new enterprises seeking government and major corporate development dollars for broader community economic development activities. These coalitions have yet to formulate and realize broader economic goals for Buffalo's East Side. Recognizing that building economic, social, and political capital is a complex integrated process, local clergy of mostly large and medium-sized congregations worked independently and collectively to build social networks fostering collective economic advancement for their churches. However, unlike many of their peers across the nation, African American churches under their leaders in Buffalo have not successfully exploited their social networks to become a strong centralized force of collective political empowerment on behalf of the community as a whole. This was seen as a source of frustration for Smith, who came with a reputation as a civil rights activist from his involvement with Rev. Dr. Martin Luther King, Jr. and the group of clergy leaders, who founded the Valley Christian Improvement Association in Cincinnati, Ohio, in the early 1960s. Smith described his initial visit to the city of Buffalo, during a 1998 revival at St. John:

> Leaving Cincinnati to come to Buffalo was a very difficult decision. . . . I saw that Buffalo presented a good opportunity to do what I was doing [in Cincinnati] on a larger scale. . . . I saw [St. John] as being large enough to be able to provide me with the creature comforts of [life]. . . . that is permit me to give my talents to the city more freely. Little did I know that the city really didn't want them! . . . I had spent from 1960 to 1972 [in Cincinnati, Ohio] doing nothing but protest and involvement with the total support of my church, the total involvement of my church with a group of clergymen that had cohesively come together to work together, and now I find here's a community where none of this is going on. None of this! Nobody wants to get involved. I just buried myself into this kind of private, personal protest.

Many of the African American ministers agreed that Smith effectively built his social networks with local clergy and politicians through political activism in both local and national campaigns in the African American community (Wallace 2001), which led to partnerships and collaboration on new developmental projects with mostly younger and educated clergy eager to participate and influence in the local political arena. In this vein, Smith mobilized "Black Social Capital" (Orr 1999) to work together with local and national African American clergy to achieve social ends. He capitalized on the historical experiences of African Americans and the cultural attachments and loyalty to the Black Church and its internal bonds and networks to build financial wealth for St. John, which was not solely independent of government funding, but certainly not totally reliant upon it. Utilizing intercommunity or "bonding" social ties among congregants, and political or "bridging" ties among local politicians and community supporters, which crossed social divides of religion, class, ethnicity, and socioeconomic status (Woolcock and Narayan 2000:230; Gittell and Vital 1998), Smith created a broader range of networks that contributed to social capital for the African American community. This "networking" model, although construed as ambiguous in its theoretical construction and policy influence in social capital literature, is the best way to explain Smith's exercise of social capital.

A Model of African American Ministerial Influence on Social Capital

Woolcock and Narayan (2000:231) surmise that the network view of social capital is characterized by two key propositions: social capital is perceived as a "double-edged sword," given the range of valuable services, from personal household favors to job referrals and emergency cash one can receive from close ties; but on the flip side, the same valuable services can incur significant negative/positive economic costs and consequences to the member/group later on by placing considerable claims on a members' sense of obligation and commitment. This is why the "sources of social capital need to be distinguished from the consequences that derived from them." The authors argue further that the logical conclusion which can be drawn from the network view is that both strong intra/intercommunity ties and weak extra-community networks are needed to avoid making redundant claims regarding the efficacy of social capital (Woolcock and Narayan 2001). Thus, given the nature of community change over time, one can reason that the costs and benefits associated with particular combinations of bonding and bridging networks with respect to community economic development activities in African American communities will change as well.

The principal goal of community economic development is to stimulate the local economy through greater integration and participation in community action or activities using local resources that foster employment opportunities and business investments in sectors that improve the community as a whole. At the heart of community economic development is a belief in self-determination, cultural appreciation, and economic empowerment. Economic empowerment depends on local economic development, a concept that has a range of definitions and goals. Woolcock and Narayan (2000:232), argue that local economic development "takes place through a mechanism that allows individuals to draw initially on the benefits of close community membership but that also enables them to acquire the skills and resources to participate in networks that transcend their community, thereby progressively joining the economic mainstream." A general graphic illustration is adapted from Woolcock and Narayan (2000), and particularized to explain how Smith used social capital through his leadership role within the church networks to bridge into the local political arena thereby bringing significant local community economic development projects to the African American community in Buffalo, New York.

Figure 8.1 demonstrates that as the social capital networks built through the leadership activities of Smith in Buffalo became more diverse, so too did the welfare of St. John Baptist Church and Smith's reputation as a leader with local and national clergy and politicians, and to some extent the African American community in Buffalo. On the left side of Figure 8.1, we view Smith building "bonding networks" as an internal "spiritual caretaker of congregation" moving toward "bridging networks" in his external political activist/leadership role as "community nurturer" of the African American community as a whole. The foundation for Smith's community economic development work was facilitated in his early days through his political protests and activism. In Figure 8.1, (1) represents the Operation PUSH activities; pulpit endorsements/voter registration drives; convention hall activities for local, state and national political candidates; and Black History Month Programs, which built his reputation in the community. This helped him to negotiate for government-sponsored housing and collaboration with other churches on commercial development; (2) represents McCarley Gardens low-to-moderate-income (LMI) and St. John Tower Senior Citizen Housing. As Smith pursued more and more government-sponsored projects/programs for his congregation (3) represents the early, now defunct Community Outreach Mission Center on Jefferson Avenue, which by the way did not necessarily result in greater social capital for his parishioners. Smith moved away from collaboration and partnerships with other local clergy toward building linkages

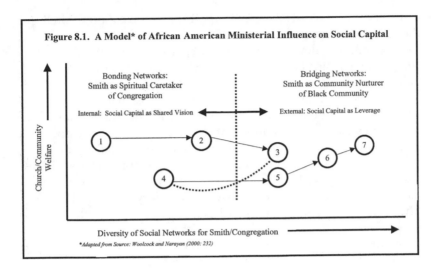

Figure 8.1. A Model* of African American Ministerial Influence on Social Capital

to national clergy and larger funding opportunities to build economic wealth through the establishment of the St. John Federal Credit Union; in Figure 8.1 (4) represents the establishment of the St. John Federal Credit Union, the Smith Child Life Foundation Fund, and the annual free Income Tax Preparation services for senior citizens and congregants. In a sense, Smith began to divest himself of local community ties to "find a potentially more diverse network where 'bridging' social capital is more abundant and economic opportunities more promising" (Woolcock and Narayan 2000:233). He did this initially through educational activities and the development of St. John Christian Academy— (5) represents the educational initiatives/programs: Early Head Start Program, Project EXCEL, Project Gift and St. John Christian Academy—then later through government-sponsored job-training activities—(6) represents the U.S. HUD-sponsored Neighborhood Network Center operated through St. John—and in a business investment partnership with national African American clergy leaders in the creation of the Revelation Corporation of America. (7) represents the collective economic advancement initiatives through the Bennett W. Smith Family Life Center for congregants with projected small business incubator and Revelation Corporation.

The Revelation Corporation of America, a credit card company, is the genius of bridging networks of five of the nation's largest African American church denominations: The National Baptist Convention, USA, The Progressive National Baptist Convention, National Baptist

Convention of America, African Methodist Episcopal Zion Church and the Christian Methodist Episcopal Church, which is designed to leverage the collective purchasing power of approximately 20 million of its congregational members across America (Smith 1996:36). The corporation plans to provide local amenities to members through homeowner's, life, and auto insurance; business, consumer and new construction loans; catalog sales and coupons for discounted food and merchandise; and national programs on single-family home ownership, multifamily rental housing, commercial, and industrial development in addition to the credit card and retail trade coupons. The goal is to develop a "reciprocal relationship between its core group of church members and major retailers across the country" (Smith 1996:36). Thus, by using local bonding social capital networks to build bridging networks nationally, these African American clergy leaders are attempting to foster collective economic advancement through the creation of economic institutions for African Americans as a whole.

Some argue that the networks' approach to social capital has the tendency to minimize the "'public good' nature of social groups, regarding any benefits of group activity as primarily the property of the particular individuals involved" (Woolcock and Narayan 2000:234), which explains the emphasis on Smith's leadership role as the locus of social capital. Often, institutional and discriminatory practices can undermine efforts by disenfranchised and disconnected African Americans to act in their collective interest, thus many rely on courageous leaders who can articulate self-help ideals that promote programs and strategies that are embedded in the African American values and cultural traditions derived from the enslavement period, but also reflect the economic interests of the masses of African Americans found in inner cities (Franklin 1984:203). Following in the leadership traditions of DuBois and King, as the social capital networks expanded for Smith, he attempted to direct his spiritual and political activities to "restore hope" in the African American community in Buffalo.

Implications for Social Capital Theory

The impetus behind President George W. Bush's recent formation and inauguration of the White House Office of Faith-Based and Community Initiatives is to release more and more federal control over social programs to state and local governments, forcing local officials to seek local partnerships/collaboration with community actors to help harness resources for social programs to deal with social problems. Many argue that the Black church is well positioned to play an even larger role in faith-based community development through the receipt of government funds for programs, but more importantly to build social capital for the disconnected and disillusioned in African American communities and neighborhoods. From enslavement through the history of legal and racial segregation, when African Americans were prevented from either building their own institutions or participating in existing mainstream institutions, black churches "developed and contained civil society for them," through politics, arts, music, education, economic development, social services, civic associations, leadership opportunities, and business enterprises (Calhoun-Brown 2000:169). Today, as the "most resource rich institution in the African-American community," African American churches also are particularly central to social capital and civic engagement in terms of creating diverse networks of visionary spiritual and energizing leadership, social services and economic investments.

In a political and social climate where American citizens hold conflicting opinions about the nature of civic engagement and participation, long-standing African American church leaders will continue to be called upon to give direction to new policies and planning efforts in their respective communities. These leaders have the unique ability to inspire "change of consciousness" as well as "mutual transformation" of individuals seeking inclusion into broader social networks (Campolo 2000:139; Walsh 1999). Social scientists should recognize that "People of African [ancestry] have always lived with a sense of hope" (Malone 1994:52), which is embedded in social action historically pursued through the African American. Putnam's (2000:408–409) challenge to America's clergy, lay leaders, theologians, and ordinary worshipers is to "spur a new, pluralistic, socially responsible 'great awakening,' so that by 2010 Americans will be more deeply engaged than we are today in one or another spiritual community of meaning, while at the same time becoming more tolerant of the faiths and practices of other Americans. . . . creating networks that bridge the racial, social, and geographic cleavages that fracture our metropolitan areas." In this vein, all community residents must take an active part in the organization, administration, and implementation of community economic development activities.

The collective strength lies with the economic wealth and moral fortitude of the African American church, particularly in inner city communities. The African American church has always been in a position to leverage the decision-making process every level in the community. It was from these mediating institutions that the collective consciousness, cultural awareness, and economic empowerment struggles began and, more importantly, fostered the activist tradition of all citizens of the African American community. As Overacker (1998:6)concludes,

> [In] gain[ing] a more comprehensive understanding of the role of the church in both the lives of its members and the social, economic and political life of the African American community as a whole (a role consistently acknowledged as central), scholars need to gather more data concerning how the church functioned at the local, community level. The study of communities, their commonalities and differences, breaks down the tendency to treat the African American community, or its churches, as monochromatic entities lacking complexity or diversity. An analysis of local situations, especially during times of historical transition, adds depth and perspective to the landscape of the African American experience.

Thus, critical examinations of social capital as it functions in a local context with respect to African American communities contribute significantly to expanding the literature on social capital and community development.

Notes

1. Rev. Dr. Bennett W. Smith, Sr., passed away on August 7, 2001, after the series of interviews was complete. For a larger discussion, see S. L. Wallace (2001).

References

Billingsley, Andrew. 1999. *Mighty like a River: The Black Church and Social Reform.* New York: Oxford University Press.

Brazier, Arthur M. 1969. *Black Self-Determination: The Story of The Woodlawn Organization.* Grand Rapids, MI: William B. Eerdmans.

Calhoun-Brown, Allison. 1996. "African American Churches and Political Mobilization: The Psychological Impact of Organizational Resources." *Journal of Politics,* 58.4:935–953.

Calhoun-Brown, Allison. 2000. "Upon This Rock: The Black Church, Nonviolence, and the Civil Rights Movement." *PS: Political Science and Politics,* 33.2:168–174.

Campolo, Tony. 2000. *Revolution and Renewal: How Churches Are Saving Our Cities.* Louisville, KY: Westminster John Knox Press.

Cisneros, Henry. G. 1996. *Higher Ground: Faith Communities and Community Building.* Washington, DC: U.S. Department of Housing and Urban Development.

Cnaan, Ram A. et al. 1998. "Bowling Alone but Serving Together: The Congregational Norm of Community Involvement." Report prepared for the Center for Research on Religion and Urban Civil Society, University of Pennsylvania, Philadelphia.

DuBois, W. E. B. 1903. *The Negro Church.* Atlanta: Atlanta University Press.

DuBois, W. E. B. 1965. *The Souls of Black Folk.* New York: Avon.

Franklin, Vincent P. 1984. *Black Self-Determination: A Cultural History of the Faith of the Fathers.* Westport, CT: Lawrence Hill.

Frazier, Edward Franklin. 1963. *The Negro Church in America.* New York: Schocken.

Gittell, Marilyn, Isolda Ortega-Bustamante, and Tracy Steffy. 2000. "Social Capital and Social Change: Women's Community Activism." *Urban Affairs Review,* 36.2:123–147.

Gittell, Ross, and Avis C. Vidal. 1998. *Community Organizing: Building Social Capital as a Development Strategy.* Thousand Oaks, CA: Sage.

Gittell, Ross, and Margaret Wilder. 1999. "Community Development Corporations: Critical Factors That Influence Success." *Journal of Urban Affairs,* 21.3:341–362.

Hanifan, Lyda J. 1916. "The Rural School Community Center." *The Annals of the American Academy of Political and Social Science,* 67:130–138.

King, Jr., Martin Luther. 1967. *Where Do We Go from Here: Chaos or Community?* Boston: Beacon Press.

Lincoln, C. Eric. 1984. *Race, Religion, and the Continuing American Dilemma.* New York, NY: Hill and Wang.

Lincoln, C. Eric. 1974. *The Black Church since Frazier.* New York: Schocken.

Lincoln, C. Eric, and Lawrence H. Mamiya. 1990. *The Black Church in the African-American Experience.* Durham, NC: Duke University Press.

Malone, Walter. 1994. *From Holy Power to Holy Profits: The Black Church and Community Economic Empowerment.* Chicago: African American Images Press.

Morris, Aldon D. 1984. *The Origins of the Civil Rights Movement: Black Communities Organizing for Change.* New York: Free Press.

Mukenge, Ida Rousseau. 1983. *The Black Church in Urban America: A Case Study in Political Economy.* Lanham, MD: University Press of America.

Naison, Mark D. 1990. "In Quest of Community: The Organizational Structure of Black Buffalo," In *African Americans and the Rise of Buffalo's Post-Industrial City, 1940 to Present,* ed. H. L. Taylor, Jr., 207–215. Buffalo, NY: Buffalo Urban League.

Nelsen, Hart M., and Anne K. Nelsen. 1975. *The Black Church in the Sixties.* Lexington: University of Kentucky Press.

Orr, Marion. 1999. *Black Social Capital: The Politics of School Reform in Baltimore, 1986–1998.* Lawrence: University Press of Kansas.

Overacker, Ingrid. 1998. *The African American Church Community in Rochester, New York: 1900–1940.* Rochester, NY: University of Rochester Press.

Owens, Michael Leo. 2000. "Political Action and Black Church-Associated Community Development Corporations." Unpublished paper delivered the 30th Annual Meeting of the Urban Affairs Association, Los Angeles, CA, May 3–6.

Putnam, Robert D. 1995. "Tuning In, Tuning Out: The Strange Disappearance of Social Capital in America." The Ithiel de Sola Pool Lecture. *PS: Political Science & Politics,* 28.4:664–683.

Putnam, Robert D. 2000. *Bowling Alone: The Collapse and Revival of American Community.* New York: Simon and Schuster.

Ramsay, Meredith. 1998. "Redeeming the City: Exploring the Relationship between Church and Metropolis." *Urban Affairs Review,* 33.5:595–626.

Reed, Gregory J. 1994. *Economic Empowerment through the Church: A Blueprint for Progressive Community Development.* Grand Rapids, MI: Zondervan.

Reese, Laura A., and Gary R. Shields. 1998. "Faith-Based Development: Economic Development Activities of Urban Religious Institutions." Paper presented at the Annual Meeting of the American Political Science Association, Boston.

Silverman, Robert Mark. 2000. "Vying for the Urban Poor: Charitable Organizations, Faith-based Social Capital, and Racial Reconciliation in a Deep South City. Unpublished paper delivered at the 65th Annual Conference of the Association of Social and Behavioral Scientists, Jackson, Mississippi, March 22–25.

Silverman, Robert Mark. 2001. "CDCs and Charitable Organizations in the Urban South: Mobilizing Social Capital Based on Race and Religion for Neighborhood Revitalization." *Journal of Contemporary Ethnography,* 30.2:240–268.

Smith, Sr., Bennett W. 1976. "Black Americans Urged to Join New Push for Excellence." *Buffalo Courier Express* 23(July):1, 16.

Smith, E. 1996. "United They Stand." *Black Enterprise* (June):36.

Special Report. 1995. "Amazing Grace: 50 Years of the Black Church." *Ebony* (April):87–96.

Thomas, June Manning, and Reynard N. Blake, Jr. "Faith-Based Community Development and African-American Neighborhoods." 1996. In *Revitalizing Urban Neighborhoods,* ed. W. Dennis Keating, Norman Krumholz, and Philip Star, 131–143. Lawrence: University Press of Kansas.

Turner, Robyn S. 1999. "Entrepreneurial Neighborhood Initiatives: Political Capital in Community Development." *Economic Development Quarterly,* 13.1:15–22.

Vidal, Avis C. 1992. *Rebuilding Communities: A National Study of Urban Community Development Corporations.* Community Development Research Center, Graduate School of Management and Urban Policy. New York: New School for Social Research.

Walker, Jr., Theodore. 1991. *Empower the People: Social Ethics for the African-American Church.* Maryknoll, NY: Orbis.

Wallace, Sherri Leronda. 2001. "Buffalo's 'Prophet of Protest': The Political Leadership and Activism of Reverend Dr. Bennett W. Smith, Sr." *Afro-Americans in New York Life and History,* 25.2:7–43.

Walsh, Joan. 1999. "Current Issues; Creative Solutions." Report prepared June 10, 1998, on the Civic Work of Congregations. Published on *Religion and Civic Culture Online* (July).

Washington, James M. 1996. "Urban Economic Development Strategies of African-American Baptist Clergy During the Cold War Era." In *Churches, Cities, and Human Community: Urban Ministry in the United States, 1945–1985,* ed. Clifford J. Green, 258–279. Grand Rapids, MI: William B. Eerdmans.

Wilmore, Gayraud S. 1983. *Black Religion and Black Radicalism.* 2nd ed. Maryknoll, NY: Orbis.

Woolcock, Michael, and Deepa Narayan. 2000. "Social Capital: Implications for Development Theory, Research, and Policy." *World Bank Research Observer,* 15.2: 225–249.

Mobilizing Social Capital through Community Struggle

Judith N. DeSena

Introduction

The concept of social capital offers social scientists a model in which ordinary people engage in civic activities through social networks and resource mobilization. Social capital is community (Etzioni 2001). By building social capital people make connections to individuals and institutions, which can be set in motion whenever necessary.

Social capital is described by characteristics of trust and cooperation, and is measured through civic behavior such as participation in voluntary associations, attendance at community meetings, voter turnout, political clubs, and membership in religious institutions (Putnam 1993). Moreover, social capital is divided into types, which are dependent upon the degree of familiarity people have with each other (those who know each other vs. those who do not) (Putnam 1993). An additional feature of social capital includes its use as leverage toward action (Temkin and Rohe 1998; Briggs 1998; Granovetter 1973, 1974). In general, the literature views social capital as a key element of neighborhood stability.

This study attempts to offer a view of social capital on a community level, in which social capital is mobilized through community organizing efforts. It focuses on the potential of community organizations in assembling and building social capital, and ultimately achieving political empowerment, while also promoting community cooperation and social unity among various ethnic and racial groups, and making local women visible and in the forefront of community affairs. This chapter demonstrates that participation in a multiethnic community coalition challenged peoples' traditional views of "how to get things done," as well as their stereotypical perceptions of race and ethnicity. Community residents expected government to respond to their concerns and problems, and moved toward mobilization when they were ignored. This transforming process politicized many residents. In addition, community members of different ethnic groups came to view each other as allies, with shared interests and common enemies. They moved beyond segregation and mutual blame for social problems, and supported each other in struggle. In addition, this chapter examines local women's participation in building social capital through community organizing. Like other studies which investigate womens' community work (Gittell, Ortega-Bustamante and Steffy 2000; Naples 1998; Pardo 1998), women in Greenpoint–Williamsburg are in the forefront of community organizing efforts.

This research extends and contributes to the thinking on social capital at the local level, among low-income groups, by analyzing the origins, events and issues, and eventual decline of a community organization in Brooklyn called the Greenpoint–Williamsburg Coalition of Community Organizations (GWCOCO). The GWCOCO was a grassroots, multiethnic, racially mixed community organization, which used a confrontational style of community action. It operated between 1976 and 1982, an earlier period of fiscal austerity in New York City. From its inception, the organization's purpose was community unity and activism. The coalition involved working class and poor residents of Greenpoint and Williamsburg, two different, but adjacent neighborhoods that worked toward improving living conditions and the quality of life within this community. The GWCOCO enhanced social capital by "build[ing] bonds and bridges in a low income community" (Gittell and Vidal 1998:15).

This research is important for two reasons. First, it shows how a progressive grassroots coalition can be formed which transcends class and color lines. This research describes how common interests, highly salient issues, and community organizing efforts were mobilized under the leadership of women to improve the quality of life in the northern Brooklyn community of Greenpoint–Williamsburg. The second reason this research is important is because it identifies the connection between the development of social capital in communities and other forms of capital. This comes through in the discussion of the decline of the GWCOCO, which occurred in response to changing regimes and support structures in broader institutions.

Greenpoint–Williamsburg

The neighborhoods of Greenpoint and Williamsburg make up northern Brooklyn, in New York City. Greenpoint is a primarily white, working class area, while Williamsburg is comprised mostly of poor Hispanics and blacks. In 1990, Greenpoint–Williamsburg had a total population of 155,972. Of those individuals, 46 percent were white (non-Hispanic), 7 percent were black (non-Hispanic), 44 percent were Hispanic, and 3 percent were Asian and other non-Hispanic groups.[1] More recent data on City Council District 34,[2] indicates that in 1997, the Williamsburg District was 8 percent white (non Hispanic), 21 percent black (non Hispanic), 4 percent Asian (non Hispanic), and 67 percent Hispanic (City Project 2000). Demographic data on City Council District 33 specifies that in 1997,[3] the Greenpoint District was 62 percent white (non Hispanic), 11 percent black (non Hispanic), 4 percent Asian (non Hispanic), and 23 percent Hispanic (City Project 2000). As the GWCOCO was forming, it divided the community into six areas to insure that the interests of ethnic and racial groups were represented. These areas were Greenpoint (mixed white ethnic groups), Northside (Polish), Central Williamsburg (Italian and African Americans), East Williamsburg (African Americans and Hispanics), Southside (Hispanic), South Williamsburg (Hasidic Jews and Hispanics, however the Hasidic community was not a regular participant in the coalition). Since the GWCOCO was a coalition of civic organizations, the organizers of this coalition recruited existing groups for membership. In other words, existing bonds were bridged. Each geographic/ethnic section elected three area vice presidents as representatives, as well as voted for the executive board members who filled the positions of president, executive vice president, sSecretary, and treasurer. Elections took place at an annual convention, and vacancies were filled at delegate assemblies, which were held four times a year. Membership in the coalition was through a local community organization, such as block, tenant, and civic associations, as well as religious, health, and housing groups. Political clubs were not accepted as members so that the coalition's work would not be directed or dominated by politicians. Moreover, politicians were often the targets of the coalition's actions. By excluding them and their clubs from membership, the GWCOCO could hold them accountable for their performance. The coalition was made up of approximately 100 community organizations.

Residents from each neighborhood bridged their ethnic and racial differences, and worked together to improve their quality of life by fighting for municipal and social services in these communities. The commitment to create the GWCOCO included an overt dedication to multi-ethnic leadership and participation. The coalition's leaders and staff were successful at rallying social capital to form a coalition because they handled the process of overcoming racial and ethnic barriers with finesse. They respected existing local organizations as vehicles for membership, and understood old conflicts, controversies, and divisions. They were able to focus people on common enemies who were decision- and policymakers and identify these elites as the source of the community's problems.

Research Methods

This research was carried out through the use of participant observation, content analysis, and interviews. I was a member of the coalition discussed, and therefore had access to other members, its meetings, and written materials. I attended meetings, analyzed reports to funding sources and the membership, and interviewed coalition leaders and staff. These major approaches were the ways in which I collected data for this analysis.

Mobilizing Social Capital through Struggle

The coalition worked on a variety of local issues including the renovation of local parks, adequate sewers, more police for public housing, the maintenance of investment practices and essential city services. This chapter will describe two actions. In all cases, the approach was one of confrontational community organizing. The coalition emulated the style of Saul Alinsky even though members had not been trained by Alinsky's legacy, the Industrial Areas Foundation (IAF). As one of the coalition's organizers described:

> It was all Saul Alinsky style organizing, that's what we were doing. Our bible was Rules for Radicals. I think what ACT UP is doing today is very similar to that type of organizing. It's very aggressive, it's militant in a way, it's very attention grabbing. We did a lot of stuff. We were good for our really wild demonstrations, which grabbed the attention we were looking for so that an issue could be hot. We did a mock car accident. We had people all bloodied up laying all over the streets. We blocked the BQE [Brooklyn-Queens Expressway] during the height of rush hour a couple of times. A few leaders were arrested for that one.

The Alinsky approach to organizing involves identifying a common enemy, target, or threat and using it to bring people together across racial and/or local geographic divisions. Once people focus on a common enemy and experience the power that comes with unified action, they are motivated to work together and build an organization (Alinsky 1971).

Redlining

One of the first issues the coalition worked on was redlining. It was quite common during the 1970s for banks to disinvest in inner city neighborhoods by refusing to offer mortgage, business, and home improvement loans. Segments of Greenpoint and Williamsburg were redlined by the major savings banks in the area, namely Anchor Savings, The Dime Savings Bank, Green Point Savings Bank, Lincoln Savings Bank, and Williamsburgh Savings Bank. The Greenpoint/Williamsburg Committee Against Redlining (GWCAR) was formed in August 1977 after a Town Hall meeting where data on redlining were presented. GWCAR was made up of staff and community leaders from a number of local groups including, the Pratt Center, Catholic Charities, Los Sures, St. Nicholas Neighborhood Preservation and Housing Rehabilitation Corp., People's Firehouse, and Neighbors of Greenpoint and Williamsburg (N.A. 1979c). A member of GWCAR described: "People came to St. Nick's saying they couldn't get mortgages. The group investigated where the banks invested. Banks like Anchor were investing outside the community. [GWCAR] met with CEO's and brought people with them who were denied mortgages." This committee was established prior to the coalition's founding convention. After the founding convention, GWCAR was considered a committee of the coalition. GWCAR demonstrated in and around banks, and met with bank officials to press for changes in the banks' lending policies in the community. GWCAR wanted banks:

> To continue taking ads for mortgage and home improvement loans; to consider each property for which a loan request is made separately and on the basis of the soundness of the building itself rather than in the context of the block it is on, which may include industry or run down buildings; to promise to use a percentage of the local deposits locally; to drop the restriction on loans going only to depositors in order to encourage more activity; and to make an agreement on the banks' policies in writing. (Jagged 1978)

One demonstration took place on October 30, 1978, and it saw about 45 anti-redlining protesters in [Halloween] masks enter the Broadway branch of the Williamsburgh Savings Bank, where they engaged in a discussion of bank policy with bank vice president Jay Jones. The protest began on the steps of the building at about 6:00; about 15 minutes later, the anti-redliners went inside, where they gave out balloons and skeletons with anti-redlining slogans (Jagged 1978). Shortly after this action, GWCAR met with Jones to persuade him to sign an agreement outlining anti-redlining practices. This case is an example of the approach taken by GWCAR with banks in the community.

The Committee's breakthrough came when Anchor Savings committed $25 million "over the next 5 years in mortgage and home improvements loans" (N.A. 1977), the largest pool of money to be invested in the community by a savings bank at the time. The Dime Savings Bank of Williamsburg pledged $1 million for local loans (N.A. 1980). A similar agreement was obtained from Lincoln Savings Bank. According to the coalition's executive director: "This was significant because it was probably the most successful redlining campaign in the country. What was unique about these fights was we got the CEO's to meet with us, and a lot of the redlining fights of that period did not get the CEO's at the table." He further explained that Anchor Savings was trying to open another branch and GWCAR and the coalition's demonstrations were holding it up. "That was the trigger that got Anchor to buy in." The other banks then followed Anchor's lead and committed money to be invested in the community.

Anti-redlining efforts in the 1970s have resulted in additional positive outcomes for Greenpoint–Williamsburg, which continued to exist through the 1990s. These are in the form of a Building Survival Program and a neighborhood credit union. A leader of the coalition explained:

> Redlining has resulted in the Building Survival Program. Banks would-n't give loans to people in city owned buildings that were abandoned. We still meet and give loans to people who need money to stay in their homes until they can get a 7A administrator. We give money for plumb-ing, roofs, boilers. It's a revolving loan fund, interest free. You must be in buildings managed by Los Sures, St. Nicholas, People's Firehouse. Another offshoot of redlining is the North Brooklyn Federal Credit Union. It still exists with $200 million. We give money to people who can not get it at a bank.

The coalition's efforts had long-term positive effects on the commu-nity. Through these local actions and the struggle against redlining, additional levels of social capital were created. People involved formed collaborative relationships, which led to associations providing more services, such as local development corporations, housing management corporations, and from the banks, more loans because of the anti-redlining campaign.

Demolition of an Abandoned Factory

A large factory owned by the Trunz Meat Corporation was located in Greenpoint–Williamsburg. In 1972 the business failed and the factory was abandoned (Editorial 1979a). Over time the building deteriorated. The roof collapsed, windows were broken and unsealed, and an entrance was open (N.A. 1979d). The building was a hazard and threatened the safety of residents living in the surrounding neighborhood. A local newspaper reported:

> The Greenpoint residents had already lived through a lot of problems created by the abandoned building. A few years ago two boys were sodomized in the building. Drug sales are reported to be a common occurrence around the rotting hulk, and those dealing the drugs are not alone at the site: rats and stray dogs call the place home and venture forth from it to disturb neighbors of the plant. Numerous fires have also struck the old factory. (N.A. 1979d: 8)

The community had made several unsuccessful attempts to have the building demolished. A number of member organizations of the coalition decided to undertake this issue once again. The groups involved included: Neighborhood Facilities Corp., Italian American Multi Service Center, Morgan Avenue Block Association, Kingsland Avenue-Herbert Street Area Block Association, North Henry Street Block Association, and the 94th Precinct Federation and Central Williamsburg, since the abandoned factory was situated on the border of these two areas. On April 18, 1979 concerned residents met and established "a committee to Demolish the Trunz Building" (N.A. 1979a: 1). Community organizers from the coalition assisted this committee. The first step taken by the committee was the submission of a list of demands to the New York City Department of Housing Preservation and Development (HPD). The committee insisted that HPD take the following action:

1. Agree to have the Trunz Building declared an "Unsafe Building" within 30 days;

2. Agree to have the building exterminated for rodents;

3. Agree in writing to this committee that the building will be scheduled for demolition within 90 days;

4. Agree to fence the property after demolition is completed. (N.A. 1979a: 1)

One week later the local state senator arranged a meeting with the community and city officials. Representatives from New York City's Department of Buildings and Public Development Corporation attended, but the person responsible for demolition was noticeably absent (Gallob 1979). At this meeting the community learned that the hold up was because of money. A local newspaper reported the following:

> At the heart of the problem is money. The building was assessed by the city at $439,000, and there are back taxes owed on it to the tune of some $800,000, the meeting was told. In addition, it would cost the city a large sum—variously estimated at between $125,000 and twice that amount to take the old building down. The city is trying to minimize its own costs and maximize the return it hopes to get. (N.A. 1979d: 8)

The overall preference from the City's point of view was to place the burden of demolition or rehabilitation on another party. The best possibility for the City was to sell the property, collect back taxes, and furnish the new owner with the community's demands. The community, however, was unwilling to wait any longer for the City to realize this best case.

By the end of the week, after this meeting with city officials, residents held a demonstration in front of the factory. "They marched into the intersection of Morgan and Meeker Avenues, bearing signs that read 'Take It Down,' and 'Koch Don't Botch This One'" (N.A. 1979d: 8). The committee planned another demonstration that would be more striking and, therefore, obtain the attention of citywide media, and include City Hall as a site. This one was held on May 11, 1979 (Gallob 1979: 16).

"A People's Demolition," equipped with sledgehammers and hard hats attracted three television stations. The action started at the factory with residents, some of whom were senior citizens, swinging sledgehammers, removing bricks from the building. These bricks were placed in a pick-up truck, which was driven to City Hall by the local state senator. Once at City Hall, residents delivered the bricks to Mayor Koch, some gift-wrapped, as a Mother's Day gift. Participants were thrilled by the demonstration and excited by the television coverage. They later watched themselves on the evening news, which featured for this story an elderly, Italian man swinging his sledgehammer at the abandoned building.

A local assemblyman was successful in obtaining a meeting with John LoCicero, Special Assistant to the Mayor. LoCicero agreed verbally to the committee's demands, sent a letter to the committee conceding to their requests. A newspaper account reported that the letter also stated that: "Bids [for demolition] would be let out on June 1st . . . in addition, the Buildings Department will seal up the structure on that day. The city hopes, LoCicero told concerned Greenpointers, to have it under the hammer within three months" (Gallob 1979: 16). By November of the same year, the Trunz factory was gone and the empty lot had been fenced. A wholesale food outlet later occupied the space. It is presently home to a drive-thru McDonald's restaurant.

Race and Ethnic Relations

The coalition built momentum with each successful area and community-wide action or resolution. In fact as one organizer expressed, "It was prestigious to be elected to the Coalition's Board of Directors." Member groups also learned that they were empowered by the participation of other residents—in other words, the larger the group attending a meeting or action, the better the qualitative outcome. The different geographic areas and ethnic communities of the coalition began to share their most precious resource: residents. An organizer stated:

> Each area developed its own needs, its own issues and presented them to the whole [coalition]. And each area was supportive of the other, and that started to break down some of the [racial] barriers. People were coming into the white neighborhoods, and the whites were going into Hispanic and black neighborhoods. They were finally coming together collectively around things that they felt were for the neighborhood . . . The Southside would come to Greenpoint saying, "look, we need help, we need your numbers to come and support us." Greenpoint people would go to the Southside. Southside would come to Greenpoint. The Coalition was a forum where people could finally come together around stuff and start to break down some of those barriers. . . . I think that the structure that we had kind of forced interaction. We made sure all [ethnic] groups were represented on the Board.

Although the organization's structure did force interaction at board meetings and delegate assemblies, it did not require them to gather at other times. However, a "rainbow coalition" did evolve.[4] One of the coalition's organizers viewed the campaign to demolish the old Trunz Meat factory a milestone for the organization: "Because it was the first time that the blacks and Hispanics really came and stood with the whites on a major fight. That's why Trunz was such a major win." On community-wide issues such as redlining, integration occurred more naturally because all groups were involved or affected by the matter and its outcome. The formation and viability of the GWCOCO indicates that local organizing efforts can promote the building of social capital across racial divisions, and thus, foster more positive race relations in communities.

Women and Social Capital

The coalition provided an arena whereby womens' unrecognized activism was supported and made visible. Women were given a place in the coalition to present their skills through activism and public forums. Through the coalition, womens' community work was moved from being "there" (Lofland 1975), in the background of community life, to more formal, public arenas. Women chaired community meetings, agitated elected officials and government representatives, and served as president and other executive officers of the coalition. Women learned to assert themselves and to engage in public speaking, a practice which is uncomfortable for most women according to Tannen (1990). With every assertion, these women were empowered.

An investigation of women in Greenpoint–Williamsburg suggests that women create community (Haywoode 1991; DeSena 1990). They do it by mobilizing social capital through their everyday activities. Women organized block associations, and fought for a day care and senior citizens centers. Women were also involved in the struggle to preserve housing in lieu of planned expansion of a local factory, and fought to maintain fire protection. Local women were the organizers, working behind the scenes. In addition, women crossed racial, ethnic, and economic boundaries when organizing around community issues. One woman commented:

> Women played a key role in leadership, but were never recognized. The ones who were usually concerned about activities in the community were women who had kids, and they always wanted life to be better for the kids. So they participated in PTA's, in civic groups, they did the fund raising, they do the issue organizing. Most of them were smart enough to do the writing, so they would do the letters and they were considered "secretaries." But we know secretaries carry a lot of power. I think the concerns of women are around children. It could be anything from a street light to being afraid of a kid getting hurt on the corner, to better police protection. I don't think their fathers go out there and fight like the women do.

In Greenpoint–Williamsburg, women are in the forefront of community involvement and activism.

One community organization, which was a member organization of the coalition, was the National Congress of Neighborhood Women (NCNW). This organization offered leadership training and a community-based college program (Haywoode 1991). This program developed the skills of its participants with an emphasis on community work.

Among the many activities involved in building community was womens' participation in the coalition. Many of the women who graduated from a locally based college program run by the National Congress of Neighborhood Women are found as leaders and activists of the coalition. These women used the skills developed in the college program for coalition activities. They were elected to the coalition's board of directors, including the position of president. Neighborhood women chaired committees on a variety of local issues, and debated with representatives of city government at public forums. They were involved in local development (Gittell, et al. 2000).

Women were empowered and also transformed by their participation in the coalition. Noschese (1991) remarks in *Metropolitan Avenue*, her film about womens' activism in Greenpoint–Williamsburg:

> These women who took leadership in their community to fight for things they believed in, and in the process . . . they developed an inner strength inside themselves. And they, regardless of whether they won or they lost, or what the issue was, it sort of changed their lives. Just the fact that they acted to fight for what they believed in. That is sort of what I guess power is about . . . But what they . . . decided was that something meant something to them . . . and they decided to work for it and work for other people and it really changed them. It changed them like nothing in their lives had changed them before.

Many maintain the multicultural relationships and networks formed by their involvement in the coalition. Moreover, many continued their community work after the coalition's decline and took with them a different view of politics, government, race relations, and the workings of a democratic system, that developed from their activism. Women leaders of the coalition have entered local electoral politics by being elected to public office, or to the school board, hired as a political aide, or appointed to the community board. They continue to be informed and shaped politically by their activist experiences.

The Coalition's Decline

In 1982 the coalition closed its doors. The major reason was lack of funding. Reagan's cuts were fully instituted, and the coalition's organizers were laid off. In fact, their last year was spent primarily in an unsuccessful attempt to raise funds. In addition, many of the community organizations that were members of the coalition were also experiencing major budget cuts or loss of funding completely. The coalition found itself in the awkward position of competing with its member organizations for funding.

As its budget decreased, the coalition's organizing staff was laid off. One of the first organizers to be furloughed was an African American woman. This caused racial conflict and divisiveness toward the end of the organization's tenure. Leaders were competing for and arguing over resources, which took the form of community organizers. The coalition faced destruction because of its dependency on powerful institutions for resources (Kraus 1984). Eventually, the coalition ran out of money and went out of business. With each period of fiscal constraint and economic recession, community organizations face few funding alternatives. The importance of financial self-sufficiency of community organizations is apparent. Organizations must look to be supported by the private sector, through grants, donations, and membership dues in which foundations, local institutions, and individuals can contribute. In this way, the work of organizations like the GWCOCO can continue with changing political climates and economic policies.

The coalition no longer exists, much to the regret of many of its leaders. According to one leader: "A lot of things that the Coalition worked on are still in effect. But there's no one out there now to bring together ethnic, racial, and economic groups. There's no solid group out there fighting for any kind funding, or fighting any of the budget issues." This investigation indicates that, when combined with other forms of capital, efforts to increase social capital through grassroots organizing can transform local institutions by including people of varied cultural backgrounds and women. Furthermore, grassroots organizations devoted to building social capital create a "local voice" which must be a part of democratic policy decisions and the allocation of capital.

Conclusions

This chapter illustrates two interrelated dimensions of the debate concerning social capital in the community development process: how social capital is accumulated on a community level, and how the mobilization of social capital is linked to the level of access residents have to resources and political support from broader institutions. In terms of the former, this chapter indicates the potential for altering peoples' awareness and perceptions of race relations by organizing existing social capital to create bridges and bonds capable of further strengthening a community. These aspects of social capital are illustrated in the sections of this chapter that describe the community organizing activities of the GWCOCO. In terms of the latter, this chapter shows how racial and ethnic conflict is a symptom of scarce resources and austerity politics (Lichten 1995). These issues, and their implications for mobilizing social capital, are illustrated in the parts of this chapter that discuss the decline of the GWCOCO.

Despite the decline of the GWCOCO, the experience of coalition building brought women out front and enhanced race relations in the community of Greenpoint–Williamsburg. In an earlier analysis of Greenpoint (DeSena 1990), it was established that residents used a series of informal strategies to "protect one's turf." Many of these same people, while defending the neighborhood, also managed to transcend their isolationist stances and participate with their neighbors in Greenpoint and Williamsburg to find solutions to local problems. Whites and people of color worked together in planning and stood together in protest. Relationships developed to a point where they supported their comrades' efforts by attending meetings and actions even when the outcome would not directly affect them. On an informal level, a number of cross-racial friendships were formed, as well as romantic and political relationships, because of the coalition experience. Residents of Greenpoint and those of Williamsburg became friends. A white, Greenpoint woman was the main campaigner for a Latina woman of Williamsburg who sought public office. White community organizers assisted black community leaders, and black community organizers worked with white community organizations. A Latina woman from Williamsburg and a Polish man from Greenpoint were married. In some cases, people moved from one neighborhood to another. The social networks formed through the coalition enabled people to obtain housing in each neighborhood. Alliances were also made across ethnic and racial lines between community organizations focusing on the delivery of services, such as summer jobs and year round training programs for youth, and the federal summer food program.

The coalition provided the opportunity for the social exchanges described, and challenged people's stereotypical thinking about race and ethnicity. The occasion to mix with people from different ethnic groups within the community may not have occurred without the existence and structure of the coalition. In part, the ability to build the GWCOCO and promote its community organizing activities was facilitated by the availability of resources and political support from larger institutions. However, patterns of race relations remained altered and an understanding of community organizing was retained for those who experienced the coalition after political regimes had changed and institutional support was withdrawn from the community.

Participants of the coalition were politically empowered by the experience. Many continued their community work after the coalition's decline, and took with them a more radical view of politics, government, and the workings of a democratic system, that developed from their activism. They also acquired skills from coalition activities, such as public speaking and analysis of the power structure, which served them as they carried on community work. Former coalition participants are presently found in various local settings. Some remained active in the community organization that they represented as members of the coalition. Others have devoted themselves to resolving environmental hazards in Greenpoint–Williamsburg. Some, who worked on planning the future of McCarren Park under the auspices of the coalition, proceed in their efforts. Leaders of the coalition have also entered local politics by being elected to public office, or to the school board, hired as a political aide, or appointed to the community board. They continue to create social capital, and are informed and shaped socially and politically by their activist experiences.

This study indicates the need for community organizations to be fiscally self-sufficient instead of falling victim to the funding whims of government and foundations. In many respects, the decline of the GWCOCO occurred as a result of its dependence on external institutions for basic financial support. The coalition's need to seek external funding after a less supportive political regime came to power led to its demise. Prior to that period, the embeddedness of the coalition in a supportive financial, political, and institutional setting facilitated community organizing and grassroots activism. Residents and local institutions, including churches and businesses, benefit from neighborhood improvements that emerged during this period. They were part of local coalition building then, and they are likely resources to be drawn upon to support community organizing efforts in the future.

Finally, this chapter raises questions regarding citizen participation. In a democratic society, ordinary people should be encouraged to participate in generating issues and setting priorities. This study demonstrates the ability of community organizations, through mobilization, to confront contemporary urban problems such as disinvestment, poverty, unaffordable housing, drug abuse, racial tension, and crime. Through models like the coalition, ordinary people can be directly involved in the formation of urban policy, while also building social capital in communities capable of cultural and gender variation. Moreover, the coalition served as an incubator for grassroots leadership. Many residents in the Greenpoint–Williamsburg community learned about the political process and developed community organizing skills through their experiences with the coalition. Greater institutional support for vehicles that empower ordinary people are crucial if citizen participation is to be expanded in the future.

Notes

1. This information was obtained from "Population Change by Race and Hispanic Origin by Selected Ages; Housing Unit Change." Brooklyn Community District 1, 1980–1990.
2. This City Council District designation includes Williamsburg and other neighborhoods.
3. City Council District 33 includes Greenpoint and other neighborhoods.
4. Jesse Jackson used the phrase "rainbow coalition" in reference to his constituents when he ran for the Presidency. GWCOCO's use of the term predated Jackson's concept.

References

Alinsky, Saul. 1971. *Rules for Radicals.* New York: Vintage.
Briggs, Xavier de Souza. 1998. "Brown Kids in White Suburbs: Housing Mobility and the Multiple Faces of Social Capital." *Housing Policy Debate,* 9:1.
DeSena, Judith N. 1990. *Protecting Ones Turf: Social Strategies for Maintaining Urban Neighborhoods.* Lanham, MD: University Press of America.
Etzioni, Amitai. 2001. "Is Bowling Together Sociologically Lite?" *Contemporary Sociology,* 30:223–224.
Gallob, Joel. 1979. "People to City: Demolish Trunz! Community Groups, Pols Demand Action." *North Brooklyn News,* May 4–10:1.
Gittell, Marilyn, Isolda Ortega-Bustamante, and Tracy Steffy. 2000. "Social Capital and Social Change: Women's Community Activism." *Urban Affairs Review,* 36:123–147.
Gittell, Ross, and Avis C. Vidal. 1998. *Community Organizing: Building Social Capital as a Development Strategy.* Thousand Oaks: Sage.
Granovetter, Mark. 1973. "The Strength of Weak Ties Hypothesis." *American Journal of Sociology,* 78:1360–1380.

Granovetter, Mark. 1974. *Getting a Job: A Study of Contacts and Careers.* Cambridge: Harvard University Press.

Haywoode, Terry. 1991. "Working Class Feminism: Creating a Politics of Community Connection and Concern." Ph.D. Dissertation, City University of New York.

Jagged, Mark. 1978. "GWCAR Trick-or Treats Bank." *North Brooklyn News,* November 3–9:15.

Kraus, Jeffrey. 1984. "Neighborhood Organizations and Resource Dependency: The Establishment in the Neighborhood." *Journal of Urban Affairs,* 6:116.

Lichten, Eric. 1995. "Fiscal Crisis and the New Class Politics: Managing Inequality in an Age of Decline." In *The Other City,* ed. Susanne MacGregor and Arthur Lipow. Atlantic Highlands, NJ: Humanities Press.

Lofland, Lynn. 1975. "The 'Thereness' of Women." In *Another Voice,* ed. Marcia Millman and Rosabeth Moss Kanter. New York: Anchor.

N.A. 1977. *Quarterly Report Submitted by Neighbors of Greenpoint and Williamsburg to the Campaign for Human Development.* May 19–August 15.

N.A. 1979a. "Community and Coalition Band Together to Demand Demolition Of Trunz Building." *Greenpoint Gazette,* April 24:1.

N.A. 1979b. Editorial, *North Brooklyn News.* May 4–10:4.

N.A. 1979c. "Housing Activists Sought Underlining Causes." *North Brooklyn News,* February 16–22:17.

N.A. 1979d. "Trunz: City's $ vs. People's Safety?" *North Brooklyn News,* May 4–10:8.

N.A. 1980. *Program of the Fourth Annual Convention of the Greenpoint–Williamsburg Coalition of Community Organizations.* Sunday, November 16:9.

Naples, Nancy A. 1998. *Grassroots Warriors: Activist Mothering, Community Work, and the War on Poverty.* New York: Routledge.

Noschese, Christine. 1991. *Metropolitan Avenue.* New Day Films.

Pardo, Mary. 1998. *Mexican American Women Activists: Identity and Resistance in Two Los Angeles Communities.* Philadelphia: Temple University Press.

Putnam, Robert D. 1993. *Making Democracy Work: Civic Traditions in Modern Italy.* Princeton, NJ: Princeton University Press.

Tannen, Deborah. 1990. *You Just Don't Understand.* New York: Ballantine.

Temkin, Kenneth, and William Rohe. 1998. "Social Capital and Neighborhood Stability: An Empirical Investigation." *Housing Policy Debate,* 9:1.

10 Conclusion

A Progressive Model

Robert Mark Silverman

Three Caveats to the Social Capital Debate

The preceding chapters have examined the relationship between institutional structure and the mobilization of social capital in community-based organizations. This examination illuminates three issues of concern to scholars and practitioners interested in the promotion of community development and grassroots activism through community-based organizations. First, scholars and practitioners need to pay greater attention to the manner in which social capital and other forms of capital are entwined. Second, there is a need for greater understanding of the manner in which social capital is embedded in broader institutional structures. Finally, greater attention needs to be paid to the degree of compatibility among various forms of social capital that exist in a setting. Each of these issues is discussed below as they relate to community development and grassroots activism. Following these discussions, a progressive model for mobilizing social capital is proposed.

INTEGRATING SOCIAL, FINANCIAL, HUMAN, AND CULTURAL CAPITAL

In their respective chapters, contributors to this book remind readers that social capital does not operate in a vacuum. Rather, social capital is entwined with other forms of capital. Ivan Light offers the most theoretically developed statement concerning this issue, where he describes the manner in which various forms of capital metamorphose into others. The essence of this argument is that no form of capital emerges or operates alone. Instead, specific forms of social, financial, human, and cultural capital are combined to forge an amalgam, known as capital, which validates a society's prevailing institutional structure. As an implication of this observation, social capital should not be viewed as a substitute for another form of capital. It should be viewed as an ingredient in the broader process of capital formation.

This theme is further developed in the chapter by Randy Stoecker, where the inherent contradictions between social capital and other forms of capital are discussed. In this chapter, Stoecker points out that social capital is increasingly identified as a missing ingredient in community development; yet, the growing emphasis placed on social capital overshadows the degree to which other forms of capital are also missing in distressed communities. In essence, Stoecker describes how all forms of capital have been withdrawn from these communities due to a shift in broader institutional structures away from values focused on place and community. Stoecker sees this as an inherent conflict between what Marx and others describe as use value and exchange value. When placed in this framework, Stoecker's argument suggests that the formation of an amalgam of social, financial, human, and cultural capital to promote use value has given way to a new amalgam of these elements that promotes exchange value.

The conflict of the mobilization of capital to build community versus the mobilization of capital to create commodities is explored further in the chapter by Kelly Patterson and me. This chapter focuses on a dispute between residents and a real estate developer over the formation of a homeowners' association. However, the heart of the dispute is over the ends to which social capital, and other forms of capital, are being mobilized. This chapter both contrasts and complements Stoecker's. As a contrast to Stoecker's focus on capital depletion in distressed communities, this chapter focuses on a local setting where all forms of capital are being deposited. As a complement to Stoecker's chapter, this one highlights the conflict between those who promote use value and those who promote exchange value. Moreover, this chapter illustrates Light's points about the mutual metamorphosis of capital, since the conflict Patterson and I describe entails multiple forms of capital. Notably, the conflict described is not about capital per se, but rather the ends to which capital is applied.

Together, these three chapters refocus the discussion of capital accumulation by highlighting the role of all forms of capital in the community development process. Each chapter reminds us that community development is a process fueled by the interaction of all forms of capital. Moreover, these chapters highlight the degree to which a consensus concerning the ends to which capital is mobilized (i.e., the promotion of use value versus exchange value respectively) is necessary for community development activities to be effective. In part, consensus building grows out of grassroots efforts. However, it also is shaped by the institutional structures in which community-based organizations are embedded. Given these structural influences on community development efforts, those interested in progressive reform need to place greater emphasis on enhancing the role of local communities in decision-making, particularly as it relates to capital formations. Without expanded space for disenfranchised groups and grassroots interests, the community development process will remain in control of organizations and institutions that emphasize exchange values over use values.

Overcoming Institutional Barriers to Community-Based Organizing

Other chapters build on these observations by highlighting the manner in which institutional structures become barriers to mobilizing social capital for progressive ends. For example, the chapter by Gina Neff describes how microfinance programs, conceived as a grassroots mechanism to promote self-sufficiency, lose much of their democratic appeal as they become institutionalized. Her analysis demonstrates that when it is embedded in the hierarchical structure of large institutions, social capital can sometimes become an impediment to the development of community-based networks. Neff describes how social capital was mobilized among an elite group of funding agencies and organizations. This produced a high degree of closure among these actors, which resulted in limited access to microfinance programs for smaller grassroots organizations. In addition, the hierarchical manner in which the funding of microfinance programs was organized limited the scope of grassroots-level control over policy and implementation. Of course, the goals of microfinance programs focus on a narrow range of community development activities related to the promotion of entrepreneurship among the poor, which may explain their limited ability to mobilize social capital for the promotion of progressive ends. However, other chapters also identify this limitation in other community-based organizations.

For example, Brian Sahd's discussion of CDCs in the South Bronx indicates that the mobilization of social capital for grassroots ends tends to subside as organizations become institutionalized. In each of the CDCs he discusses, community control fell out of favor as the organizations became incorporated into broader institutional networks. In part, this transformation is the byproduct of an increased scope of CDC functions in areas such as physical development and social service delivery. However, it is also an outgrowth of organizations becoming embedded in broader institutional structures that emphasize the creation of commodities over the building of community. This shift becomes more visible in Sahd's work due to its historical focus. This shift represents three distinct phases of capital mobilization in the South Bronx. First, all forms of capital flee the South Bronx. Then, residents who remain in the community mobilize capital at the grassroots level in order to build community. Finally, institutional actors return to the South Bronx in order to create commodities, and subsequently displace grassroots activists.

The identification of a link between the embeddedness of community-based organization in broader institutional networks and the atrophy of grassroots control in the community development process has several implications for progressive reform. For instance, this situation indicates that there is a need to formalize the role of community members in the decision-making processes of organizations and institutions with which community-based organizations interact. Additionally, the manner in which planning and decision-making processes are organized requires modification. Progressive reform requires that decision-making related to local community development take place in an increasingly democratic manner with community members having the ultimate decision-making power. In essence, power relations in the institutional networks within which community-based organizations are embedded need to be less hierarchical, and the goals of community development must emphasize the expansion of democratic decision making in addition to traditional community development activities.

BLENDING FRAGMENTED FORMS OF SOCIAL CAPITAL

In addition to considering the manner in which various forms of capital interact, and the role of institutional structure in the mobilization of social capital, it is important to recognize that social capital can take several forms. Moreover, there is no guarantee that distinct forms of social capital are compatible with others. In part, this is because various forms of social capital are embedded in institutional networks that focus on potentially contradictory ends. For instance, some forms of social capital are more amenable to the pursuit of use value, while others promote structural arrangements driven by exchange value relations. In addition to these limitations, social capital is often organized around specialized constituencies. This aspect of social capital mobilization is illustrated in the chapters focused on race, gender, and religion.

Perhaps the most extreme example of the mobilization of social capital around specialized constituencies comes from my chapter dealing with black CDCs in Jackson, Mississippi. In this chapter, racial identity is identified as one foundation from which social capital can be mobilized. The chapter describes how the use of race-based social capital in the black community was instrumental to CDC formation, particularly in a setting where other forms of capital had been systematically withdrawn. However, it is also argued that the focus on a single form of social capital has its downside. By restricting social capital to a narrow constituency, it is argued that the scope of capital formation is truncated. If social, financial, human, and cultural capital are drawn from a single source, then less overall capital accumulation will result.

This dilemma is examined from another perspective by Sherri Wallace. Her chapter focuses on the role of social capital based on black church affiliation in the community development process. She argues that by mobilizing social capital through the Black Church, ministers were able to attract capital for community development projects in distressed communities of Buffalo, New York. Wallace's treatment of social capital adds a dimension to my work, by indicating that a single form of social capital can be used effectively to leverage external resources for community development efforts. However, the degree to which these efforts produced broad-based participation at the grassroots level remains somewhat ambiguous. Although the ministers Wallace writes about were adept at mobilizing social capital to attract resources for their church's development projects, these efforts did not appear to stem from grassroots mobilization within individual churches or through coalitions among them. As a result, her analysis raises questions about the need for the creation of broad-based coalitions as a strategy for enhancing capital accumulation and citizen participation in the community development process.

In contrast to my and Wallace's chapters, the chapter by Judith DeSena describes how a group of neighborhood organizations came together to form a coalition for community building in Brooklyn, New York, during the late 1970s and early 1980s. From her chapter it is clear that this coalition was broad-based, grassroots oriented, multiracial, and woman-led. Moreover, the coalition focused on mobilizing social capital for the purpose of enhancing use value in the community. DeSena points out that the emergence of this coalition was an outgrowth of a specific set of structural conditions. In particular, there was sustained external support for grassroots organizing coming from political, economic, and institutional actors during the time that the coalition was active. This was the case despite the fact that neighborhoods where the coalition formed faced accelerated decline. However, by the 1980s, external support for grassroots organizing began to wane as national institutions shifted toward a greater focus on promoting exchange value. The result was a weakening of the coalition that DeSena studied. In the end, it was not possible to sustain a broad-based coalition on social capital alone.

Three lessons are learned from the chapters in this book. First, it is necessary to combine all forms of capital in order to pursue specific community development ends. Second, those ends must be well defined and supported by broader institutional structures in society. Finally, the ability to combine various forms of social capital is a function of the magnitude of other forms of capital that are combined to forge an amalgam (i.e., the accumulation of capital). In essence, a great deal of financial, human, and cultural capital is required if many forms of social capital are to be mobilized simultaneously. Furthermore, there is a need for external institutional support to sustain efforts to mobilize capital in a manner that promotes use value. Of course, that requires that local organizations and external institutions be structured in a manner that allows them to share such a focus and emphasizes democratic decision-making in the community development process.

A Progressive Model for Mobilizing Social Capital

A unifying theme across the chapters in this book is that there is a need for further research on the relationships that exist among the mobilization of social capital, the promotion of community development, and democratic decision-making at the grassroots level. In the light of the preceding discussion, future research should focus on furthering the development of progressive models for mobilizing social capital based on three elements. The first element draws from the need to combine all forms of capital for the purposes of building community and enhancing use value. At a minimum, this aspect of a progressive model would entail the creation of mechanisms to transfer financial capital and human capital to democratically run, community-based organizations. For instance, a progressive model would call for legislation to be enacted at the federal, state, and municipal levels of government to earmark a portion of revenues from property, sales, and income taxes for democratically structured, community-based organizations. This would allow for such organizations to have greater economic stability and lessen their dependence on grants and other external funds. It would also create a pool of autonomous financial resources for organizations to draw from in order to develop human capital that contributes to local use value.

In addition to earmarking revenue to democratically run, community-based organizations, a progressive model would include mechanisms that leverage institutional resources in order to assist these organizations in the development of technical expertise and human capital. In the context of such a model, public universities, trade associations, and other tax-exempt organizations would provide democratically run, community-based organizations with training and technical assistance. A requirement to provide assistance would be linked to an organization's tax-exempt status. In this way, organizations committed to grassroots activism would be able to combine existing social capital with stable sources of financial capital and opportunities to develop human capital. A focus on bringing all of the elements of capital formation to local organizations for community development purposes is central to progressive reform, since the redistribution of resources to the local level promotes the concept of community controlled development and increases the emphasis on use values in public policy.

The second element of a progressive model for mobilizing social capital would require the creation of political mechanism to increase the level of access that community-based organizations have to the policy-making process, particularly in areas of policy and development that affect residents at the neighborhood level. Strategies for community review, amendment, and approval of policy and local development proposals need to be instituted so that grassroots constituencies have greater input in the policy-making process. These strategies entail the infusion of community interests in a number of policy-making arenas. In state and local government, progressive reform would give community members greater access to the policy development process. In the private and nonprofit sectors, progressive reform would require organizations engaged in community development to elevate the role of community members on their boards of directors and in other aspects of internal governance. At the neighborhood level, progressive reform would give residents the power to vote in community referendums on proposed community development projects. Giving residents greater voice and veto power over public policy and development decisions that conflict with the promotion of use values is essential if democratic decision-making at the grassroots level is to influence the activities of institutional actors in a meaningful way.

The final element of a progressive model for mobilizing social capital is the requirement for community-based organizations to incorporate a cross-section of community members into each organization's decision-making process. Residents from across race, gender, and class lines should have equal access to grassroots decision-making as a condition of receiving funding and participating in the local policy development process. In this way, democratic decision-making at the grassroots level would be linked to obtaining greater access to resources and policymaking. More importantly, democratically run, community-based organizations must be required to define the boundaries of the communities that they represent in a manner that maximizes diversity. Progressive reform entails that community boundaries are drawn so they are inclusive of diverse populations along the lines of race, class, gender, and religion. By promoting diversity, progressive reform brings a spectrum of voices to the dialogue concerning community development. Furthermore, progressive reform would require that democratic decision-making processes be driven by the principle of diversity as promoted in community development activities and outcomes.

Together the three elements of a progressive model for mobilizing social capital would facilitate the emergence of a multidimensional and inclusive approach to community development. This model would promote capital formation that is sensitive to use values; infuse financial resources and technical knowledge in communities for capacity building; act as a mechanism for empowering residents and infusing existing institutional structures with democratic processes; and promote an ethos of egalitarianism and diversity in contemporary communities. Of course, the model outlined above merely sets a foundation for the further articulation of a progressive agenda for community-based organizations in contemporary urban society. It is now incumbent upon scholars, policymakers, practitioners, and individual citizens to develop a more detailed articulation of specific reforms and the emerging progressive movement in society.

Selected Bibliography

Abrahamson, Mark. 1996. *Urban Enclaves: Identity and Place in America*. New York: St. Martin's Press.

Alinsky, Saul. 1969. *Reveille for Radicals*. New York: Vintage.

Alinsky, Saul. 1971. *Rules for Radicals*. New York: Vintage.

Arnove, Robert F., ed. 1980. *Philanthropy and Cultural Imperialism*. Boston: G. K. Hall.

Arnstein, Sherry R. 1969. "A Ladder of Citizen Participation." *Journal of the American Institute of Planners*, 35.4:216–224.

Baron, Stephen, John Field, and Tom Schuller. 2001. *Social Capital: Critical Perspectives*. New York: Oxford University Press.

Barton, Stephen E., and Carol J. Silverman, eds. 1994. *Common Interest Communities: Private Governments and the Public Interest*. Berkeley: Institute of Governmental Studies Press.

Bates, Timothy. 1989. "Small Business Viability in the Urban Ghetto." *Journal of Regional Science*, 29.4:625–643.

Bates, Timothy. 1997. *Race, Self-Employment, and Upward Mobility: An Illusive American Dream*. Baltimore: Johns Hopkins University Press.

Beck, Ulrich. 1992. *Risk Society: Towards a New Modernity*. London: Sage.

Becker, Gary S. 1993 [1964]. *Human Capital*. 3d ed. Chicago: University of Chicago.

Becker, Gary S. 1996. *Accounting for Tastes*. Cambridge: Harvard University.

Blakely, Edward J., and Mary Gail Snyder. 1997. *Fortress America: Gated Communities in the United States*. Washington, DC: Brookings Institution Press.

Bockmeyer, Janice L. 2000. "A Culture of Distrust: The Impact of Local Political Culture on Participation in the Detroit EZ." *Urban Studies*, 37.13:2417–2440.

Bourdieu, Pierre. 1979. *La Distinction: Critique sociale du jugement*. Paris: Editions de Minuit.

Bourdieu, Pierre. 1980. "Le Capital Social." *Actes de la recherche en sciences sociales*, 31:2–3.

Bourdieu, Pierre. 1986. "The Forms of Capital." In *Handbook of Theory and Research for the Sociology of Education*, ed. John G. Richardson, 241–258. New York: Greenwood Press.

Borocz, Jozsef, and Caleb Southworth. 1996. "Decomposing the Intellectuals'

Class Power: Conversion of Cultural Capital to Income in Hungary, 1986." *Social Forces,* 74:797–821.

Bowles, Samuel. 1999. "Social Capital and Community Governance." *Focus* 20:6–10.

Burt, R. 1992. *Structural Holes: The Social Structure of Competition.* Cambridge: Harvard University Press.

Burt, Ronald. 1997. "The Contingent Value of Social Capital." *Administrative Science Quarterly,* 42:339–365.

Capek, Stella M., and John I. Gilderbloom. 1992. *Community versus Commodity Tenants and the American City.* Albany: State University of New York Press.

Chang, Edward T., and Jeannette Diaz-Veizades. 1999. *Ethnic Peace in the American City: Building Community in Los Angeles and Beyond.* New York: New York University Press.

Chang, Hedy Nai-Lin. 1997. "Democracy, Diversity, and Social Capital." *National Civic Review,* 86.2:141–147.

Chung, Angie Y., and Edward Taehan Chang. 1998. "From Third World Liberation to Multiple Oppression Politics: A Contemporary Approach to Interethnic Coalitions." *Social Justice,* 25.3:80–100.

Clavel, Pierre, Jessica Pitt, and Jordan Yin. 1997. "The Community Option in Urban Policy." *Urban Affairs Review,* 32.4:435–458.

Coleman, James S. 1988. "Social Capital in the Creation of Human Capital." *American Journal of Sociology,* 94S:S95–S120.

Coleman, James S. 1990. *Foundations of Social Theory.* Cambridge: Harvard University Press.

Collins, Patricia Hill. 1993. "Toward a New Vision: Race, Class, and Gender as Categories of Analysis and Connection." *Race, Sex, and Class,* 1.1:25–45.

Counts, Alex. 1996. *Give Us Credit.* New York: Random House.

Cowan, Spencer M., William Rohe, and Esmail Baku. 1999. "Factors Influencing the Performance of Community Development Corporations." *Journal of Urban Affairs,* 21.3:325–340.

Dasgupta, Partha, and Ismail Serageldin, eds. 1999. *Social Capital: A Multifaceted Perspective.* Washington, DC: World Bank.

DeFilippis, James. 2001. "The Myth of Social Capital in Community Development." *Housing Policy Debate,* 12.4:781–806.

Delgado, Gary. 1986. *Organizing the Movement: The Roots and Growth of ACORN.* Philadelphia: Temple University Press.

DeSena, Judith N. 1990. *Protecting One's Turf: Social Strategies for Maintaining Urban Neighborhoods.* Lanham, MD: University Press of America.

DeSena, Judith N. 1998. "Low-Income Women and Community Power." *Sociological Spectrum,* 18:311–332.

Dilger, Robert Jay. 1992. *Neighborhood Politics: Residential Community Associations in American Governance.* New York: New York University Press.

Dionne, E. J., Jr., ed. 1998. *Community Works: The Revival of Civil Society in America,* Washington, DC: Brookings Institution Press.

Duncan, Cynthia M. 1999. *Worlds Apart: Why Poverty Persists in Rural America.* New Haven, CT: Yale University Press.

Durlauf, Steven N. 1999. "The Case 'Against' Social Capital," *Focus,* 20.3:1–5.

Edwards, Bob, Michael W. Foley, and Mario Diana. 2001. *Beyond Tocqueville: Civil Society and the Social Capital Debate in Comparative Perspective.* Hanover, NH: University Press of New England.

Evans, Sara M., and Harry C. Boyte. 1986. *Free Spaces: The Sources of Democratic Change in America.* New York: Harper and Row.

Farkas, George. 1996. *Human Capital or Cultural Capital?* New York: Aldine de Gruyter.

Feagin, Joe R., and Robert Parker. 1990. *Building American Cities: The Urban Real Estate Game.* New York: Prentice Hall.

Feagin, Joe R., and Hernan Vera. 2001. *Liberation Sociology.* Boulder, CO: Westview Press.

Fernandez Kelly, M. Patricia. 1994. "Towanda's Triumph: Social and Cultural Capital in the Transition to Adulthood in the Urban Ghetto." *International Journal of Urban and Regional Research,* 18.1:88–111.

Fernandez Kelly, M. Patricia. 1995. "Social and Cultural Capital in the Urban Ghetto: Implications for the Economic Sociology of Immigration." In *The Economic Sociology of Immigration: Essays on Networks, Ethnicity, and Entrepreneurship,* ed. Alejandro Portes, 213–247. New York: Russell Sage Foundation.

Fish, John Hall. 1973. *Black Power/White Control: The Struggle of the Woodlawn Organization in Chicago.* Princeton, NJ: Princeton University Press.

Fligstein, Neil. 1996. "Markets as Politics: A Political-Cultural Approach to Market Institutions." *American Sociological Review,* 61.3:656–673.

Foley, Michael W., and Bob Edwards. 1999. "Is It Time to Disinvest in Social Capital?" *Journal of Public Policy,* 19.2:141–173.

Ferguson, Ronald F., and William T. Dickens, eds. 1999. *Urban Problems and Community Development.* Washington, DC: Brookings Institute Press.

Garreau, Joel. 1988. *Edge City: Life on the New Frontier.* New York: Anchor.

Gittell, Marilyn. 1980. *Limits to Citizen Participation.* New York: Sage.

Gittell, Marilyn, Kathe Newman, Janice Bockmeyer, and Robert Lindsay. 1998. "Expanding Civic Opportunity: urban Empowerment Zones." *Urban Affairs Review,* 33.4:530–559.

Gittell, Marilyn, Isolda Ortega-Bustamante, and Tracy Steffy. 2000. "Social Capital and Social Change: Women's Community Activism." *Urban Affairs Review,* 36.2:123–147.

Gittell, Ross, and Avis Vidal. 1998. *Community Organizing, Building Social Capital as a Development Strategy.* Newbury Park, CA: Sage.

Gittell, Ross, and Margaret Wilder. 1999. "Community Development Corporations: Critical Factors that Improve Success." *Journal of Urban Affairs,* 21.3:341–362.

Glickman, Norman J., and Lisa Servon. 1998. "More than Bricks and Sticks: Five Components of Community Development Corporation Capacity." *Housing Policy Debate,* 9.3:497–539.

Granovetter, Mark S. 1972. "The Strength of Weak Ties." *American Journal of Sociology,* 78.6:1360–1380.

Granovetter, Mark. 1974. *Getting a Job: A Study of Contacts and Careers.* Cambridge: Harvard University Press.

Granovetter, Mark S. 1985. "Economic Action and Social Structure: The Problem of Embeddedness." *American Journal of Sociology,* 91.3:481–510.

Gratz, Roberta Brandes. 1994. *The Living City: How America's Cities Are Being Revitalized by Thinking Small in a Big Way.* 2nd ed. Washington, DC: Preservation Press.

Greeley, Andrew. 1997. "Coleman Revisited, Religious Structures as a Source of Social Capital." *American Behavioral Scientist,* 40.5:587–594.

Grogan, Paul S., and Tony Proscio. 2000. *Comeback Cities: A Blueprint for Urban Neighborhood Revival.* Boulder, CO: Westview Press.

Hartigan, John. 1999. *Racial Situations: Class Predicaments of Whiteness in Detroit.* Princeton, NJ: Princeton University Press.

Hayduk, Ron, and Ben Shepard, eds. 2001. *From ACT UP to the WTO: Urban Protest and Community Building in the Era of Globalization.* New York: Verso.

Indergaard, Michael. 1997. "Community-Based Restructuring? Institution Building in the Industrial Midwest." *Urban Affairs Review,* 32:5:662–682.

Immergluck, Daniel. 1999. "Intrametropolitan Patterns of Small-Business Lending." *Urban Affairs,* 34:787–804.

Jacobs, Jane. 1961. *Death and Life of Great American Cities.*

Johannisson, Bengt. 2000. "A Tripolar Model of New-Venture Capitalising: Financial, Human and Social Capital." Paper presented at the 11th Nordic Conference on Small Business Research, Aarhus, Denmark, June 18.

Keating, W. Dennis, Norman Krumholz, and Philip Star, eds. 1996. *Revitalizing Urban Neighborhoods.* Lawrence: University Press of Kansas.

Kochinsky, Julia. 1998. "Challenging the Third Sector Housing Approach: Impact of Federal Policies (1980–1996)." *Journal of Urban Affairs,* 20.2:117–135.

Kretzman, John P., and John L. McKnight. 1993. *Building Communities from the Inside Out: A Path Toward Finding and Mobilizing Community Assets.* Chicago: ACTA.

Lang Robert E., and Steven P. Hornburg. 1998 "What Is Social Capital and Why Is It Important?" *Housing Policy Debate,* 9.1:1–16.

Light, Ivan. 1972. *Ethnic Enterprise in America.* Berkeley: University of California.

Light, Ivan, and Steven J. Gold. 2000. *Ethnic Economies.* New York: Academic Press.

Lin, Nan, Karen S. Cook, and Ronald S. Burt. 2001. *Social Capital: Theory and Research.* New York: Aldine de Gruyter.

Lin, Nan. 2002. *Social Capital: A Theory of Social Structure and Action.* Cambridge: Cambridge University Press.

Logan, John R., and Harvey L. Molotch. 1987. *Urban Fortunes: the Political Economy of Place.* Berkeley: University of California Press.

Massey, Douglas S. 1999. "Why Does Immigration Occur? A Theoretical Synthesis." In *The Handbook of International Migration,* ed. Charles Hirschman, Philip Kasinitz, and Josh DeWind, 34–52. New York: Russell Sage Foundation.

McKenzie, Evan. 1996. *Privatopia: Homeowner Associations and the Rise of Residential Private Government.* New Haven, CT: Yale University Press.

Molotch, Harvey. 1976. "The City as a Growth Machine: Toward a Political Economy of Place." *American Journal of Sociology,* 82.2:309–332.

Naples, Nancy A. 1998. *Grassroots Warriors: Activist Mothering, Community Work, and the War on Poverty.* New York: Routledge.

Nyden, Philip, Anne Figert, Mark Shibley, and Darryl Burrows. 1997. *Building Community: Social Science in Action.* Thousand Oaks, CA: Pine Forge Press.

Nye, Nancy, and Norman J. Glickman. 2000. "Working Together: Building Capacity for Community Development." *Housing Policy Debate,* 11.1:163–198.

Orr, Marion. 1999. *Black Social Capital: The Politics of School Reform in Baltimore, 1986–1998.* Lawrence: University Press of Kansas.

Pardo, Mary S. 1998. *Mexican American Women Activists: Identity and Resistance in Two Los Angeles Communities.* Philadelphia: Temple University Press.

Pattillo-McCoy, Mary. 1999. *Black Picket Fences: Privilege and Peril Among the Black Middle Class.* Chicago: University of Chicago Press.

Paxton, Pamela. "Is Social Capital Declining in the United States? A Multiple Indicator Assessment." *American Journal of Sociology,* 105.1:88–127.

Perry, Stewart E. 1987. *Communities on the Way: Rebuilding Local Economies in the United States and Canada.* Albany: State University of New York Press.

Peterman, William. 2000. *Neighborhood Planning and Community- Based Development: The Potential and Limits of Grassroots Action.* Thousand Oaks, CA: Sage.

Piven, Frances Fox, and Richard A. Cloward. 1977. *Poor People's Movements: Why They Succeed, How They Fail.* New York: Pantheon.

Portes, Alejandro. 1998. "Social Capital: Its Origins and Applications in Modern Sociology." *Annual Review of Sociology,* 24:1–24.

Portes, Alejandro, and Patricia Landolt. 2000. "Social Capital: Promise and Pitfall of its Role in Development." *Journal of Latin American Studies,* 32:529–547.

Portes Alejandro, and R. Bach. 1985. *Latin Journey: Cuban and Mexican Immigrants in the United States.* Berkeley: University of California Press.

Portney, Kent E., and Jeffrey M. Berry. 1997. Mobilizing Minority Communities: Social Capital and Participation in Urban Neighborhoods. *American Behavioral Scientist,* 40.5:632–644.

Putnam, Robert D. 1993. *Making Democracy Work: Civic Traditions in Modern Italy.* Princeton, NJ: Princeton University Press.

Putnam, Robert D. 1995. "Bowling Alone: America's Declining Social Capital." *Journal of Democracy,* 6.1:65–78.

Putnam, Robert D. 2000. *Bowling Alone: The Collapse and Revival of American Community.* New York: Simon and Schuster.

Rabrenovic, Gordana. 1996. *Community Building: A Tale of Neighborhood Mobilization in Two Cities.* Philadelphia: Temple University Press.

Robinson, Tony. 1996. "Inner-City Innovator: The Non-Profit Community Development Corporation." *Urban Studies,* 33.9:1647–1670.

Rubin, Herbert J. 2000. *Renewing Hope within Communities of Despair: The Community-Based Development Model.* Albany: State University of New York Press.

Ryan, William. 1976. *Blaming the Victim.* New York: Vintage.

Saegert, Susan, J. Phillip Thompson, and Mark Warren. 2001. *Social Capital and Poor Communities.* New York: Russell Sage Foundation.

Sampson, Robert J., Jeffrey D. Morenoff, and Felton Earls. 1999. "Beyond Social Capital: Spatial Dynamics of Collective Efficacy for Children." *American Sociological Review,* 64:633–660.

Schneider, Jo Anne. 1999. "Trusting that of God in Everyone: Three Examples of Quaker-Based Social Service in Disadvantaged Communities." *Nonprofit and Voluntary Sector Quarterly,* 28.3:269–295.

Servon, Lisa J. 1999. *Bootstrap Capital: Microenterprise and the American Poor.* Washington DC: Brookings Institution Press.

Servon, Lisa J., and Timothy Bates. 1998. "Microenterprise as an Exit Route From Poverty: Recommendations for Programs and Policy Makers." *Journal of Urban Affairs,* 20.4:419–441.

Silverman, Robert Mark. 1999. "Black Business, Group Resources, and the Economic Detour: Contemporary Black Manufacturers in Chicago's Ethnic Beauty Aids Industry." *Journal of Black Studies,* 30.2:232–258.

Silverman, Robert Mark. 2001. "Neighborhood Characteristics, CDC Emergence and the Community Development Industry System: A Case Study of the American Deep South." *Community Development Journal,* 36.3:234–245.

Silverman, Robert Mark. 2001. "CDCs and Charitable Organizations in the Urban South: Mobilizing Social Capital Based on Race and Religion for Neighborhood Revitalization." *Journal of Contemporary Ethnography,* 30.2:240–268.

Silverman, Robert Mark. 2002. "Vying for the Urban Poor: Charitable Organizations, Faith-Based Social Capital, and Racial Reconciliation in a Deep South City." *Sociological Inquiry,* 72.1:151–165.

Simonsen, William, and Mark D. Robbins. 2000. *Citizen Participation in Resource Allocation*. Boulder, CO: Westview Press.

Sirianni, Carmen, and Lewis Friedland. 2001. *Civic Innovation in America: Community Empowerment, Public Policy, and the Movement for Civic Renewal*. Berkeley: University of California Press.

Smith, David Horton. 2000. *Grassroots Associations*. Thousand Oaks, CA: Sage.

Stabile, Donald L. 2000. *Community Associations: The Emergence and Acceptance of a Quiet Innovation in Housing*. Westport, CT: Greenwood Press.

Stall, Susan, and Randy Stoecker. 1998. "Community Organizing or Organizing Community? Gender and the Craft of Empowerment." *Gender and Society,* 12.6:729–756.

Starr, Roger. 1985. *The Rise and Fall of New York City*. New York: Basic.

Stoecker, Randy. 1994. *Defending Community: The Struggle for Alternative Redevelopment in Cedar-Riverside*. Philadelphia: Temple University Press.

Stoecker, Randy. 1997. "The CDC Model of Urban Redevelopment: A Critique and an Alternative." *Journal of Urban Affairs,* 19.1:1–22.

Stoll, Michael A. 2001. "Race, Neighborhood Poverty, and Participation in Voluntary Associations." *Sociological Forum,* 16.3:529–557.

Stoutland, Sara E. 1999. "Levels of the Community Development System: A Framework for Research and Practice." *Urban Anthropology and Studies of Cultural Systems and World Economic Development,* 28.2:165–191.

Suttles, Gerald D. 1972. *The Social Construction of Communities*. Chicago: University of Chicago Press.

Swanstrom, Todd. 1993. "Beyond Economism: Urban Political Economy and the Postmodern Challenge." *Journal of Urban Affairs,* 15:55–78.

Taub, Richard P. 1988. *Community Capitalism: The Southshore Bank's Strategy for Neighborhood Revitalization*. Cambridge: Harvard University Press.

Temkin, Kenneth, and William Rohe. 1998. "Social Capital and Neighborhood Stability: An Empirical Investigation." *Housing Policy Debate,* 9.1:61–88.

Thomas, June Manning, and Reynard N. Blake, Jr. 1996. "Faith-Based Community Development and African-American Neighborhoods." In *Revitalizing Urban Neighborhoods,* ed. W. Dennis Keating, Norman Krumholz, and Philip Star, 131–143. Lawrence: University Press of Kansas.

Twelvetrees, Alan. 1989. *Organizing for Neighborhood Development: A Comparative Study of Community Development Corporations and Citizen Power Organizations*. Brookfield, VT: Avebury.

Velez-Ibanez, Carlos G. 1983. *Bonds of Mutual Trust: The Cultural Systems of Rotating Credit Associations Among Urban Mexicans and Chicanos*. New Brunswick, NJ: Rutgers University Press.

Vidal, Avis C. 1995. "Reintegrating Disadvantaged Communities into the Fabric of Urban Life." *Housing Policy Debate,* 6.1:169–230.

Vidal, Avis C. 1997. "Can Community Development Re-Invent Itself? The Challenge of Strengthening Neighborhoods in the 21st Century." *Journal of the American Planning Association*, 63.4:429–438.

Wacquant, Loic. 1998. "Negative Social Capital: State Breakdown and Social Destitution in America's Urban Core." *Netherlands Journal of Housing and the Built Environment*, 13.1:25–40.

Waldinger, Roger. 1999. *Still the Promised City?: African-Americans and New Immigrants in Postindustrial New York*. Cambridge: Harvard University Press.

Wallis, Allan. 1998. "Social Capital and Community Building: Part Two." *National Civic Review*, 87.4:317–336.

Wallis, Allan, Jarle P. Crocker, and Bill Schechter. 1998. "Social Capital and Community Building: Part One." *National Civic Review*, 87.3: 253–271.

Wasserman, Stanley, and Katherine Faust. 1994. *Social Network Analysis: Methods and Applications*. Cambridge: Cambridge University Press.

Wilson, Patricia. 1997. "Building Social Capital: A Learning Agenda for the Twenty-First Century." *Urban Studies*, 34.5/6:745–760.

Wilson, William Julius. 1999. *The Bridge over the Racial Divide: Rising Inequality and Coalition Politics*. Berkeley: University of California Press.

Wood, Richard L. 1997. "Social Capital and Political Culture: God Meets Politics in the Inner-City." *American Behavioral Scientist*, 40.5:595–605.

Woodard, Michael D. 1986. "Voluntary Association Membership Among Black Americans: The Post–Civil Rights Era." *Sociological Quarterly*, 28:285–301.

Woolcock, Michael. 1998. "Social Capital and Economic Development: Toward a Theoretical Synthesis and Policy Framework." *Theory and Society*, 27:151–208.

Wuthnow, Robert. 1998. *Loose Connections: Joining Together in America's Fragmented Communities*. Cambridge: Harvard University Press.

Wylie, Jeanie. 1989. *Poletown: A Community Betrayed*. Urbana: University of Illinois Press.

Yin, Jordan S. 1998. "The Community Development Industry System: A Case Study of Politics and Institutions in Cleveland, 1967–1997." *Journal of Urban Affairs*, 20.2:137–157.

Yoo, Jin-Kyung. 2000. "Utilization of Social Networks for Immigrant Entrepreneurship: A Case Study of Korean Immigrants in the Atlanta Area." *International Review of Sociology*, 10:347–363.

Yunus, Muhammed, with Alan Jolis. 1998. *Banker to the Poor*. London: Aurum Press.

Zhou, Min, and Carl L. Bankston. 1998. *Growing Up American: How Vietnamese Children Adapt to Life in the United States*. New York: Russell Sage.

Contributors

Judith N. DeSena is a professor in the Department of Sociology and anthropology at St. Johns University. She received her Ph.D. in sociology from City University of New York. Her research focuses on the social structure of community, women's community activism, and gentrification. She is the author of *Protecting One's Turf: Social Strategies for Maintaining Urban Neighborhoods* (University Press of America, 1990) and *People Power: Grassroots Politics and Race Relations* (University Press of America, 1999). She is editor of *Contemporary Readings in Sociology* (Kendall-Hunt, 1989) and co-editor of *Italian Americans in a Multicultural Society* (Forum Italicum, 1994, with Jerome Krase). Her articles have been published in *Sociological Spectrum, Journal of Urban Affairs, Sociological Inquiry,* and other social science journals.

Ivan Light is a professor in the Department of Sociology at the University of California, Los Angeles. He received his Ph.D. in sociology from the University of California, Berkeley. His research focuses on immigration, ethnic entrepreneurship, and urban sociology. He is the author of *Ethnic Entrepreneurs in America* (University of California Press, 1972), *Cities in World Perspective* (Macmillan, 1983), *Immigrant Entrepreneurs: Koreans in Los Angeles* (University of California Press, 1988, with Edna Bonacich), *Immigration and Entrepreneurship* (Transactions, 1993, with Parminder Bhachu), *Race, Ethnicity and Entrepreneurship in America* (Aldine Gruyter, 1995, with Carolyn Rosenstein), and *Ethnic Economies* (Academic Press, 2000, with Steven Gold). In addition, he has published various articles in *International Migration Review, International Journal of Urban and Regional Research, Ethnic and Racial Studies,* and other academic journals.

Gina Neff is a doctoral student in the Department of Sociology at Columbia University and a research associate in the Center on Organizational Innovation. Her research focuses on the nonprofit sector, the Internet, and organizational change. Since 1997 she has been conducting in-depth interviews and field research in New York's "Silicon Alley." Neff's dissertation research on economic uncertainty and flexible organizations in the internet industry has been cited in *Fortune* and the *Industry Standard*. Her writing on microcredit and economic policy has appeared in such publications as *Working Woman, Utne Reader, Nation, Left Business Observer,* and *Dissent.*

Kelly L. Patterson is a visiting assistant professor in the Department of Urban and Regional Planning and a senior research associate at the State University of New York, Buffalo. Her research focuses on African American women, well-being, and mental health in the African American community, the Black Church, and urban sociology.

Brian Sahd is an affiliated research associate in the Community Development Research Center at New School University, and he is the director of the New York Garden Trust for the New York Restoration Project. He received his Ph.D. in urban planning from Columbia University. His research focuses on community development, grassroots organizations, and urban planning.

Robert Mark Silverman is an associate professor in the Department of Urban and Regional Planning and a senior research associate at the State University of New York, Buffalo. His research focuses on community-based organizations, citizen participation, race relations, ethnic entrepreneurship, and urban inequality. He is the author of *Doing Business in Minority Markets: Black and Korean Entrepreneurs in Chicago's Ethnic Beauty Aids Industry* (Garland, 2000). He has also published articles in a variety of social science journals such as: *Sociological Inquiry, Community Development Journal, Journal of Contemporary Ethnography, Journal of Black Studies,* and *Journal of Social History.*

Randy Stoecker is a professor in the Department of Sociology and Anthropology at the University of Toledo. He received his Ph.D. in sociology from the University of Minnesota, Twin Cities. His research focuses on community organizing, urban redevelopment, community networks on the internet, and participatory action research. He is the website manager for COMM-ORG: the On-Line Conference on Community Organizing and Development <http://comm-org.utoledo.edu>. He is the author of *Defending Community: The*

Struggle for Alternative Redevelopment in Cedar-Riverside (Temple University Press, 1994). He has published articles in *Journal of Urban Affairs, Sociological Practice, American Behavioral Scientist, Gender and Society, Journal of Community Practice, Journal of Sociology and Social Welfare,* and other social science journals.

Sherri Leronda Wallace is an assistant professor in the Department of Political Science at the University of Louisville. Her research focuses on community economic development, the African American Church, and elder care in the African American community. In 2002 she was the recipient of the *William Wells Brown Award* from the Afro-American Historical Association of the Niagara Frontier, Inc. She has published articles in *Economic Development Quarterly, Review of Black Political Economy, Journal of Developmental Entrepreneurship, Journal of Community Development Society,* and *Afro-Americans in New York Life and History.*

Index